Longman Exam Guides
Business Law

Longman Exam Guides

Series Editors: Stuart Wall and David Weigall

Titles available:

Bookkeeping and Accounting
Business Law
Economics
English as a Foreign Language: Intermediate
English Literature
Monetary Economics
Office Practice and Secretarial Administration
Pure Mathematics
Secretarial Skills

Forthcoming:

Accounting: Cost and Management
             Financial
             Standards
Biology
British Government and Politics
Business Communication
Business Studies
Chemistry
Commerce
Computer Science
Electronics
Elements of Banking
English as a Foreign Language: Preliminary
                                  Advanced
French
General Principles of Law
General Studies
Geography
Mechanics
Modern British History
Physics
Quantitative Methods
Sociology
Taxation

Longman Exam Guides

BUSINESS LAW

Jillinda Tiley
Suzanne Bailey

LONGMAN
London and New York

Longman Group Limited
Longman House, Burnt Mill, Harlow
Essex CM20 2JE, England
Associated companies throughout the world

Published in the United States of America
by Longman Inc., New York

First published 1986
Second impression 1986

British Library Cataloguing in Publication Data
Tiley, Jillinda
    Business law.—
    (Longman exam guides)
    1. Corporation law—Great Britain
    I. Title   II. Bailey, Suzanne
    344.106′66   KD2079

ISBN 0-582-29678-1

Library of Congress Cataloging in Publication Data
Tiley, Jillinda, 1942–
    Business law.
    (Longman exam guides)
    Includes index.
    1. Commercial law—Great Britain—Outlines,
    syllabi, etc. 2. Commercial law—Great Britain—
    Examinations, questions, etc.
    I. Bailey, Suzanne.   II. Title   III. Series.
    KD1629.3.T55 1986   346.41′07′076
    85-23398
    ISBN 0-582-29678-1   344.1067076

Set in 9½ on 11pt Linotron Times
Printed and Bound in Great Britain by
The Bath Press, Avon

Contents

Editors' Preface

Much has been said in recent years about declining standards and disappointing examination results. Whilst this may be somewhat exaggerated, examiners are well aware that the performance of many candidates falls well short of their potential. Longman Exam Guides are written by experienced examiners and teachers, and aim to give you the best possible foundation for examination success. There is no attempt to cut corners. The books encourage thorough study and a full understanding of the concepts involved and should be seen as course companions and study guides to be used throughout the year. Examiners are in no doubt that a structured approach in preparing for and taking examinations can, together with hard work and diligent application, substantially improve performance.

The largely self-contained nature of each chapter gives the book a useful degree of flexibility. After starting with Chapters 1 and 2, all other chapters can be read selectively, in any order appropriate to the stage you have reached in your course. We believe that this book, and the series as a whole, will help you establish a solid platform of basic knowledge and examination technique on which to build.

Stuart Wall and David Weigall

Acknowledgements

We would like to thank Pat Babington-Smith, Barbara Mornin and Margaret Nichols for their help in typing the manuscript and B J and his word processor. Thanks also to the Computing Section at Cambridgeshire College of Arts and Technology for compiling the index.

We are indebted to the following Examining Boards for permission to reproduce questions from past Examination papers:

The Associated Examining Board; The Chartered Association of Certified Accountants; The Institute of Chartered Secretaries and Administrators; The Institute of Cost and Management accountants; The Institute of Legal Executives; The Royal Society of Arts Examinations Board.

The answers provided are the sole responsibility of the authors.

Chapter 1   **The Examinations**

Law is increasingly being taught on a wide range of professional and inter-disciplinary courses and in schools, as well as at degree and diploma level. The purpose of this book is to act as a guide to examinees taking such courses, some of which are identified in Table 1.1. It is our hope that the book will be of use to a student of law at any level since its purpose is not to become a surrogate textbook but to give guidance in the essential techniques required in coping successfully with law examinations.

These could be identified as the ability:

1. To extract the relevant from the irrelevant;
2. To analyse a problem;
3. To apply rules to a fact situation, distinguishing the relevant facts where necessary.

In order to give such guidance we have tried to identify and define the key points for the topic area covered in each chapter. We have reproduced some recent examination questions on the topic and provided outline or tutor's answers.

It is in no way intended that this guide should take the place of a standard textbook. Cases have been cited as authority, where appropriate, without discussion and very often their facts are only to be found at the back of the chapter in the section on useful applied materials. There are innumerable cases we could have cited – no attempt has been made to be exhaustive – we have had to select in the same way that an examinee must choose to support his or her case.

At the end of each chapter we have suggested some further reading or made other suggestions intended to be helpful to a varied group of readers familiar in differing degrees with the law. The reading is divided into basic student texts and more advanced works. Students taking 'A' Level or professional examinations would probably find the first group gives adequate cover. Those taking

Table 1.1 Topics and Courses

Chapter and Topic	AAT Business Law (Intermediate)	ACCA Law (Level 1)	BTEC National Diploma/Certificate — OE	BTEC National Diploma/Certificate — Business Law	GCE 'A' Level Law	ICA Law (Foundation)	ICMA Business Law (Foundation B)	ILE (Part 1)	ICSA — Intro to English Law (Part 1)	ICSA — Eng. Bus. Law (Part 2)	IOB — GP of Law (Stage 1) Law re-Banking (Stage 2)	IOM Cert/Dip in Marketing Legal Aspects	LCCI Higher Group Diploma in Law	RICS Law Part 1	RSA (DPA) Legal Aspects
3. Sources	√	√	√		√	√	√	√	√		√	√	√	√	√
4. Administration	√	√	√		√	√	√	√	√		√	√	√	√	√
5. Formation of contract	√	√	√	√	√	√	√	√	√	√	√	√	√	√	√
6. Contents of contract	√	√	√	√	√	√	√	√	√	√	√	√	√	√	√
7. Discharge of contract	√	√	√	√	√	√	√	√	√	√	√	√	√	√	√
8. Sale of goods	√	√	√	√	√	√		√		√		√	√	√	√
9. Agency	√	√		√	√		√				√	√	√	√	√
10. Partnerships and companies	√	√	√	√	√			√	√	√	√	√	√	√	√
11. Employment: creation and content of contract		√	√			√	√	√				√	√	√	√
12. Employment: termination of contract		√	√			√	√	√				√	√	√	√
13. Negotiable instruments	√	√		√	√			√		√	√			√	
14. General principles of tort		√	√		√	√	√	√	√		√	√	√	√	√
15. Negligence		√	√		√	√	√	√	√		√	√	√	√	√
16. Defamation			√			√	√	√			√		√		√

AAT – Association of Accounting Technicians
ACCA – Chartered Association of Certified Accountants
BTEC – Business and Technician Education Council
ICA – Institute of Chartered Accountants
GCE – General Certificate of Education
ICMA – Institute of Cost and Management Accountants
ICSA – Institute of Chartered Secretaries and Administrators
ILE – Institute of Legal Executives
IOB – Institute of Bankers
IOM – Institute of Marketing
LCCI – London Chamber of Commerce & Industry
RICS – Royal Institute of Chartered Surveyors
RSA – Royal Society of Arts

degree examinations or specialising in a particular area might prefer one of the more detailed texts.

Although varying in their depth of coverage, the textbooks suggested all cite a number of cases, both in the text and in footnotes, to which you may make direct reference in the reports. Each case will itself contain the names of all the cases cited in argument. This will provide you with excellent source material.

Where it is difficult to obtain access to the reports themselves, you should be able to get hold of a casebook. There are a number of these which contain excerpts from the judgments of the major cases. In reading the judgments you will not only learn the facts and the decision in the case, but you will learn, from the style of the judgment, how to approach and unravel problems. Frequently in giving a decision a judge will consider a variety of circumstances. While these comments are obiter dicta, i.e., not part of the judgment, they are very helpful in understanding the judge's view of the law. A judge will frequently review a whole series of past decisions which can operate as excellent revision, as well as helping to forecast what future decisions might be.

In addition to the specific books suggested at the end of each chapter, readers are recommended to consult the current (fourth) edition of *Halsbury's Laws of England*. This is an encyclopaedic work containing many volumes. Topics are dealt with alphabetically. Use the index in the appropriate volume and the supplements, published annually and monthly, to keep the material up to date.

Current Law, published monthly by Sweet & Maxwell, provides simple access to all recent developments, including some unreported cases. You will find there references, by subject index, to new statutes and to other delegated legislation, as well as articles published during the month in the major legal journals. These include the *Law Quarterly Review, Modern Law Review, Cambridge Law Journal, New Law Journal, Solicitors' Journal* and specialist journals.

Statutes can be found in most public libraries; *Halsbury's Statutes* or *Current Law Statutes* give you the text and explanatory notes. Statutes can be bought from bookshops or direct from Her Majesty's Stationery Office (HMSO), 49 High Holborn, London WC1.

Chapter 2

Examination Preparation and Technique

In preparing for an examination there is no substitute for *hard work*! Law demands knowledge of a body of rules and the ability to apply them to a problem situation. Simple, clear notes which you understand, listing the main points to remember and the authorities which support the rules, are probably the best revision aid. It cannot be stated too often that there is a *lot* of material to be covered for a law examination – simple notes should *remind* you of more complex problems and act as a focus for your thoughts – they will not, of *themselves*, necessarily give you all you will need.

There are two kinds of question usually asked on law papers – the 'straight' essay question 'Discuss . . .', 'Explain . . .', and the problem question – where you will be asked to apply rules to a practical situation. In either case *read* the question carefully; take time to find out what you are being asked to do. No marks will be given for irrelevant information – they may even be lost. It is very unlikely you will be asked to 'write all you know about . . .'!

You should find that you are not too pressed for time – time spent *thinking* and planning the final presentation of your answer is time well spent. It is a good idea to jot down on some rough paper names of cases which flash into your mind, or the points you immediately think are important in case you forget them. Then prepare either an essay plan for an essay question, or an analysis for a problem question.

An essay should always have an introduction, presenting an outline of your proposed discussion, a development (plus illustrations) and a conclusion. A busy examiner will get an immediate 'feel' for the quality of your answer from the introduction and be 'left' with your conclusion. So, do make sure that these are pertinent and well presented.

Authorities should always be quoted where possible – but for a reason, such as support for a legal principle; the examiner does *not* want a video re-run of the story. If you have forgotten the name of the case but can remember the facts a *brief* reference will indicate that you do *know* the case but have temporarily forgotten its name. An examiner will forgive this much more readily than a long detour into all the details in an attempt to compensate.

Cases should usually be cited after the rule for which they are authority. There is generally no need to discuss the facts unless you wish to refer to a case whose name you have forgotten, or unless you are using the facts by way of *illustration* of a principle rather than as an authority. For example, *Donoghue* v. *Stevenson* is the usual authority for the proposition that a manufacturer owes a duty of care to the ultimate consumer. In a question on defective goods you could start with the general proposition 'A manufacturer owes a duty of care to the ultimate consumer', then add, '*Donoghue* v. *Stevenson*', after your proposition. No facts are needed. If you have forgotten the name you could refer simply to 'the decision in the House of Lords in the snail in the bottle case'.

If you wish to use a case as an illustration, make sure the examiner can see clearly the *point* you are trying to make, that is, what relevance your illustration has to the problem you are dealing with. Be careful *not* to say of a problem 'this is *Smith* v. *Bloggs*' – a problem may be based on, or similar to, a decided case, but is most certainly *not* 'the' case!

In a problem question, look carefully at what you are asked to do. Sometimes 'Discuss', sometimes 'Advise B'. Clearly you will get no marks if you advise *C* instead! In order to give advice you will have to 'unravel' the problem, but do remember to conclude – as with a mathematical problem – with the advice asked for.

It is a good idea in answering a problem to tackle it in stages:

1. Who is the plaintiff *or* plaintiffs? – look out for more than one!
2. Who is the defendant *or* defendants?
3. What is the *kind* of damage of which the plaintiff is complaining?
4. What is the plaintiff's cause of action?

You may find there are several defendants, several kinds of damage, and several causes of action. Jot all this down on a piece of rough paper or you will very easily get in a muddle!

5. Define/explain the cause(s) of action which you have identified, i.e. state the relevant legal rules and give their authority.
6   Apply 5 to the facts.
7. Consider any defences available.
8. Conclude. 'In the light of the above, A should be advised . . .'

Then write a presentable layout on your exam paper.

Where you have several plaintiffs/defendants you may find it easier to deal with each case/cause of action in a separate paragraph. It is perfectly acceptable to use initials for your parties and much more preferable to 'he', which can be confusing.

An examiner will frequently not give you all the facts. This is deliberate. It is up to you to raise the issues omitted. This can be done quite simply and briefly, by the use of 'if'. You should have stated the legal rules in stage 5 above; when you come to stage 6 (apply to facts), you can say 'if X broke the duty of care . . .'; 'if X did *not* break the duty of care . . .'; 'if X was fraudulent . . .'; or 'if X was merely negligent . . .'.

If you are really hard pressed for time, a lot of information can be put across in staccato note form. Don't waste time making excuses!

It is helpful to underline names of cases, e.g. *Hadley* v. *Baxendale*. There is no need to give a date for a case, although you should always do this for a statute, e.g. Sale of Goods Act 1979.

An examiner will be much more impressed by a brief answer, clearly written in a logical way, even though it omits some fine point, than with a much longer recital which is not *directed* to the question.

Finally, write clearly, give cases and statutes capital letters, avoid verbosity or personal involvement. 'It is submitted' is preferable to 'I think'.

Chapter 3

Sources of Law

When asked to describe the sources of English law a student might question exactly what he is required to discuss. This is because the word 'source' can have different meanings in the study of law. It can refer to the social, political and economic conditions which influence the lawmaking process, to the historical origins of legal rules, to the authority which gives law its validity or to where the law can be found. More importantly, for the purposes of this chapter, the term sources of law can refer to the processes by which English law is created.

This topic is liberally sprinkled with distinctively English legal phrases, such as the common law, equity and judicial precedent. To understand these terms the student must acquire some appreciation of the historical development of the unique legal system which is English law.

ESSENTIAL PRINCIPLES

This chapter is divided into three sections. Section 1 concentrates on the development of English law through the courts. It includes a discussion of the doctrine of judicial precedent, the common law and equity. Section 2 looks at both statutory and delegated legislation, including EEC legislation, together with a discussion of the rules of statutory interpretation. Section 3 briefly describes some of the other, now minor, sources of English law; custom, Roman law, canon law, the law merchant and books of authority.

A. THE DOCTRINE OF JUDICIAL PRECEDENT

(*stare decisis* – let the decision stand) The traditional view is that English judges do not make law but simply apply legal rules to the particular case before them. This assessment of the judicial role is known as the *declaratory theory*. Although it is now accepted that judges do make laws, this view is the basis of the doctrine of judicial precedent.

The essence of judicial precedent is that a court, depending on its position within the court hierarchy, is bound to follow a legal principle formulated by another court in an earlier similar case. The operative word is 'bound'. The later court may disagree with the other court's decision and may even consider it to be bad law but, in theory, it has no alternative but to apply the precedent.

Judicial precedent is dependent on three elements:

1. the court hierarchy;
2. that a particular legal principle (the *ratio decidendi*) was the reason for the decision; and
3. that the case before the court is similar to the one in which the ratio was stated.

The doctrine of judicial precedent is thus founded on the application of legal rules to later analogous cases. We shall deal with each element in turn.

THE COURT HIERARCHY	**The position of each court determines whether it is bound by another court's decisions.** The order within the hierarchy is as follows (you may find it helpful to refer to Fig. 4.1, p. 22):
1. House of Lords	This court makes decisions which bind *all* lower courts. It was previously bound by its own decisions, which meant that a House of Lords' decision could only be changed by Parliament. Now, however, the House can depart from its earlier decision if it is in the interests of justice to do so (Practice Statement, 1966).
2. Court of Appeal (civil division)	This court is bound by the House of Lords and in turn binds all lower courts. Generally it is bound by its own decisions unless the exceptions in *Young* v. *Bristol Aeroplane Co* 1944 apply: (a) there are two conflicting Court of Appeal decisions; (b) a previous Court of Appeal decision conflicts with a later House of Lords' decision; or (c) the previous decision was given *per incurian*, that is incorrectly, without taking into account relevant statute or case law.
3. Court of Appeal (criminal division)	This court is bound by the House of Lords and binds all lower courts. However, because it is dealing with the liberty of the subject, it does not necessarily consider itself bound by its own previous decisions. Neither division of the Court of Appeal is bound by the other.
4. High Court	The divisional courts of the High Court are bound by the House of Lords and by the Court of Appeal, and in turn bind all lower courts. Their decisions bind later divisional courts in the same division on the

same basis as the Court of Appeal divisions are bound by their previous decisions.

High Court judges sitting alone are bound by all higher courts, and their decisions will in turn bind lower courts. They do not bind each other.

5. County Court and Magistrates Court

These courts are bound by all other courts. They are *not* bound by their own previous decisions.

THE RATIO

The term *ratio decidendi* (usually shortened to ratio) has never been formally defined but is accepted as meaning the legal principle of a case. This is distinct from the finding of facts which binds only the parties.

As mentioned above, a judge sitting in a certain court is bound by another court's ratio. Therefore he must be able to identify the ratio of any particular case. This is not always so simple. A judge is not obliged to indicate where the ratio of his judgment is to be found. Further, in appeal courts where several judges sit, although they may all come to the same conclusion they may do so for different reasons. Each judge's ratio may, therefore, be slightly or even substantially different. There is also no limit to the number of *rationes* which may be formulated in any one case.

Because of these potential difficulties it is frequently up to later courts to determine the exact ratio of an earlier case. This provides an opportunity for later courts to control the influence of any particular ratio. For example, the neighbour principle formulated in *Donoghue* v. *Stevenson* 1932 (see Ch. 15) has been used by later courts as a general principle to determine when a duty of care arises in the tort of negligence.

A case may contain other legal statements besides the ratio. These are known as *obiter dicta*, being statements said 'by the way'. *Obiter dicta* are made, for example, when a judge states what he considers the law would have been if the facts of the case before him had been different or when he gives a dissenting judgment. *Obiter dicta* are not binding on later courts but they are persuasive and can have great influence. Probably one of the most famous *obiter dictum* was given in the case of *Hedley Byrne & Co Ltd* v. *Heller & Partners Ltd* 1964 which created liability for negligent misstatements (see Ch. 15). It is sometimes difficult to distinguish a *ratio decidendi* from an *obiter dictum*.

That the case before the court is similar to the one in which the ratio was stated

If the case which is being heard is similar to a case in which a particular ratio was stated, then, if that court is bound by the other court's judgments, that ratio must be applied. However, as no two cases are identical in their facts, a later court may decide that the cases are not similar. If the facts of the two cases are considered to be *materially different* the cases will be *distinguished* and the earlier court's ratio will not be applied.

| **How flexibility is retained** | The requirement that later courts must apply the ratios of previous decisions could lead to stagnation. The system has, however, developed certain devices so that some flexibility can be retained. A court will not be bound if a precedent: |

1. *Was reversed on appeal by a higher court.*
2. *Was overruled by a later court.* If a precedent is overruled it is no longer good law. However, this does not affect the decision given in the earlier case as once a judgment has been given the case is closed, subject to any appeal. **This is the principle of *res judicata*, (the thing has been judged).**

    A court may also '*disapprove*' of an earlier precedent considering it to be incorrect. This does not affect the validity of that precedent which is still good law.
3. *Can be distinguished.* A later court can distinguish if the facts of the earlier case and the case before the court are materially different.
4. *Is only persuasive.* In this category are obiter dicta, judgments pronounced by inferior courts, and decisions given by courts not directly involved in the making of English law; i.e., Scottish, Irish, Commonwealth and foreign courts. The Privy Council's judgments, for example, are only persuasive but can be extremely influential as illustrated by the *Wagon Mound* case which established one of the basic rules of remoteness in tort (see Ch. 15).

In addition, flexibility is maintained by allowing the House of Lords to depart from its previous decisions (Practice Statement 1966) and by the need for later courts sometimes to decide what the exact ratio of an earlier case was.

ADVANTAGES OF JUDICIAL PRECEDENT

The doctrine of judicial precedent is unique to the common law and it has certain advantages:

1. *It gives certainty to the law.* Because potential litigants are aware of previous decisions they are able to settle their disputes without the necessity of going to court.
2. As the system is dependent on actual cases *the law adapts to meet socio-economic changes* and is based on real situations not just theoretical ones.
3. *The system allows a detailed body of law to develop naturally.*

DISADVANTAGES OF JUDICIAL PRECEDENT

On the other hand judicial precedent also has disadvantages:

1. *The system can create rigidity in the law*;
2. *The law may develop slowly and haphazardly* as it is dependent on the chance of litigation;
3. In order to avoid applying a particular precedent *a court may distinguish to a fine degree*;

4. *The amount of case law may become excessive;*
5. *There is no necessary advance warning that a precedent will be changed.*

LAW REPORTS

The system of judicial precedent can only work if previous decisions are *known* by later courts. Law reports, at least until the last century, fluctuated in their reliability. Now reports are regularly published by the Incorporated Council of Law Reporting and by private firms. Some of the more famous reports are the Weekly Law Reports and the All England Laws Reports. However, the law report is only a record of the precedent and therefore an unreported case can be cited as a precedent if it is vouched for by a barrister who was present in court when the decision was given.

COMMON LAW AND EQUITY

These two historical sources of English law were both developed through the application of judicial precedent. Although the term **common law** can mean simply case law, it really stands for that body of law which was created and administered by the common law courts.

Originally the common law derived from local customs but gradually a body of law developed which was distinct from custom and which applied to all Englishmen. In certain respects the common law was harsh. For example, if a litigant could not fit his claim into a particular writ form he was unable to bring his claim. Further, the common law was increasingly concerned with procedure rather than with the merits of the case. In addition, the only remedy available at common law was damages. Because of the inadequacies and difficulties of the common law, litigants frequently petitioned the king for justice. The king passed these petitions onto his chancellor who eventually granted these petitions in his own name. Thus was created the **Court of Chancery** where the rules of the system of law known as **equity** were developed.

Equity made certain substantial contributions to English law, for example:

1. *It recognised a beneficiary's interest in property held for him on trust.* A trust is a relationship whereby property is vested in one person (the trustee) who is bound to deal with that property for the benefit of another person (the beneficiary);
2. It created the '*equity of redemption*' which allowed a mortgagor to redeem his land after the date of redemption had passed;
3. It developed new remedies such as the *injunction*, being a court order prohibiting or compelling certain action, and *specific performance* which requires that the terms of a contract or trust be fulfilled. All equitable remedies are discretionary; the court does not have to award them to an applicant, in contrast to damages which are given as of right if the applicant can establish his claim.

Equitable decisions are based on the maxims of equity such as 'he who comes to equity must come with clean hands', requiring that a plaintiff must have a clear conscience, and 'equity looks at the intent and not the form'. The latter maxim was the basis for equity's development of the principle of 'equity of redemption'.

The Judicature Acts 1873–75 created a new court structure, the Supreme Court of Judicature, through which both the principles and remedies of the common law and equity could be applied and dispensed. This does not mean that the common law and equity became one system, for they did not. Their separate rules still apply. Thus, a litigant wishing to obtain an equitable remedy must still comply with the maxims of equity. If the common law and equity conflict, equity prevails.

B. STATUTES AND DELEGATED LEGISLATION

Parliament is unrivalled as a source of English law. No limits can be placed on Parliament's powers and none of its laws can be declared unconstitutional. Any *statute* enacted by Parliament overrides any legal rules which may conflict with it, whether they be common law or statute.

The process by which Parliament creates general laws is relatively straightforward. A *bill*, being a prospective piece of legislation, is introduced either in the House of Commons or the House of Lords, unless it is concerned with the collection of revenue when it must be introduced in the Commons. If the bill is supported by the government it is called a *Public Bill*. If such a bill is introduced by a private Member, the Bill is a *Private Member's Bill*. There are also Bills which deal with private interests known as *Private Bills*.

When a public or private member's bill is introduced it receives a formal first reading. It then has a second reading which is really the first opportunity for a general debate on the bill's provisions. If the bill passes its second reading it goes to a committee, where it is discussed in detail. If the bill is extremely important it may be discussed by a Committee of the Whole House. The committee then reports back and at this Report Stage any amendments suggested by the committee are voted on. Finally the bill receives a third reading whereupon it is sent to the other House where it goes through the same procedure. If passed by both Houses the bill becomes law once it receives the Royal Assent, which is never withheld. The law thus created will then be enforceable unless the statute states otherwise. Once enacted, a statute remains law until it is repealed by another Act of Parliament.

Parliament may pass legislation for a variety of reasons.

1. *To create new laws.*
2. *To amend existing legislation.*
3. *To repeal legislation.*
4. *To consolidate* into one act all the pieces of legislation affecting a specific area of law. The Employment Protection (Consolidation) Act 1978 is an example of such a statute.
5. *To codify* by bringing together all the law, case law and statute,

on a particular subject. The Sale of Goods Act 1893 (now 1979) was enacted for this purpose.

Various bodies have been established to assist Parliament in keeping the law under review. The most important of these bodies is the **Law Commission** which submits an annual report to the Lord Chancellor.

Statutory interpretation

The function of the courts is to put into effect the intention of Parliament. If the words used in a statute are clear and unambiguous, there will be no problem but, if this is not the case, the courts must interpret the meaning of the words used.

To assist them in interpreting a statute the courts can refer to the Act's *long title*, i.e. its section headings, any schedules included with the Act or the Act's interpretation section, if it has one. The court is allowed to make use of only a limited number of external aids. Judges are allowed to use dictionaries to determine the meaning of non-legal words, to consider the Reports of Royal Commissions and of the Law Commission and other such bodies, and to refer to the Interpretation Act 1978. One thing that courts cannot do is to consult Hansard, the record of Parliamentary debates, or to ask anyone in Parliament for the meaning of an Act, for no one person or group can speak for Parliament as a whole.

Certain rules of interpretation have been developed to assist the courts. These are known as the *literal, golden* and *mischief rules*.

Literal rule

The literal rule **requires that words should be given their ordinary, natural meanings and sentences their grammatical meanings, even if the result is absurd or harsh.** The reason for this is that the courts can only interpret the meaning of an Act from the words used in the statute. Thus, when Parliament made it an offence to 'offer' flick knives for sale under the Restriction of Offensive Weapons Act 1959 it did not make it an offence for a shopkeeper to display flick knives, for that is not an offer but an invitation to treat (see p. 17). (*Fisher* v. *Bell* 1961).

Golden rule

It may happen that when words are given their literal meaning the result is manifestly absurd. If that is the case the court may use the golden rule, i.e. **interpret the words to avoid such an absurdity.** Thus, in *R.* v. *Allen* 1872 the courts interpreted the offence of bigamy, contrary to s.57 of the Offences Against the Person Act 1861, as going through a ceremony of marriage while still being married to another person, although the actual wording of the Act is 'whosoever being married shall marry another person during the life of the former husband or wife'. If the literal rule was applied it would be impossible for anyone to commit bigamy as under English law no one can legally be married to more than one person at any one time.

Mischief rule

The application of the mischief rule, (the rule in *Heydon's Case*), allows the courts more latitude than the other rules in interpreting statutes. Under this rule **the judge considers what the law was before**

the statute was passed and what mischief Parliament was trying to prevent by passing the legislation. The court then interprets the statute in such a way as to remedy the mischief.

The mischief rule was used in the case of *Smith* v. *Hughes* 1971. Parliament had made it an offence under the Street Offences Act 1959 for prostitutes to solicit men in public places. Although the prostitute prosecuted in this case had propositioned men from a private house and not in the street, she was still convicted. The mischief which the Act was trying to remedy, as the court saw it, was molestation by common prostitutes of people walking the city's streets.

These rules of interpretation are undoubtedly necessary. Problems arise, however, because it is never certain which rule a judge will use. Further, the use of the golden and mischief rules involves, to a greater or lesser extent, subjective judgments.

Interpretive aids

In addition to the above rules, the courts have *other interpretive aids*. These include *the rules of construction and certain presumptions*.

The rules of construction include the following.

1. A statute must be read as a whole and every section read in the light of every other section.
2. General words following specific words must be construed in the context of the specific words and no further. This is known as the *ejusdem generis rule*. Thus, if the phrase used in a statute is 'cats, dogs and other animals' the phrase 'other animals' would not include lions, wolves, and grizzly bears.

In interpreting a statute the courts make the following rebuttable presumptions.

1. Legislation is not intended to have retrospective effect.
2. Legislation is not intended to impose liability, unless the defendant is at 'fault'. Fault in this context means the defendant acting intentionally, recklessly or negligently when committing the wrong.
3. Acts of Parliament are not intended to bind the Crown.
4. The court's jurisdiction is not to be ousted.

The system of precedent applies to statutory interpretation. For example, once the House of Lords has given its interpretation of the meaning of the words in a statute all other courts must accept that meaning. The House of Lords is itself bound by the EEC's European Court of Justice concerning the interpretation of Community legislation (see below).

Delegated legislation

A complex body of legal rules is required by the modern state. For various reasons Parliament is incapable of producing all the legislation which is needed and it may delegate the power to make laws to other persons or bodies. This is done by passing an enabling act which outlines the general purpose of the law, leaving the details to be filled in by the body or person to whom power has been delegated. The laws thus produced are known as delegated legislation and have the same authority as if they had been enacted by Parliament itself.

Delegated legislation can take a variety of forms. The most important are:

1. *Ministerial regulations known as statutory instruments;*
2. *Orders in Council* made by the Privy Council under the Royal prerogative;
3. *Local authority by-laws.*

It is argued that EEC legislation is a form of delegated legislation (see below).

Delegating legislative power to others has certain advantages.

(a) it saves Parliamentary time;
(b) it allows for changes in the law to be made quickly;
(c) it increases the possibility of experimentation;
(d) it allows those who have specialised knowledge to create laws.

Yet, there are disadvantages as well. For example:

(a) it allows non-elected persons to make laws;
(b) the body of delegated legislation is so vast that ignorance of the law may be no defence but it is certainly a reality.

Controls

Because of the possibility that delegated powers may be misused, legislative and judicial controls have been created. Legislative controls include the following:

1. Some types of delegated legislation have to be 'laid' before Parliament.
2. Ministers may be called upon to answer questions in Parliament on delegated legislation made by their offices.
3. There exists a Select Committee on Statutory Instruments as well as a committee which looks at EEC legislation.
4. Parliament can, of course, simply withdraw the power to make delegated legislation.

Judicial controls include:

1. Although the courts cannot question an Act of Parliament, they can declare delegated legislation to be *ultra vires* and therefore null and void because the delegated body was not given the power to make such laws.
2. The courts must be satisfied that the delegated legislation must be reasonable to be valid, particularly in the case of local by-laws.

EEC Legislation

The United Kingdom became a member of the EEC by the Treaty of Accession 1972 but it was with the passing of the European Communities Act 1972 that EEC legislation became part of English law. It is argued that by passing this Act Parliament gave up some of its sovereignty. To counter this it is said that Parliament could always repeal the 1972 Act.

The Treaty of Rome 1957 established the general objectives of the Community. The law-making bodies of the EEC, the Council and the Commission, create various types of legislation. These are:

1. *Regulations*. These are 'self executing' and become part of the law of all member states without the need for any state's legislative body to take any action.
2. *Directives*. These are addressed to one or more member states and require that a state's law be brought into line with community law. It is left to the individual state to make such alterations as are necessary. In Britain this is done by statutory instrument.
3. *Decisions*. These are binding without the need for further legislation on those to whom they are addressed.

In addition, the Council and the Commission may publish *recommendations* and *opinions* which are persuasive only.

If there is a conflict between the internal laws of a member state and EEC legislation, then the legislation of the EEC will prevail.

The European Court of Justice, the EEC's judicial body, is not a law-making body as such. Its importance lies in settling disputes and in interpreting community legislation. Any court of a member state may request the Court of Justice to give a ruling on the meaning of Community law, but a member state's final court of appeal must do so if such an interpretion is necessary. The European Court's ruling is binding.

C. OTHER SOURCES OF ENGLISH LAW

CUSTOM

The common law was founded on *local* custom. Now custom is an exception to the common law. In order to be enforceable a local custom must be 'judicially noted'. To be recognised by the courts a custom must be shown to:

1. Have existed from 'time immemorial' (1189). A custom is accepted as being of such antiquity if no evidence is submitted which proves that the custom was only practised after that date.
2. Have been exercised with consent, openly and continuously, as of right;
3. Be certain both as to content and locality;
4. Be consistent with any other local customs;
5. Be obligatory if a duty is imposed; and
6. Be reasonable.

Another form of custom, although not a direct source of English law, is *commercial* custom. The courts will take note of such business practices and, if appropriate, will apply them as implied contractual terms.

ROMAN LAW

Although extremely influential in the development of Continental and Scottish law, Roman law had little direct influence on English law. Its principles formed part of the body of canon law and the law merchant and in this way it had some indirect influence.

| **CANON LAW** | This was the body of law dispensed by the ecclesiastical courts. It influenced the development of matrimonial law and probate. Also, because the early chancellors were churchmen, the rules of canon law had some effect on the development of equity. |

| **LAW MERCHANT** | The law merchant was the first code of international mercantile law and was applied in commercial medieval courts. From the law merchant English law acquired the foundations of the law of partnership and agency and the concept of negotiability. |

| **BOOKS OF AUTHORITY** | Textbooks are expressions of opinion and although persuasive are not accepted as sources of law. There are some books, however, written before there was adequate law reporting which are accepted as sources of English common law. These include the writings of Glanvill, Bracton, Coke and Blackstone. |

| **USEFUL APPLIED MATERIALS** | The cases listed below illustrate certain points made in this chapter. |

STATUTORY INTERPRETATION

Literal rule

1. *Fisher* v. *Bell* 1961. The Restriction of Offensive Weapons Act 1959 made it an offence to offer an offensive weapon for sale. A shopkeeper was charged with displaying flick knives in his window. He was found not guilty as the display was an invitation to treat, not an offer. The Act was changed after this case.
2. *IRC v. Hinchy* 1960. The Income Tax Act 1952 s.25(3) required that those who did not file a correct income tax return were subject to pay ' . . . treble the tax he ought to be charged . . . '. Held D had to pay treble the total tax payable not simply treble the unpaid tax which is what Parliament really intended. Section 25(3) was repealed.

Golden rule

3. *R.* v. *Allen* 1872. D charged with bigamy. The court interpreted s.57 of the Offences Against the Person Act 1861 to mean it is an offence to go through a ceremony of marriage while married to another who is still alive at the time the ceremony takes place.

Mischief rule

4. *Smith* v. *Hughes* 1971. Section 1 of the Street Offences Act 1959 says 'It shall be an offence for a common prostitute to loiter or solicit in a street or public place for the purposes of prostitution.' Held that a prostitute who opportuned men in the street from her window was guilty.

The following are examples of typical examination questions. It may be helpful if you spend around ten minutes planning an answer to each question before turning to the outline answers.

Question 1.

(a) What do you understand by the term 'statute law'? State the advantages and disadvantages of this kind of law.

(b) Discuss the rules which govern the interpretation of statutes. (ACCA 1981).

Question 2.

(a) Explain the meaning and purpose of delegated legislation using examples of a business nature.

(b) In what ways may the use of delegated legislation be controlled? (ICMA 1982)

Question 3.

Evaluate the part played by equity both historically and today in the development of English law. (AEB 1984)

Question 4.

In what circumstances may a judge avoid applying a precedent? Why should he wish to do this? (ILE 1983)

OUTLINE ANSWERS

Answer 1.

(a) 'Statute law' is law enacted by the Queen in Parliament – the majority of the House of Commons and the House of Lords together with the consent of the Queen. A statute is legally enforceable when it receives the Royal Assent, unless otherwise stated, and remains enforceable until repealed by a later Act. Where there is a conflict between case law and statute, statute prevails.

The advantages of statute are that it is made by elected representatives together with members of the Lords many of whom hold life peerages because of their contribution to the community. Also, Parliament, by passing legislation, can make radical innovative changes in the law. The disadvantages are that no Parliamentary Act can be declared unconstitutional, that statutes frequently need to be interpreted and that the passage of a bill is a lengthy process.

(b) The courts must put into effect the intention of Parliament. The three rules of interpretation are:

   (i) *Literal Rule* – the words in a statute must be given their ordinary natural meaning and sentences their grammatical meaning;

   (ii) *Golden Rule* – if the literal interpretation of the words of a statute lead to a manifest absurdity the courts may interpret those words to avoid such an absurdity;

   (iii) *Mischief Rule* – the statute is interpreted to remedy the mischief being the purpose of the legislation.

The courts also use rules of construction, e.g. the *ejusdem generis* rule and presumptions of interpretation.

Answer 2.

(a) Parliament can delegate to another person or body the power to make law which has the same authority as if it were made by Parliament. The purpose of delegated legislation is to keep the law flexible, to save Parliamentary time and to allow persons to make law in an area in which they have specialised knowledge. Examples of delegated legislation include the statutory instruments by which EEC directives are incorporated into English law and ministerial regulations made under the provisions of the Health and Safety at Work etc. Act 1974 and the Consumer Credit Act 1974.

(b) Delegated legislation is controlled by Parliament and the courts. Parliamentary controls include questions to ministers, the requirement that some delegated legislation be 'laid' before Parliament and Parliamentary Standing Committees. The ultimate control is a withdrawal of the power by Parliament. The courts can declare delegated legislation to be null and void if made outside the delegate body's powers or if made unreasonably.

Answer 3.

Equity is the body of law developed through the Court of Chancery to mitigate the harshness of the common law. Equity's contributions to English law included recognition of the beneficiary's interest in trust property, developing the concept of the 'equity of redemption' and various discretionary remedies such as the injunction and specific performance. The rules of equity are applied according to the equitable maxims.

Equity and the common law are now administered by the same courts, although they are still separate bodies of law. Any litigant wishing to rely on an equitable principle or to obtain an equitable remedy must comply with the rules of equity. If the common law and equity conflict, equity prevails. The rules of equity have now become as rigid as those of the common law.

A TUTOR'S ANSWER

Question **4** is typical of questions asked on judicial precedent, a favourite topic of examiners. A student must first discuss the doctrine of judicial precedent before he can answer the question.

According to the doctrine of judicial precedent a court in certain circumstances is bound to follow the legal principle established in an earlier court. This is the principle of *stare decisis* (let the decision stand). A court is bound if the case being heard is similar to the case in which the legal principle (*ratio decidendi*) was pronounced and the earlier court stands in a particular relationship within the court structure to the later court. Thus a decision by the House of Lords will bind all lower courts.

The development of case law through the application of judicial precedent provides stability and certainty to the law, but it may also cause stagnation. A judge may therefore wish to avoid a precedent if it does not reflect modern conditions. In order to enable the law to be sufficiently flexible to meet changes and challenges a court may wish to avoid applying a precedent. A judge is not bound to apply a precedent when:

1. A higher court has reversed on appeal a lower court's decision. For example, the decision given by the Court of Appeal in *McLoughlin* v. *O'Brian* 1982 (see Ch. 15) was reversed by the House of Lords;

2. A later court which occupies a superior position in relation to the court which created the precedent may overrule the earlier court's decision. Thus, the House of Lords, applying the Practice Statement 1966 in *British Railways Board* v. *Herrington* overruled its own previous decision in *Robert Addie & Sons (Collieries) Ltd* v. *Dumbreck* 1929;

3. If there is a material difference between the case which established the ratio and the case before the court. Thus *Stilk* v. *Myrick* 1809 was distinguished from *Hartley* v. *Ponsonby* 1857.

4. If the precedent is only persuasive, for example it is an obiter statement, or it is made by a court inferior to the one hearing the case or by a court outside the English court hierarchy such as the Privy Council.

5. If the precedent is inconsistent with an Act of Parliament.

In addition to the above, the fact that frequently the precise meaning of a case's ratio is uncertain allows a later court to interpret the earlier case's ratio in the way it considers to be the most suitable.

A STEP FURTHER

BASIC READING

There are various textbooks which discuss the sources of English law. These include:

General Principles of Law (3rd edn.) Clive R. Newton, Concise College Texts, Sweet & Maxwell, 1983;
Introduction to Law L. A. Rutherford, I. A. Todd and M. G. Woodley, Sweet & Maxwell in association with The Institute of Legal Executives, 1982.

FURTHER READING

Students who are interested in the development of English law might read the reports of the Law Commission and the various Royal Commissions. These reports usually contain a summary of the law and proposals for change. A list of all reports and working papers of the Law Commission is contained in the *Law Commission's Annual Report* issued as a House of Commons paper.

A student might also wish to look at *Hansard* for a record of what was said in Parliamentary debates. Developments in case law can be traced through the law reports such as the *All England Law Reports*.

A catalogue of government publications can be obtained from Her Majesty's Stationery Office: HMSO, 49 High Holborn, London, WC1V 6HB.

Chapter 4

Administration

One of the primary functions of any legal system is to provide forums where remedies can be obtained or penal sanctions imposed. This chapter looks at the framework of the English legal system; the areas where disputes are settled and the personnel, lawyers and laymen, who administer the law. We should note that Scotland has its own separate legal system.

Aspects of this topic are frequently the subject of essay questions. A student might be asked to explain the appeal process, to give his views on whether the English legal profession should remain divided or to discuss the contribution of laymen. Alternatively the student might need to demonstrate knowledge of the court structure when answering a question which is primarily concerned with another aspect of law, such as obtaining a remedy for breach of contract.

It is essential for anyone interested in the law to appreciate *how* the system operates, since it is important that you both understand the rules of law *and* know where grievances can be aired and settled.

ESSENTIAL PRINCIPLES

A. THE COURTS

The English courts can be classified in a number of ways.

1. Whether they deal with criminal or civil matters.
2. Whether they have original or appellate jurisdiction; in other words whether the court hears cases being decided for the first time or hears cases on appeal from other courts.
3. Whether the court's jurisdiction is limited (an inferior court) or unlimited (a superior court). This classification will be used as the basis for discussion in this chapter. You may find it helpful to refer to Fig. 4.1 during this discussion.

Civil Proceedings

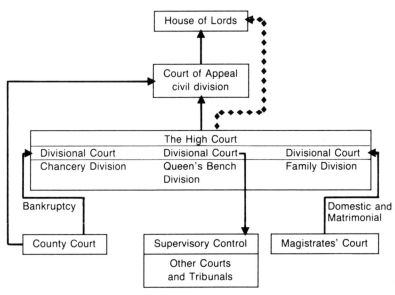

◆ ◆ ◆ ◆ ◆ ◆ leapfrog procedure

Criminal Proceedings

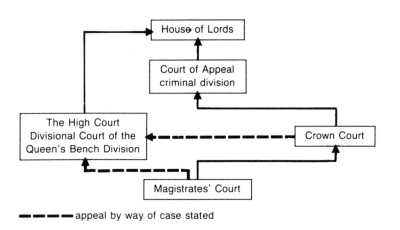

▬ ▬ ▬ ▬ appeal by way of case stated

Fig. 4.1 Routes of appeal

THE INFERIOR COURTS	The two main inferior courts are the magistrates' court and the county court; another inferior court is the small claims court.

The Magistrates' Court

The magistrates' court has both civil and criminal jurisdiction. Its jurisdiction is limited to hearing cases which have never been tried before. It hears no appeal cases. Magistrates' courts are local courts dealing generally with matters which have occurred within the vicinity of the court. Each magistrates' court is a separate court from all other magistrates' courts; thus the Cambridge magistrates' court is in no way connected with the Oxford magistrates' court.

Except in the larger cities where legally qualified lawyers known as stipendiary magistrates sit, cases heard in magistrates' courts are decided by lay magistrates, sometimes referred to as justices of the peace. At least two but usually three magistrates hear a case and then give their verdict and, in criminal cases, pass sentence. They never sit with a jury. Lay magistrates are advised on the law by the clerk of the court who must be a solicitor or barrister having at least five years' experience.

Criminal jurisdiction

It could be argued that the magistrates' court is the most important of all the criminal courts since almost all criminal cases must start in this court, although some offences must be tried at the Crown Court.

Offences can be divided into three types.

1. *Summary offences.* These are offences which can only be tried in the magistrates' court. Driving offences fall mainly in this category.
2. *Hybrid offences.* These offences may be tried in the magistrates' court, if the defendant elects to be tried in that court and the magistrates agree to hear the case, or in the Crown Court. Because the defendant has a choice as to where he wishes the matter to be tried, these offences are also referred to as 'triable either way'. Theft is an example of a hybrid offence.

    The magistrates' powers of sentencing are limited to a fine of not more than £2000 or six months' imprisonment.
3. *Indictable offences.* These are the more serious offences such as murder and rape and can only be tried at the Crown Court. In such cases the magistrates must first sit as examining justices to decide whether the prosecution has an apparently reasonable or *prima facie* case against the accused. These hearings are known as committal proceedings. No defendant can normally be tried at the Crown Court until he has been committed for trial by a magistrates' court.

Civil jurisdiction

The magistrates' court has the following civil jurisdiction.

1. Domestic and matrimonial proceedings. This includes, for example, power to make maintenance orders, custody orders, and affiliation orders.
2. Application for liquor and gaming licences.
3. The enforcement of certain debts, such as local council rates arrears.

Appeals from the Magistrates' Court	1.	*Criminal.* A defendant has a right of appeal against either conviction or sentence to the Crown Court. An appeal can also be made to the Divisional Court of the Queen's Bench Division of the High Court 'by way of case stated' on point of law. The term 'case stated' means that the magistrates are required to write a statement detailing their findings based on the facts of the case.
	2.	*Civil.* The Divisional Court of the Family Division of the High Court hears appeals in domestic matters such as affiliation proceedings. Licensing and gaming appeals are heard by the Crown Court.

The Juvenile Court

Children and young persons (between the ages of 14 and under 17) are dealt with by this special court which consists of three magistrates selected from a special panel. Magistrates from both sexes must hear the case.

Proceedings in juvenile courts are closed to the public. Juvenile courts have various functions including:

1. Deciding criminal charges brought against young offenders (over the age of 10).
2. Making care orders placing children of any age who are at risk or uncontrollable into the care of the local authority.
3. Making adoption orders.

The County Court

The county court was established by the County Courts Act 1846 to deal with small civil claims. It is a local court hearing actions having some connection with the district within which each court is situated. For example, to bring an action for breach of contract the defendant must either reside or carry on business within the locality of the particular county court or the plaintiff must show that the contract was made within that area. Further, the court's jurisdiction is limited by the size of the claim. For instance, it can only hear claims in contract or tort not exceeding £5000. Claims exceeding that amount must normally proceed in the High Court.

The county court deals with a variety of work. It hears claims in contract and tort, undefended matrimonial proceedings and ancillary matters related to those proceedings, applications for adoptions, landlord and tenant disputes and applications for bankruptcy and the winding up of small companies. There is a large overlap between the types of matters which this court hears and those matters heard by the High Court, particularly the Queen's Bench Division.

In some areas the county court has sole jurisdiction. For example, it hears claims under the Sex Discrimination Act 1975, the Race Relations Act 1976 and the Consumer Credit Act 1974.

Each county court is staffed by a registrar and a judge or recorder. The registrar is the chief administrative officer of the court and also acts as a deputy judge. He must be a solicitor of at least seven years' standing. Although it is possible for a jury of eight laymen to be used, normally the judge, recorder or registrar hears cases sitting alone.

Appeals from the County Court	All appeals, except in bankruptcy matters, proceed to the Court of Appeal (civil division). Bankruptcy appeals go to the Divisional Court of the Chancery Division of the High Court.

The Small Claims Court

This court was established to help those with relatively small claims, such as consumers, conduct their own cases. All claims which are for not more than £500 must be referred to the small claims court unless there are special considerations, such as a difficult question of law to be decided. Claims over £500 may be referred to the small claims court if the parties so wish.

Disputes in the small claims court are decided by arbitration. The atmosphere is informal, the hearings being in a private room (known as chambers) and not in open court, and the rules of evidence and procedure are relaxed.

THE SUPERIOR COURTS

1. The Supreme Court of England and Wales

The superior courts are not limited, as the inferior courts are, by locality and jurisdiction. They are not local courts. Although a superior court may sit in various places it is the same court. Thus the Central Criminal Court (the Old Bailey) is in London but that is only one location of the Crown Court.

The courts making up the Supreme Court of England and Wales are: The Crown Court; the High Court; the Court of Appeal.

The Crown Court

The primary business of the Crown Court is criminal. Its work can be divided into three categories.

1. Trials of defendants who have been committed to the Crown Court.
2. Sentencing defendants who have been convicted by magistrates who consider their powers of sentencing to be insufficient; and
3. Hearing appeals against conviction or sentence from the magistrates' court.

Crown Court judges are either High Court judges, circuit judges or recorders. The Crown Court is itself divided into three tiers; the more senior judges sitting in the first tier hearing the more serious cases such as murder and rape.

If the defendant pleads not guilty, a jury of 12 laymen must be empanelled. The jury determines questions of fact, such as whether the defendant is guilty or not guilty. The judge decides questions of law. Although a unanimous verdict is desirable, if the judge consents a majority verdict of 10 to 2 is acceptable.

If the defendant pleads guilty or is found guilty or is committed for sentence to the Crown Court, the judge determines sentence.

When hearing an appeal from the magistrates' court the judge together with up to four magistrates who have not heard the case before will decide whether to uphold, vary or quash the original conviction or sentence.

Appeals from the Crown Court	Appeals against conviction or sentence can be made to the Court of Appeal (criminal division) or on a point of law to the Queen's Bench Division of the High Court.

The High Court

The High Court is composed of three equal but separate divisions: (a) Queen's Bench Division; (b) Chancery Division and (c) Family Division. Each division is staffed by judges known as puisne judges. The court's work is not limited by considerations of quantum or locality.

The work of each division is of two types:

1. Cases being heard for the first time which are heard by a single judge.
2. Appellate and other specialised actions which are heard by a divisional court where cases are heard by at least two judges.

(a) The Queen's Bench Division

This is the largest division and is headed by the Lord Chief Justice. Its original jurisdiction is principally concerned with claims based on contract or tort. Usually a case is heard by a judge sitting alone but sometimes a jury is used, for example, in actions based on defamation, false imprisonment or fraud.

Two special courts sit within the Queen's Bench Division; the **Admiralty Court** dealing with salvage claims and the **Commercial Court** deciding commercial disputes.

Divisional Court The Divisional Court of the Queen's Bench Division handles the only criminal cases heard by the High Court; hearing appeals 'by way of case stated' from either the magistrates' court or the Crown Court. In addition, this court exercises supervisory control over inferior courts and tribunals by means of judicial review determining whether there has been a breach of the rules of natural justice or if a body has acted *ultra vires* (outside its powers). If so, the court has the power to grant one of the **prerogative orders;** *certiorari, prohibition* or *mandamus.* The court may also be asked to give its opinion on the legality of a particular course of action by making a declaratory judgment. Finally, this court can order the release of someone unlawfully detained by issuing the **prerogative writ** of *habeas corpus.*

(b) The Chancery Division

The official head of the Chancery Division is the Lord Chancellor but it is the Vice-Chancellor who conducts the affairs of this court. This division is the vestige of the Court of Chancery in which the rules of equity were created and its jurisdiction reflects that heritage. It is concerned with matters of trusts, mortgages, partnership and company law, bankruptcy and liquidation, contentious probate and orders for specific performance of contracts. When the court is asked to make an order as to the administration of a mentally disordered person's property it is known as the *Court of Protection.* It is the *Patents Court* when hearing patent actions.

	Divisional Court The Chancery Division's divisional court hears appeals from the county court on bankruptcy matters as well as appeals from the Commissioners of Inland Revenue.
(c) The Family Division	The head of this division is known as the President. The division has jurisdiction over matrimonial causes including defended divorce petitions, wardship applications and adoptions.

Divisional Court   This court hears appeals from the magistrates' court. |

The Court of Appeal

The Court of Appeal	The Court of Appeal, as its name indicates, deals only with appeals. It has two divisions; civil and criminal. Both divisions are staffed by Lords Justices of Appeal. Usually three Lords Justices hear a case.
The civil division	This is headed by the Master of the Rolls. It hears appeals from the county court and the High Court. It also hears appeals from the Restrictive Practices Court, the Employment Appeal Tribunal and the Lands Tribunal.
The criminal division	The head of the criminal division is the Lord Chief Justice. This division hears appeals from the Crown Court against conviction or sentence.
2. The House of Lords (Appellate Committee of the House of Lords)	This is the final court of appeal in the United Kingdom headed by the Lord Chancellor. It hears civil appeals from the Court of Appeal and from the High Court by means of the 'leapfrog' procedure created by the Administration of Justice Act 1969 which enables the Court of Appeal to be bypassed. It hears criminal appeals from the court of Appeal and from the Divisional Court of the Queen's Bench Division. The court is staffed by Lords of Appeal in Ordinary.
OTHER COURTS	In addition to the inferior and superior courts, there are other judicial bodies which are part of, but not directly linked into, the court structure. These courts include the following:

1. *Judicial Committee of the Privy Council.* This court is composed of Privy Councillors who hold or have held senior judicial positions such as Lords of Appeal in Ordinary. This Committee acts as the final court of appeal for some Commonwealth countries as well as determining questions of law referred to it by the Crown.
2. *Special courts having High Court status.* The Restrictive Practices' Court which decides actions concerning restrictive trade agreements and the Employment Appeal Tribunal which hears appeals from industrial tribunals.
3. *Coroner's Court.* The main work of this court is in the conduct of inquests to determine the cause of death. Usually the coroner sits alone but sometimes he may be assisted by a jury of seven to eleven laymen. This court also decides cases concerning treasure trove.

4. *Military Courts.* Courts Martial hear cases alleging breaches of military regulations. Appeals are heard by the Court Martial Appeals Court and then the House of Lords.

5. *Ecclesiastical Courts.* These courts decide Church disputes. Appeals lie to either the Provincial Court of Canterbury or York and then to the Judicial Committee of the Privy Council.

B. TRIBUNALS

One consequence of the increase in the amount of social legislation in Great Britain, such as the Social Security Acts, has been the need for methods to be devised to settle disputes regarding the application of such legislation. Numerous administrative tribunals have been established to satisfy this need. Their advantages are as follows:

1. *Cases are heard quickly and with less emphasis on procedure* than in the ordinary courts. This is essential, as disputes regarding the payment of benefits, for example, must be settled as soon as possible in order to avoid additional distress to the applicant. Further, tribunals were designed to enable the layman to bring his own claim *without* the assistance of a lawyer.

2. *The jurisdiction of each type of tribunal is well defined*; for example, an industrial tribunal hears only cases involving employment law. The lay members of the tribunal are selected because of their special knowledge of the area over which the tribunal has jurisdiction. In addition, many of the cases coming before a tribunal have more than just legal aspects making them inappropriate as matters to be decided by the ordinary courts.

3. *Tribunals are cheap and take pressure of work off the ordinary courts.*

Administrative tribunals are usually composed of a legally qualified chairman and two laymen. Some tribunals, such as the Lands Tribunal which hears appeals on rating valuations and compensation for compulsory purchase, are concerned with matters relating to the activities of national or local government departments. Other tribunals, such as the Rent Tribunal, are involved in settling disputes between individuals.

Certain controls are used to ensure that administrative tribunals act fairly. These include:

1. *Council on Tribunals* – created by the Tribunals and Inquiries Act 1958 (now 1971). It has, as its brief, to keep under review the procedural rules used in tribunals. It also makes recommendations as to the membership of certain tribunals and prepares an annual report which the Lord Chancellor must lay before Parliament.

2. *If requested, a tribunal must provide a written statement of the reasons for its decision.*

3. *The Queen's Bench Division Divisional Court exercises supervisory control by means of judicial review* to ensure that no tribunal acts outside its powers or in breach of the rules of natural justice.

In addition to administrative tribunals, there are also domestic tribunals. These bodies are used by professional organisations to decide complaints against members of that profession. An example of a domestic tribunal is the Solicitors' Disciplinary Tribunal.

C. PUBLIC INQUIRIES

To the layman's eye public inquiries are a close relative of tribunals because they, like tribunals, hear evidence on an issue in dispute, such as the site of a new airport or whether planning permission should be given. However, unlike tribunals, the recommendations which are made by the chairman of an inquiry do not have to be accepted by the minister.

Public inquiries are normally conducted by a civil servant appointed by the minister concerned. The procedure used at inquiries is kept under review by the Council on Tribunals.

D. ARBITRATION

Commercial and building contracts frequently contain clauses requiring the parties to settle any dispute by arbitration. The arbitrator's decision is binding upon the parties.

Arbitration has certain advantages, particularly for the businessman.

1. *The matter is heard in private.* This allows for disputes to be aired without becoming public knowledge which could be injurious to business interests.
2. *The time and place of the hearing is arranged to suit the parties.*
3. *The arbitrator is appointed by the parties and he will normally have some special expertise* relevant to the matter in dispute. For example, an architect or a surveyor would be selected to hear a building dispute.
4. *Hearings are less formal and usually less expensive* than litigation conducted through the courts.

Because of the above, it is more likely that the parties will be able to remain on good terms following the dispute than would be the case if the matter proceeded through the ordinary legal processes.

Arbitration is also used to solve industrial disputes through the Advisory Conciliation and Arbitration Service (ACAS).

E. LEGAL PERSONNEL

The judiciary

The body of judges who preside over the English courts is known as the judiciary. Most judges are appointed from the ranks of barristers, usually Queen's Counsel, although it is possible for a solicitor to become a circuit judge.

Judges are expected to be neutral and impartial. In order to achieve this, government control and interference with their work must be kept to a minimum. This is achieved in the following ways.

1. Judges are not criticised in Parliament for anything done in their judicial capacity.
2. Their salaries are charged on the Consolidated Fund which is not debated in Parliament.

3. A High Court judge or above can only be removed by a petition to the Crown presented by both Houses of Parliament.
4. Judges have immunity for acts done within their jurisdiction.

The various judicial offices are described in 'Useful Applied Materials' (p. 32).

Magistrates and jurors

Laymen participate in the legal process in various ways; as magistrates, jurors, members of tribunals, coroners and arbitrators. Magistrates and jurors represent probably the most obvious public involvement.

Lay magistrates hear cases in the magistrates' court. They are appointed by the Lord Chancellor on the advice of local select committees and are unpaid. To be appointed as a magistrate the applicant must live within 15 miles of the area in which he would act as a magistrate. Although not legally trained, once appointed they are given basic training in the law. The Lord Chancellor can remove a magistrate. They must retire at 70.

Juries are used in both civil and criminal trials but they are most commonly found in trials in the Crown Court. To be selected for jury service a person must be on the electoral register, be aged between 18–65 and be resident in the United Kingdom for at least five years. Selection for jury service is by random ballot. Certain persons such as practising lawyers and police officers cannot act as jurors and certain convicted criminals are disqualified from serving. Others, such as doctors, may be excused jury service. If, however, a person summoned for jury service refuses to serve and has not been excused, he is liable to be punished for contempt of court.

The legal profession

One of the unique features of the English legal system is that it is divided into two 'branches'; solicitors and barristers.

Solicitors

Solicitors are sometimes referred to as the general practitioners of the legal profession although in larger firms they frequently specialise. After passing the Law Society's examinations and doing articles (a form of apprenticeship) under the supervision of a qualified member of the profession, application can be made for the trainee solicitor's name to be entered onto the Rolls of Solicitors. He can also apply for a practising certificate allowing him to act for clients. Solicitors are employed in industry and in local government to name only two areas. However, they are most commonly found practising as sole practitioners or in partnership with other solicitors.

Their work includes advising and acting for clients on contentious and non-contentious matters. They are allowed to represent their clients in open court in magistrates' courts and in county courts and to a limited extent in the Crown Court.

Unlike barristers, solicitors are in a contractual relationship with their clients and can be sued for breach of contract. They are also in a fiduciary relationship with their clients whereby they are obliged to act in their client's best interests. It is a relationshp of trust.

The controlling body of the profession is the Law Society.
Disciplinary matters are heard by the Solicitors' Disciplinary Tribunal.

Barristers

Every barrister must be a member of one of the Inns of Court; Lincoln's Inn, Gray's Inn, Middle Temple and Inner Temple. After passing the professional examinations, the student will be 'called to the Bar'. If he wishes to practise as a barrister he must then find a place in chambers and complete one year's practical training as a pupil under a practising barrister. After that year, known as pupillage, he may then practise independently.

Chambers are a set of rooms occupied by a number of barristers and administered by their clerk. The barristers are not in partnership but share the chambers' expenses.

The chief occupation of barristers is advocacy and they have rights of audience in all courts. Thus, if a client wishes to be represented in the High Court a barrister must be instructed. Only a solicitor can instruct a barrister; the barrister does not have any direct relationship with the client and thus cannot be sued in contract. Their liability in negligence is also limited; they cannot be sued for the negligent conduct of a case in court.

In addition to their work as advocates, barristers also give advice on legal questions known as opinions and draft pleadings.

The controlling body for the profession is the Senate of the Inns of Court and the Bar, although each Inn is in charge of its own members. The Professional Conduct Committee hears complaints against barristers. The Bar Council acts as a public relations body for the profession.

Should there by a united profession?

It has been argued that it is not in the public's interest for the profession to remain divided. The reasons given to support *unification* include the following:

1. In many cases a barrister as well as a solicitor must be instructed, thus doubling the cost. If a Queen's Counsel is instructed the costs will increase since he will usually be accompanied by a junior barrister;
2. Frequently, instructing both a solicitor and a barrister means that the work is duplicated;
3. Because a barrister may not be instructed until just before the hearing the quality of work may suffer.

Arguments to retain a *divided* profession include:

1. The high level of advocacy is maintained by retaining a group of specialist advocates;
2. A barrister can be instructed by any solicitor on behalf of any client. If the profession was unified, barristers might be tempted to join the larger city firms and thus could only be used by those firms' clients.

It has been suggested that the problems of a divided profession could be corrected by allowing solicitors full rights of audience in all courts or by making it a requirement that all lawyers first qualify as solicitors and, after practising as such, those that wished could take a further set of examinations to qualify as barristers. These suggestions will, however, probably not be taken up for some time and for the foreseeable future the profession will remain divided.

USEFUL APPLIED MATERIALS

This section contains a glossary of terms which a student may find useful.

PARTIES TO A CIVIL ACTION

Plaintiff: The party who commences proceedings.
Defendant: The party against whom the plaintiff brings proceedings.
Applicant: The party who commences an originating application, such as for an injunction.
Respondent: The party against whom an originating application is brought.
Appellant: The party who appeals against a decision.
Respondent: The party against whom the appeal is brought.

PARTIES TO A CRIMINAL ACTION

Prosecution: The party who commences the action, usually the state via the police.
Accused/Defendant: The person who is charged or summoned to appear because of an alleged criminal offence.
    The parties to a criminal appeal are known by the same terms as used in civil matters; appellant and respondent.

LEGAL OFFICERS

Lord Chancellor: The head of the English legal system. As well as being the head of the House of Lords, the Judicial Committee of the Privy Council and the titular head of the Chancery Division of the High Court, he is also in charge of court administration and appoints and removes magistrates and advises the Prime Minister on other judicial appointments. He is a member of the Cabinet.
Lord Chief Justice: This judicial officer is the head of the Queen's Bench Division and the Court of Appeal (criminal division).
Master of the Rolls: The head of the Court of Appeal (civil division). He also has supervisory control over solicitors including keeping the Rolls of Solicitors.
Attorney-General: He is the head of the English bar and has the job of advising the Government on points of law. He appears on behalf of the Crown in important civil and criminal actions. He also decides whether certain prosecutions, such as under the Official Secrets Act, can be brought. He supervises the work of the Director of Public Prosecutions.
Solicitor-General: This barrister is the Attorney-General's deputy and has similar duties.
Director of Public Prosecutions: The DPP works under the Attorney-General. His chief functions are in the area of criminal law

including commencing prosecutions for serious offences, consenting to prosecutions being brought for certain offences, and advising whether a prosecution should be continued. He represents the Crown in criminal appeals made to the Court of Appeal or the House of Lords.

Official Solicitor: This post is occupied by a solicitor who is appointed by the Lord Chancellor. His duties include representing the interests of minors and mental patients.

JUDICIAL APPOINTMENTS

Recorders: Either a solicitor or barrister of 10 years' standing can be appointed to this part-time judicial office. Appointment is by the Queen on the advice of the Lord Chancellor.

Circuit Judges: Appointed from the ranks of barristers of 10 years' standing or those who have been recorders for five years by the Queen on the advice of the Lord Chancellor.

Puisne Judges: Barristers of 10 years' standing who are appointed to this judicial office by the Queen on the advice of the Lord Chancellor.

Lords Justices of Appeal: Barristers of at least 15 years' standing or puisne judges can be appointed by the Queen on the advice of the Prime Minister.

Lords of Appeal in Ordinary: Appointed from barristers of 15 years' standing or senior members of the judiciary. Appointed by the Queen on the advice of the Prime Minister. These judges are known as the Law Lords.

RECENT EXAMINATION QUESTIONS

It may be helpful if you spend around ten minutes planning an answer to each question before turning to the outline answers.

Question 1.

(a) Outline the criminal jurisdiction of the magistrates' courts.
(b) State **three** advantages of tribunals as a means of settling disputes, and give an example of a tribunal.
(c) What are the prerogative orders? What purpose do they serve?
(DPA 1981/83)

Question 2.

(a) Which court or tribunal would hear the following cases:
  (i) a prosecution for breach of the Factories Act;
  (ii) a claim for breach of contract to supply goods to the value of £5000
  (iii) an action for unfair dismissal;
  (iv) an action to re-possess goods following the breach of a hire-purchase agreement?

State in each instance the court to which an appeal might lie.

(b) In what circumstances might a commercial dispute be more appropriately settled by arbitration rather than a court action?
(ICMA Specimen Question)

Question 3.

Compare (a) the work and (b) the training of barristers and solicitors.
(ILE 1983)

Question 4.	Explain and assess the contribution made by lay people to the administration of justice.
	(ILE 1983)

OUTLINE ANSWERS   The following are outline answers to questions 1, 2 and 3. A full answer is presented to question 4 in 'A Tutor's Answer' (p.35).

Answer 1.

(a) The criminal jurisdiction of the magistrates' court includes:
   (i)   committal proceedings – the magistrates determine if there is a case for the defendant to answer in the Crown Court.
   (ii) trials – summary offences which must be heard in this court and those offences where the defendant elects trial in the magistrates' court. In such cases the magistrates decide the verdict and sentence.

A special panel of magistrates sits in the juvenile court hearing cases brought against children (10–14) and young persons (14–17). All defendants aged 17 or over are tried in the adult court.

(b) Three advantages of tribunals as a means of settling disputes:
   (i)   their speed in hearing cases;
   (ii) informality – making it easier for the layman to represent himself;
   (iii) their use of layman as 'judges' with specialised knowledge in the area in which the tribunal deals.
An example of a tribunal – Lands Tribunal

(c) Prerogative orders (certiorari, prohibition and mandamus) are orders obtainable from the Divisional Court of the Queen's Bench Division. The court grants these orders, as appropriate, in exercising its supervisory control over inferior courts, tribunals and other such bodies which have acted outside their powers and/or in breach of the rules of natural justice.

Answer 2.

(a) (i)   Magistrates' court – appeal to either the Crown Court or the Divisional Court of the Queen's Bench Division;
   (ii) County court or High Court (Queen's Bench Division) – appeal to the Court of Appeal (civil division);
   (iii) Industrial Tribunal – appeal to the Employment Appeal Tribunal;
   (iv) County court – appeal to the Court of Appeal (civil division)

(b) Circumstances where a commercial dispute would be more appropriately settled by arbitration include:
   (i)   the parties want the dispute settled in private and quickly;
   (ii) the parties want the dispute settled by someone who has special knowledge of the area of the dispute;
   (iii) the parties wish to continue to have commercial dealings with each other after the dispute is finished.

A commercial contract, for the above reasons, may contain a term requiring a dispute to be settled by arbitration.

Answer 3.

(a) Solicitors specialise in advising and doing paperwork in all general areas of law, e.g. conveyancing, probate, company and commercial problems, matrimonial and criminal and civil litigation. They have contractual arrangements with their clients.

Barristers are primarily advocates and have rights of audience in all courts. They also give opinions on legal problems when asked to advise by solicitors. Barristers can only act when instructed by a solicitor.

(b) Solicitors – professional examination followed by two years of articles.

Barristers – professional examination followed by one year of pupillage.

A TUTOR'S ANSWER

Answer 4.

Lay people take an active part in the administration of justice in various capacities. As lay magistrates, otherwise known as justices of the peace, they issue warrants for the arrest of persons wanted by the police and search warrants for the searching of premises. They sit in the magistrates' courts hearing both criminal and civil cases. Their principal work is in dealing with criminal cases either as examining magistrates to determine whether a matter should be committed to trial at the Crown Court, or hearing prosecutions and deciding the guilt or innocence of the accused and, if guilty, pronouncing sentence. They also hear appeals with a judge in the Crown Court.

Lay people are also called upon to act as jurors in both civil and criminal hearings, although they are more commonly used in trials in the Crown Court. They determine questions of fact while the judge decides questions of law.

Outside the main court structure lay people participate in administrative tribunals. The usual composition of an administrative tribunal is a legally qualified chairman hearing cases together with two laymen. Laymen also hear cases in the Restrictive Practices Court and the Employment Appeal Tribunal together with lawyers.

Laymen, usually doctors, are also appointed as coroners giving decisions as to causes of death and the ownership of treasure trove.

Outside the judicial system, but still deciding legal issues, laymen are frequently used as arbitrators in commercial cases.

There are certain underlying reasons why laymen are used in all of the above. They bring specialised knowledge and skills which are not often found in lawyers, they are inexpensive to use as they usually volunteer their services, and they allow for public participation in the legal processes. Because of their contribution much pressure of work is taken off the higher courts. The legal system, to function effectively, therefore must assume the presence of laymen.

A STEP FURTHER

BASIC READING

There are a number of textbooks available which describe the administration of the English legal system. A student could look at:

Introduction to English Law (10th edn) Philip S. James, Butterworth, 1979.

A First Book of English Law (7th edn) O. Hood Phillips, Sweet & Maxwell, 1977.

Learning the Law (11th edn) Glanville Williams, Stevens, 1982.

FURTHER RESEARCH

The best way to learn about a legal system is to watch it in action. Courts and tribunals are open to the public and a student is well advised to go to court to watch cases being tried. Newspaper reports of legal proceedings are also a means to learn more about how disputes are settled. A student might also want to obtain copies of business agreements containing arbitration clauses. It may also be possible for a student to spend some time in a solicitor's office or in a barrister's chambers.

USEFUL ADDRESSES

Law Society, 113 Chancery Lane, London, WC2.

(a) Senate of the Inns of Court; (b) Bar Council, both at – 11 South Square, London, WC1.

The Institute of Legal Executives, Kempston Manor, Kempston, Bedford, MK42 7AB.

Chapter 5

Formation of Contract

Contract is the foundation of all commercial transactions. There are many rules governing individual types of business dealing, some of which are dealt with in this book, but all the specific rules are merely additional to the basic rules of the law of contract.

GETTING STARTED	Contract is essentially a common law area of law. Although there are statutes it is predominantly based on custom and practice upheld in court. There is no statutory definition of contract. Textbook writers have offered a range of permutations. Here is a very simple definition: **a contract is an agreement intended to be legally binding and supported by consideration.** A contract is a bargain, a tit-for-tat deal from which both parties expect to benefit. The business world is built on the ability to make an agreement and to know that it will be carried out or that some remedy will be obtained instead. It is essential to distinguish those agreements which *are* contracts and legally enforceable from those which are not. There are therefore legal rules on when and how a contract is made. Each part of the definition will be examined below in 'Essential Principles'. Some definitions may help before looking at the rules in detail.
A valid contract	This is an agreement which the law will recognise and enforce.
A void contract	This is a contract which has no legal effect. A contract may be void for a number of reasons; it may lack certain essential form, it may be contrary to public policy or it may be no true agreement and void for mistake. Any money or property transferred under the agreement is prima facie recoverable.

A voidable contract	This is a contract, valid when made, but because of some defect, usually fraud on the part of one of the parties, is liable to be set aside by the innocent party if he wishes. Unless and until the contract *is* avoided it is a valid contract and property passing under it may not be recovered from a bona fide purchaser (a purchaser taking in good faith).
An unenforceable contract	This is a contract which fails to comply with some special rules as to the form in which it ought to be made, or one where the right of action has lapsed because of the rules on limitation of actions. Such a contract is perfectly legal; if the parties choose to carry out their obligations they will be bound by them, if they do not, the court will not enforce the contract.
A simple contract	This is an agreement not under seal. It may be in writing, or oral.
A contract under seal or a specialty contract	This is a contract signed sealed and delivered as a deed. It takes its strength from the form in which it is made. No consideration is needed. The limitation period is 12 years compared to the normal six.

ESSENTIAL PRINCIPLES

All contracts are agreements but not all agreements are contracts. A contract requires, in addition to agreement, intention to create legal relations and consideration.

AGREEMENT

This sounds deceptively simple, in practice it is not so easy. The agreement the law requires is not subjective agreement, i.e. a meeting of minds, but *objective* agreement evidenced by behaviour, i.e. would a reasonable person believe an agreement had been reached?

The two elements required are:

(a) offer; and
(b) acceptance.

Offer

The following rules should be learnt:

1. *An offer must be clear and certain*, it may be made orally or in writing or by conduct.
2. *An offer must be communicated before it can be accepted.*
3. *An offer may be made to one person, to a group*, or *to the world at large.* (*Carlill* v. *Carbolic Smoke Ball Co.* (1) 1893.)
    Where an offer is made to an individual, or to a group, only that individual or a member of the group may accept the offer. (*Boulton* v. *Jones* (2) 1857.)
4. *An offer must be distinguished from an invitation to treat.* This rule often causes confusion. What shopkeepers may call a 'special offer' may in legal terms be merely an invitation to treat; i.e. an invitation to make offers. Goods on display on supermarket shelves and goods in a shop window have been held to be invitations to treat (*Fisher* v. *Bell* (3) 1961). Whatever the publicity

material may say, the seller is inviting offers from the public rather than committing himself to anyone and everyone who accepts. This distinction is especially important where long negotiations may be going on. It is the final terms of the offer which will be the subject of the contract. An offer may be compared to a head on the chopping block waiting for the axe to fall – when accepted it becomes binding – no further reservations are permitted.

5. *An offer may be revoked at any time before acceptance.* Unless and until the offer is accepted there is no binding contract. Where one party wishes to keep an offer open, perhaps where he wishes to have time to think about it, he may buy an option i.e. pay for the right to have the offer kept open for an agreed period. Without payment, or consideration of some kind, an informal agreement to keep an offer open is not binding.

6. *Revocation becomes effective when it is received*, either direct from the offeror or via a third party, *Dickinson* v. *Dodds* (4) 1876. This can lead to odd results in which it is very difficult to find any mutual agreement, but where the law nevertheless sees a contract e.g. in *Byrne* v. *Van Tienhoven* (5) 1880 the offer was revoked in England before the offer reached New York, nevertheless the acceptance completed the contract before the revocation was received. There was no moment when the parties were actually subjectively agreed.

7. *An offer will lapse by;*
   (a) *Death of either party*;
   (b) *Lapse of time*, either the agreed time or a reasonable time;
   (c) *Rejection*, including a counter-offer, (*Hyde* v. *Wrench* (6) 1840.)

Acceptance

To be effective the acceptance must be unconditional and correspond exactly to the terms of the offer.

Acceptance subject to a condition is not clear acceptance of the offer and in fact operates as a counter-offer revoking the original offer. A offers B his car for £500. B accepts *if* the car passes its MOT test. This is *not* unconditional acceptance and there is therefore no completed contract. Be careful to distinguish a request for further information from a counter-offer (*Hyde* v. *Wrench* (6) 1840). A request does not revoke the original offer, e.g. if B had asked 'does the car have a current MOT certificate?'

The terms of the offer may relate simply to the time within which the acceptance should be made or may extend to the time or manner of acceptance. Any deviation from the terms of the offer vitiates the effect of the acceptance. You may find it easy to think of offer and acceptance as pieces of a jigsaw, they must fit together exactly. **As a general rule acceptance must be communicated**, however, there are some exceptions which examiners often ask for:

1. *Where acceptance by conduct is expected*, e.g. offers to the world at large as in *Carlill* v. *Carbolic Smoke Ball Co* (1) 1893. Where

goods are ordered from a supplier by letter, it is frequently expected that there will be no formal acknowledgement of the order, it is sufficient merely to send the goods.

2. *Where acceptance is by post acceptance takes effect as soon as the letter is posted* (*Byrne* v. *Van Tienhoven* (5) 1880). This is so, even if it never arrives. The sender will have to prove that the letter was sent to the right address and with the correct postage. For this reason businessmen will frequently require acceptance to be *received* in writing before it is binding. This rule applies only to posting; in the case of acceptance by telephone, or telex, acceptance is only effective when it is received (*Entores* v. *Miles Far East Corporation* (7) 1955). *N.B.* **Silence will not normally amount to acceptance**, i.e. an offeror cannot say, 'if I hear no more from you I will take that as acceptance'. This was the rule laid down in the old case of *Felthouse* v. *Bindley* (8) 1863, and now reproduced in the Unsolicited Goods and Services Act 1971.

INTENTION TO CREATE LEGAL RELATIONS

There are many occasions where agreements are made, and intended to be kept, but where the parties do not intend the agreement to be legally binding. Whether there is such an intention is a question of fact. Unless the court can infer such an intention there will be no contract. The following presumptions apply:

1. *In the case of domestic and social or family agreements, there is no intention to create a legally binding agreement.*
2. *In the case of business or commercial deals there is such an intention.*

N.B. These are only presumptions or starting points; they may be rebutted by evidence to the contrary. You will find several examples where the courts have found an intention to create a binding agreement in apparently social situations, (e.g. *Simpkins* v. *Pays* (9) 1955 (winnings in a newspaper competition held divisible among three members of a household)), and even in commercial cases a clear statement that the agreement is not to be legally binding will be upheld (*Jones* v. *Vernon's Pools Ltd* (10) 1938).

CONSIDERATION

Consideration is what distinguishes a bargain or contract from a gift. To make a legally enforceable agreement, English law does not generally require any special form, e.g. writing, it merely seeks to distinguish a bargain, which the parties intend should be enforceable, from a gift which is voluntary and is not enforceable (unless under seal). There is no statutory definition of consideration, various judges have tried to explain and define it. The simplest way to think of it is perhaps as 'tit-for-tat' or 'quid pro quo'. Where the court cannot find this element of reciprocity it will not uphold a one-sided promise.

Consideration may be seen as the *reason* for the promise. *It may be either executory*, i.e. a promise to do something in the future, *or executed*, i.e. completed performance of the bargain. Where a promise is made after services have been rendered the consideration is past. By definition where a promise is made *after* an act has been carried out, the act was not carried out in return for the promise (*Re McArdle* (11) 1951). *Past consideration is no consideration* (unless there was a request for services before they were rendered).

The following rules apply to consideration; they are frequently asked for by examiners:

1. *Consideration must be real or sufficient* (in the sense of being recognised by law).

   There must be some genuine undertaking of an obligation in return for the other party's promise, i.e. a party must do or give something which he would not otherwise have done. Problems occur where the consideration is a promise to do something the promisor is already bound to do. In principle this is no consideration because nothing extra has been undertaken (*Stilk* v. *Myrick* (12) 1809). The courts will sometimes find, however, that even where an existing duty was owed an additional burden has been undertaken. For example in *Glasbrook Bros.* v. *Glamorgan County Council* (13) 1925, the police were held to have given more than their public duty and therefore to have earned the agreed fee. In *Ward* v. *Byham* (14) 1956, a promise by the mother of an illegitimate child to keep the child happy was held to be sufficient consideration to support a promise of maintenance by the father, even though she, as the mother, was under a statutory obligation to maintain the child.

2. *Consideration need not be adequate*, i.e. of equal value on both sides.

   Provided *something* is promised or given the court will not question its adequacy. It is up to the parties to make their own bargains. Too gross a discrepancy in value may be evidence of fraud or a mistake negating agreement, but in the absence of such evidence it is of no consequence that the relative contributions of the parties are not equal.

3. *Consideration must move from the promisee.* In line with the basic philosophy that the law enforces bargains not gifts, only a person who has given something may enforce a promise made to him. It is irrelevant that some other person may have given consideration unless he acted as the agent of the promiser.

   N.B. This rule is entirely separate from the basic rule of *privity of contract*, i.e. that only the parties to the agreement acquire rights or liabilities under it.

4. *Part payment of a debt.* Examiners frequently ask the question 'in what circumstances is part payment of a debt good consideration for discharge of the debt?' In principle under rule (1) above the answer is there is no consideration here because the debtor is only doing what he is legally obliged to do, i.e. pay the debt. In an action of debt in 1602 the court in *Pinnel's Case* (15) held that a debt was not discharged by payment of a lesser sum on the due day. Accordingly in *D & C Builders* v. *Rees* (16) 1966 the court

held an agreement to pay part of an outstanding debt was not consideration for the creditor's promise not to sue for the balance. However, there are important exceptions to this rule. For commercial convenience a creditor may prefer to offer some incentive to obtain prompt payment and this would be ineffective if he could later recover any outstanding sum. The exceptions are where the debtor makes payment of a smaller sum at the creditor's request:

(a) *Before the due date.* (see rule in *Pinnel's Case*). It is a very frequent practice of firms to offer a discount either for cash, or payment earlier than it would otherwise be due.

(b) *At a different place or in a different manner.* Payment by cheque is not regarded as different from payment in cash.

(c) *With some additional token.* This is the X factor. The court will not enquire into its value, i.e. its adequacy, it is enough that the creditor is willing to accept it.

In each of these situations the original debt has been varied and the variation is seen as the benefit to the creditor, i.e. the consideration for his releasing the debtor from the full sum. Additionally, a composition agreement among all creditors whereby each accepts a small sum, is a defence to any creditor seeking to recover his unpaid balances.

Although consideration is needed to support a promise to distinguish a bargain from a gift, do remember that where a contract is signed, sealed and delivered it is effective as a deed and there is no need for consideration. A debt could always be released in this way.

N.B. A promise unsupported by consideration cannot be sued upon. It may sometimes, however, be used as a defence to an action. This is the doctrine of **equitable estoppel** – where a promise is made by the promisor to the promisee which is intended to be acted upon and which is acted upon to the detriment of the promisee the promisor will be estopped or prevented from going back on it. *Central London Property Trust* v. *High Trees House* (17) 1947.

FORM

In principle a contract may be made in any form, orally, in writing or by conduct. However, there are certain important exceptions to this rule.

1. *Contracts which must be made under seal.* The most important of these are conveyances of land, leases for more than three years, and promises not supported by consideration.

 Partnership agreements are frequently made under seal but there is no legal obligation that they should be.

2. *Contracts which must be made in writing.* These include bills of exchange, cheques and promissory notes, contracts of marine insurance, legal assignment of debts, the transfer of copyright and shares in a company, and HP and consumer credit

agreements under the Consumer Credit Act 1974. Contracts of employment are frequently made in writing but the *legal obligation is only to give a written statement* of the terms. Contracts of apprenticeship, however, *must* be in writing.

3. *Contracts which must be evidenced in writing.* There are only two of this type: contracts of guarantee under s.4 Statute of Frauds 1677, and contracts for the sale or other disposition of land under s.40 Law of Property Act 1925.

Consequences of lack of correct form

Where a contract in group (1) or (2) above is not under seal in writing the contract is void. Where there is no written evidence for the contracts in group (3) the contract is not void but unenforceable, i.e. the obligation is still owed but the court will not enforce it.

A contract of guarantee is a contract of secondary liability where the guarantor stands behind the original debtor and becomes liable to pay only if the primary debtor defaults, e.g. a father might guarantee his son's bank overdraft. Distinguish a contract of indemnity. This is a contract of primary obligation independent of the original debt. Only contracts of guarantee must be evidenced in writing.

CAPACITY

In principle everyone has capacity to make a contract. However, there are certain groups whose capacity is restricted, by law or by physical problems. They are:

1. Infants or minors.
2. Drunkards and lunatics.
3. Companies and corporations.

Infants or minors

(defined as persons under 18)

A very young child may lack capacity to contract because he is unable to form the necessary intention. Additionally the Infants Relief Act 1874 **renders certain contracts made by a minor 'absolutely void'.** You should learn these carefully. Under s.1 the following contracts are absolutely void:

(a) Contracts for the repayment of money, lent or to be lent.
(b) Contracts for goods other than necessaries.
(c) All accounts stated, i.e. IOU's.

Even if the minor promises to repay a loan after he has reached majority, unless there is new consideration, the promise is void. A guarantee of a loan made to a minor is as void as the principal debt (*Coutts* v. *Browne-Lecky* (18) 1947). Where a minor has obtained a loan, or non-necessary goods, by fraudulently misrepresenting his age the contract is still void (*Leslie* v. *Sheill* (19) 1914) but the minor may be prosecuted under the Theft Act 1968. If the minor is still in possession of the goods, the court may order their return to the rightful owner.

Exceptionally, where money has been borrowed and spent on necessaries, the lender may recover a reasonable price. The Bills of

Exchange Act 1882 provides that an infant may never be liable on a cheque even if it is given to purchase necessaries. **At common law there are two categories of infants' contracts; valid and voidable.** The following are **valid**:

(a) Contracts for necessaries – but liability is limited to a 'reasonable' price: s.2 SGA 1979.
(b) Beneficial contracts of service.

'Necessaries' are defined in the Sale of Goods Act 1979 s.2 as goods suitable to the condition in life of the infant and to his actual requirements at the time of sale and delivery (*Nash* v. *Inman* (20) 1908).

Whether a contract of service is for the infant or minor's benefit is a question of fact. An overall look at the contract has to be taken. A single clause providing a sanction against the infant did not prevent the contract being held on the whole to be for the infant's benefit in *Doyle* v. *White City Stadium Ltd* (21) 1935.

N.B. Where the contract is a trading contract, i.e. buying and selling, even if it is beneficial to the minor, the minor will not be bound by it (*Cowern* v. *Nield* (22) 1912).

The following are **voidable**:

(a) Contracts of a continuing nature, e.g. a share in a partnership.
(b) Contracts under which a minor acquires an interest in property of a permanent kind, e.g. a lease.

These contracts may be avoided by a minor during his minority or shortly thereafter. If he fails to repudiate them they become binding on his reaching majority. Until avoided they are valid and money paid under them cannot be recovered unless there was a total failure of consideration (*Valentini* v. *Canali* (23) 1889).

Drunkards and lunatics

A person who is drunk, or insane, by definition lacks the necessary contractual intent. His contracts are voidable but he is liable to pay a reasonable price for necessaries sold and delivered under s.2 SGA 1979. The party seeking to avoid the contract must prove that at the time of making it he was incapable of understanding the transaction and that the other party knew this.

Companies and corporations

A company or corporation is not a natural person and therefore cannot make personal contracts. The limitation on their capacity stems from the charter or statute which created them, or the memorandum of association under which they were incorporated. These different documents will have established the purposes for which the corporation was formed. Its powers are limited to carrying out those purposes. Any contract made in excess of those powers is ultra vires and void, (*Re Jon Beauforte* (24) 1953).

USEFUL APPLIED MATERIALS

The rules on contract are almost all based on mercantile custom and practice. Over the years the judges have pronounced on issues coming before them, so the authorities are the decided cases. Many of them are old cases because, of course, once a case has been decided there is no further need to argue the point. Some of the more important cases are outlined in this section; there are many other cases which could be used as illustrations. Other suggestions will be given in the section 'A Step Further' (see p. 52). A student should remember that whenever he states a rule of law an authority should be given for it. The section on examination technique gives you further help in how to use cases.

1

Carlill v. *Carbolic Smoke Ball Co* 1893
An offer may be made to the world at large.

The Carbolic Smoke Ball Company advertised that it would give £100 to anyone who caught influenza after buying and using their smokeballs as directed. Mrs C bought a smokeball, used it as directed and caught influenza. She claimed £100 from the company. The company claimed there was no contract because no offer had been made to Mrs C, and even if there had, she had not accepted it. The House of Lords held that an offer to the world had been made and Mrs C had accepted by conduct, which was impliedly what the offer required her to do.

2

Boulton v. *Jones* 1857
An offer made to one person may not be accepted by another.

J sent an order to X, the previous owner of B's business. B executed the order and sent goods to J even though the order had not been addressed to him. The court held there was no contract, B could not accept an order not meant for him.

3

Fisher v. *Bell* 1961
Goods in a shop-window are not an offer for sale.

The display of goods in a shop-window was held not to be an offer for sale but merely an invitation to treat. Therefore a criminal prosecution alleging an offer for sale of an offensive weapon failed.

4

Dickinson v. *Dodds* 1876
Revocation of an offer may be communicated by a third party as well as the offeror.

In this case a house had been offered for sale, before accepting the offer the prospective purchaser was told by a third party that the house had been sold to someone else. The court held the revocation effective and there was therefore no contract.

5

Byrne v. *Van Tienhoven* 1880
Revocation is not effective until it is received. Acceptance by post takes effect as soon as it is posted.

In this case V offered goods for sale to B, by letter. V was in

Cardiff and B was in New York. Before the letter reached New York, V wrote again cancelling the original order. However, on receipt of the original letter, B had telegraphed acceptance. The court held there was a valid contract on the terms of the original letter, the revocation was not effective until it was received, at that time the acceptance was already complete.

6

Hyde v. *Wrench* 1840
A counter-offer revokes the original offer.
    W offered to sell a farm to H for £1000. H offered £950 in reply. W declined; H then agreed to pay £1000. W refused to sell. The court would not enforce the sale holding there was no contract because the effect of the counter-offer was to end the original offer.

7

Entores v. *Miles Far East Corporation* 1955
Acceptance by telex takes effect where and when it is received, unlike acceptance by post, which is effective on posting.

8

Felthouse v. *Bindley* 1863
An offeror cannot make silence on the part of the offeree amount to acceptance.
    F wrote to X offering to buy a horse saying if he heard nothing he would consider the horse his. The court held there was no contract because silence cannot be made acceptance.

9

Simpkins v. *Pays* 1955
The general rule that domestic or social agreements are not binding may be rebutted by evidence of contrary intention.
    Three parties regularly entered a weekly fashion competition. One week the combination won. The court found an intention that any winnings should be shared.

10

Jones v. *Vernon's Pools Ltd* 1938
Here an agreement involving money, which looked like a commercial deal, was held not legally binding because the agreement clearly stated it was to be binding in honour only. There was therefore no intention to be legally bound.

11

Re McArdle 1951
Past consideration is no consideration.
    A promise to pay for work done on decorating a house after it had been carried out was held unenforceable for lack of consideration.

12

Stilk v. *Myrick* 1809
A promise to do what the promisor is already legally bound to do is not good consideration.
    The captain of a ship offered the crew extra wages to sail the ship home after there was some dissension. The court found there was no consideration, the men were already legally bound to sail the ship home.

13

Glasbrook Bros. v. *Glamorgan County Council* 1925
A promise to do *more* than the promisor was already legally bound to do is good consideration.

G B asked the local police force for protection during a strike which was provided. The C C claimed for the cost of providing for such protection. G B refused to pay saying the police were already bound to give protection and had therefore given no consideration for their claim. The court found that the police had done *more* than they were legally obliged to do and the payment was due.

14

Ward v. *Byham* 1956
Consideration may consist of very little provided it is something extra over and above the promisee's existing obligations.

In this case the promise of an unmarried mother to keep her illegitimate child happy was held to be sufficient to support the father's promise to pay £1 per week in return.

15

Pinnel's Case 1602
A straightforward action of debt in which it was laid down that payment of lesser sum than the sum due, on the day appointed, is no satisfaction for the whole debt.

16

D & C Builders Ltd v. *Rees* 1966
Payment of a smaller sum does not discharge a debt.

D & C were allowed to recover the balance of a debt due from R, even though they had earlier accepted a smaller sum in final settlement under pressure from R.

17

Central London Property Trust Ltd v. *High Trees House Ltd* 1947
Where a promise is given without consideration, it cannot be enforced but it may be available as an equitable defence.

C let a block of flats to H at a fixed rent. Because of wartime conditions, few flats were relet. The parties entered into a second agreement under which C agreed to accept a lower rent from H for the duration of the war. After the war C tried to recover the shortfall in the rent. The House of Lords held that their promise could be set up as a defence and the shortfall in the rent for the period of the war was held not recoverable.

18

Coutts v. *Browne-Lecky* 1947
A guarantee is a contract of secondary liability.

A guarantee of a loan to an infant was held void on the ground that a contract of guarantee is a contract of secondary liability. Where the principal debt is void (here a loan to an infant, void under the Infants Relief Act 1874) any guarantee of such a debt is also void.

19

Leslie v. *Sheill* 1914
An infant's contract void under the Infants Relief Act 1874 may not be indirectly enforceable in tort.

An infant borrowed money after fraudulently misrepresenting his age. The court held the debt was absolutely void under the Infants Relief Act 1874. The money was held to be irrecoverable as damages in the tort of deceit.

| 20 | *Nash* v. *Inman* 1908 |

An infant is only liable to pay for goods which are necessary to his condition in life both at the time of sale and delivery.

I, an undergraduate at Trinity College, Cambridge, an infant, ordered 11 fancy waistcoats from N, a Savile Row tailor. The court found that fancy waistcoats could be necessary to I's condition in life. However, at the time of their delivery, I was already adequately supplied, therefore the goods were not necessary, and I was not liable to pay for them under the Infants Relief Act 1874.

| 21 | *Doyle* v. *White City Stadium Ltd* 1935 |

An infant is bound by a contract of education and training which is overall for his benefit.

D was an infant boxer. He claimed not to be bound by a training contract under which prize money could be withheld if he were disqualified for certain reasons. The court held his contract of service was on the whole beneficial and he was bound by it.

RECENT EXAMINATION QUESTIONS

It may be helpful if you spend around ten minutes planning an answer to each question before turning to the outline answers.

Question 1.

A contract comes into being when an offer is accepted.
Discuss:
(a) the forms that an acceptance may take;
(b) when an acceptance may be effective without actual communication to the person making the offer.   (ICMA 1983)

Question 2.

(a) Define consideration, and distinguish between past and executed consideration.
(b) Wendy owns the Sunnyside Boarding Kennels and Cattery. Advise Wendy as to her liability in contract in the following situations:
  (i) Wendy asks Jayne, a student, to help her during the summer holidays and says she will pay her £300. Jayne agrees and works all summer. Wendy fails to pay her the £300.
  (ii) Jayne offers to help Wendy during her summer holidays. At the end of the summer Wendy says she will give her £300, but she later changes her mind and fails to pay.   (DPA 1983

Question 3.

Distinguish between contracts of indemnity and contracts of guarantee and explain why the distinction is important.(ACCA 1981)

| Question 4. | (a) How may a contractual offer be terminated? |
| | (b) On 1 October Andrew wrote to Basil offering to sell goods to Basil. Later Andrew learnt he could sell his goods for a higher price. On 8 October Andrew wrote revoking his offer to sell. On 7 October Basil posted a letter accepting Andrew's offer. Andrew's letter of revocation arrived on 10 October. Basil's letter of acceptance arrived on 11 October. Discuss whether there is a valid contract. (ACCA 1982) |

| Question 5. | Advise Helen whether she has any legal remedy in the following situations:
Helen is invited for lunch in a local restaurant by her friend Mary. Helen takes a taxi to the restaurant and waits for over an hour but Mary never arrives. Helen decides to go shopping and she sees a leather handbag in a shop-window with a price tag of £15. She goes into the shop to buy the handbag and is told the correct price is £25. Later, Helen meets her cousin Sandra, aged 16. Sandra persuades Helen to lend her £10 to buy a camera; Sandra never repays Helen the money. (DPA 1981) |

OUTLINE ANSWERS

Answer 1.

What is wanted in this question is a fairly straight statement of the rules relating to acceptance. Be careful to answer the question in the way it is asked, i.e. in two parts.

(a) An acceptance must be unconditional and correspond to the terms of the offer. Subject to that it may be in any form; by words, by conduct or by writing. The normal rule is that acceptance should be communicated to the offeree and it is ineffective until it has been so communicated. Where the offer prescribes no particular form acceptance should take the form of the offer, i.e. an offer by letter should be accepted by letter, an offer by telex should be accepted by telex. Where speed is important the form of the acceptance should be the fastest possible.

(b) The normal rule is that an acceptance must be communicated unless the offer invites acceptance by conduct as in *Carlill* v. *Carbolic Smoke Ball Co* 1893.

An acceptance by post takes effect as soon as it is posted, this is so even if the letter does not arrive. *Adams* v. *Lindsell* 1818. However, the normal rule applies to acceptance by telephone or telex, *Entores Ltd* v. *Miles Far East Corporation* 1955. Silence may not be made to amount to acceptance, *Felthouse* v. *Bindley* 1862. An acceptance given to the authorised agent of the offeror is valid.

Answer 2.

Again, a straightforward looking question but not an easy one to answer. The judges have tried many times to give a simple definition of consideration. Try to keep your answer to the point, you are not asked for all you know about consideration! In a two part question like this there is very often some overlap between the two halves. A clear statement in the first part will make it much easier for you to cope well with the second part.

(a) Consideration is the tit-for-tat or quid pro quo which distinguishes a two sided bargain from a gift. It is the reason for the promise which may take the form of some benefit to the promisee or detriment to the promisor.

Past consideration is no consideration, *Re McArdle* 1951. Past consideration is some benefit or detriment received or given *before* the promise was made. Since the consideration was given in advance of the promise by definition it was not given in return for, or as the price of, the promise.

Executed consideration is good consideration. It means that one side of the bargain carries out his side immediately the contract is entered into, as opposed to promising to perform at a later date.

(b) (i) If there was an intention that this should be a legally binding agreement there was a breach of contract by W.
There was an agreement, for which both sides gave consideration.
J worked all summer, in return for W's promise to pay. J's consideration was executed, W's was executory. W should be advised she is liable to pay J £300.

   (ii) J worked voluntarily, not in return for a promise by W. J's help had already been given when W said she would pay J. J's consideration is past and therefore not good consideration. W is under no obligation to pay J.

Answer 3.

This is a point which comes up quite often in different formats, here as a simple 'compare' question, at other times, in a short compulsory question, you might be asked to 'define' the terms.

A contract of guarantee is a contract of secondary obligation in which the guarantor undertakes the same liability as the original debtor. If the original debt is void or unenforceable, so is the guarantee, *Coutts* v. *Browne-Lecky* 1947. A contract of guarantee is unenforceable unless evidenced in writing under the Statute of Frauds 1677 s.4.

A contract of indemnity is a contract of primary obligation under which the party making it undertakes to make good losses incurred by the creditor in the agreed circumstances. There is no special form required and no dependence on the original debt.

Answer 4.

In the first part a straight list is called for with application in part (b).

(a) An offer may be terminated by:
Death of either party.
Lapse of time, either what is reasonable or what is agreed.
Rejection, either outright or a counter-offer, *Hyde* v. *Wrench* 1840.
Revocation, when received by the offeree.

(b) Acceptance by post takes effect as soon as it is posted. Revocation takes effect when it is received, *Byrne* v. *Van Tienhoven* 1880. B's acceptance was posted and therefore took effect on 7 October. A's letter of revocation was not received until 10 October, at which time the contract was already binding. The revocation was ineffective, and there is a valid contract.

A TUTOR'S ANSWER

Answer 5.

I have chosen to give a fuller answer to this question to give an illustration of how to tackle a slightly longer problem question. Some examinees are put off at the sight of what may look like a long and complicated set of facts. The secret of a question like this is to read it carefully and then to break it down into parts. The more information there is in a question the easier it will be to answer it! Having split it up into parts, present it to the examiner as a series of problems identified and principles applied.

THE INVITATION TO LUNCH

H has accepted an invitation to lunch from her friend M. H has spent money on a taxi fare to reach the restaurant and has had to wait in vain for over an hour for M. Whether H has any legal remedy in this situation will depend on whether there was a legally binding contract between her and M. A contract is an agreement which is intended to be legally binding. This is a question of fact. The courts apply certain presumptions, in the case of social arrangements there is presumed to be no intention to be legally bound. The presumption may be rebutted on proof of contrary intention. On the facts of this case there is nothing to suggest that the agreement was anything more than a social date agreed between friends. In the circumstances H should be advised she has no legal remedy against M.

THE HANDBAG

A contract comes into force when there is an offer which is unconditionally accepted. Goods in a shop-window are not an offer to the public, they are an invitation to the public to come into the shop and make an offer for the goods which the shop-keeper can then either reject or accept. *Fisher* v. *Bell* 1961. On the facts the leather handbag which H saw in the shop-window with a price-tag of £15 is an invitation to treat, not an offer which she can accept. The shop-keeper is therefore under no obligation to sell it to her for £15 and is quite entitled to refuse to sell the bag for less than £25.

N.B. There may be liability under the Trade Descriptions Act 1968.

THE LOAN

H has lent money to S who at 16 is an infant. Loans to infants are held absolutely void under s.1 Infants Relief Act 1874. Where money is borrowed for necessaries the lender stands in the same position as the seller of the necessaries, i.e. he may recover the loan. There is no evidence that a camera is necessary for S. Therefore H should be advised she has no legal remedy against S to recover the money.

A STEP FURTHER

Look carefully at advertisements in the press, mail-order catalogues and advertisers' brochures. Distinguish an invitation to treat from an offer and notice what is required to constitute acceptance, and when and how it is to be made/communicated.

If you turn to the end of Chapter 7, you will find an outline of suggested reading on the topic of Contract.

Chapter 6 # Contents of a Contract

GETTING STARTED

This chapter will look at the legal rules which govern the contents of a contract. In principle it is up to the parties to draw up their own bargains.

The bulk of the rules on the content of a contract concern the terms and their interpretation. It can often be a difficult question of fact to determine what was said or meant by the parties. There are a number of rules to help. In addition there are some contracts which the law will not enforce on the grounds of policy, and others which may be avoided by the innocent party where there has been some undue pressure.

ESSENTIAL PRINCIPLES

TERMS

The actual content of the agreement, the details of what the parties have agreed to do, is contained in the *terms* of the contract. There are various kinds of terms:

1. Express terms.
2. Implied terms.
3. Conditions.
4. Warranties.
5. Exclusion or exemption clauses.

Express terms

Express terms are the terms the parties have literally spelled out, e.g. the description or specification of goods required or work ordered, the arrangements for delivery and payment etc. Express terms are always the first place to look to determine a party's contractual rights and obligations. As long as the terms are clear they may normally be expressed in any way the parties wish, in writing or orally. To be enforceable the term must be complete and unambiguous. Subject to the rules on illegality discussed later, there are very few limitations on a party's right to define his own terms. Special mention will be made below of the provisions of the Unfair Contract Terms Act 1977 in relation to the exclusion of liability in some cases.

Implied terms

Implied terms are terms which the parties by definition have not expressly mentioned but which the law nevertheless includes. Terms are implied by:

(a) *Custom*, where it is assumed that the parties wish their agreement to be on the usual terms of trade or area;
(b) *Statute*, e.g. in the sale of goods and H.P. and in contracts for the supply of goods or services;
(c) *The court*, if the court finds it necessary to make the agreement work.

While it is not the job of the court to write a contract for the parties, it may be willing to fill in some apparent gaps where the purpose of the contract is clear (*The Moorcock* (1) 1889).

As a general rule the express terms of the contract always take precedence over the implied terms, only if the contract is silent will there be room for implied terms. The parties may normally expressly exclude the terms which the law would imply. However, in some very important cases the Unfair Contract Terms Act 1977 has restricted the ability of the parties to restrict or exclude the terms implied into contracts for the sale of goods and hire purchase by the Sale of Goods Act 1979 (see Ch. 8 for more details). All terms, whether express or implied, are either conditions or warranties.

Conditions

A condition is a term which is said to go to the root of the contract. It is a requirement so fundamental that the party who inserted it would not have made the contract without it. *Breach of condition entitles the innocent party to repudiate the contract*, that is to treat the contract as at an end. The innocent party is then relieved of his obligations under the contract and is entitled to recover damages for the breach from the guilty party.

Warranties

A warranty is a less vital term which is merely collateral to the main terms of the contract. Breach of warranty entitles an innocent party to damages but does not relieve him of his obligations.

It is often difficult to tell whether a particular term is a condition or a warranty. It is obviously important because of the different remedies for breach. In the event of dispute the court has to decide as a question of fact whether a term is a condition or a warranty. This is a matter of intention to be gleaned from what the parties did or said and the apparent importance the terms had at the time the contract was made.

If you get a question in which certain terms were certainly broken, the first thing you have to do, having identified the obligation, is to categorise it. It may not always be clear, in which case you can simply say 'if this term is a condition . . .' and 'if this term is a warranty . . .', making it clear that this is a question of fact, i.e. what was the parties' intention? It is much better to raise the problem than dogmatically state that the term is e.g. a condition. Remember the crucial difference is in the remedy.

Exclusion or exemption clauses

In the course of drafting their agreements, parties quite properly seek to define their obligations. This may take the form of an explicit clause stating that they will not be liable for certain losses or that their liability will be limited in certain cases. Over the years the courts have built up a body of rules on the interpretation of such clauses, giving the benefit of the doubt, if any, to the party prejudiced by the exclusion clause. In the Unfair Contract Terms Act 1977, Parliament has taken this a step further by positively prohibiting exclusion of liability in some cases and limiting it in most others.

The effect of an exclusion clause in a particular situation is a favourite examination question. You should learn carefully the following criteria which the court will apply in construing the validity of such a clause:

1. Reasonable notice of the exemption clause must have been given (*Parker* v. *SE Ry Co* (2) 1877).
2. The notice must be given at or before the time of the making of the contract (*Olley* v. *Marlborough Court* (3) 1949).
3. A clause printed on a receipt will not be effective unless the receipt is part of the Contract e.g. a railway ticket. Mere evidence of payment is not part of the contract (*Chapelton* v. *Barry* (4) 1940).
4. Where the effect of the exclusion clause has been misrepresented by the party seeking to rely on it, it will not be binding. This is so even if the original clause was in writing and the misrepresentation was purely oral (*Curtis* v. *Chemical Cleaning & Dyeing Co* (5) 1951).
5. Where the terms have been signed the parties will be bound by them even if the terms have not been read (*L'Estrange* v. *Graucob* (6) 1934). It is possible for party to have a defence to a signed document known as the plea of 'non est factum' but this is very difficult to prove. (See below p. 59).
6. If there is any doubt as to the meaning of an exclusion clause, it will always be construed *against* the party who inserted it.
7. If the clause is clear enough, there is no rule of law which prevents an exclusion taking effect (*Suisse Atlantique Case* 1966).

In addition to the common law rules, the Unfair Contract Terms Act 1977 has restricted the use of exemption clauses **in business transactions** in a number of ways. Briefly you should remember the following points:

1. No one acting in the course of business may exclude his liability for death or bodily injury arising from negligence. Clauses

attempting to exclude liability for other loss, e.g. damage to property, will only be valid insofar as they are held to be fair and reasonable: s.2.

2. Where a business contracts on its own standard terms, or deals with a consumer whether or not on standard terms, it cannot exclude or vary its liability for breach of contract unless the exemption is fair and reasonable: s.3.

3. In a contract for the sale or supply of goods s.12 SGA 1979 may never be excluded. In a consumer sale, ss.13–15 may never be excluded and in other sales may only be excluded insofar as is fair and reasonable. (See Ch. 8). Whether such a term is 'fair and reasonable' is a question of fact, taking into account all the relevant circumstances, such as the relative bargaining power of the parties, and any inducements offered.

MISREPRESENTATION

A misrepresentation is a false statement of fact made by one party to a contract to the other, at or before the time the contract was made, which induces the other to enter into the contract. Such a statement is by definition not part of the contract – if it were, it would be either a condition or a warranty. Where an agreement has been made on what is obviously a false premise the law will sometimes grant relief. The relief obtainable depends on whether the misrepresentation was innocent or fraudulent.

This is another area favoured by examiners. The rules themselves are not difficult, but students often have difficulty in analysing the problem adequately. Look at the definition of misrepresentation and apply it stage by stage to the facts of your problem.

Elements of definition

1. *A misrepresentation is a statement of fact.* A statement of law, a statement of opinion, an advertiser's 'puff', or a statement of intention is therefore not covered.

2. *The statement must be false.* Clearly if the statement is true the contracting party has no claim for redress.

3. *The representation must be made by one party to the contract to the other.* The essence of the complaint is that one party misled the other, where the plaintiff has relied on false information from another source, he cannot blame the contracting party.

4. *The representation must have induced the other party to enter the contract.* If he did not make the contract, or did not rely on the representation, the plaintiff has no cause for complaint. Thus he cannot plead that he relied on the misrepresentation if he did not know of it, or if he knew it to be untrue.

5. *As a general rule silence does not amount to misrepresentation.*

Silence

There are the following exceptions. Silence may amount to misrepresentation where:

(a) There is a positive duty to disclose, e.g. in fiduciary relationships and contracts of insurance;

(b) Where what has been said *is* true, but it amounts to a half-truth (e.g. *Dimmock* v. *Hallett* (8) 1866 where a vendor accurately reported that certain farms were let but omitted to say that the tenants had given notice).

(c) Where the original statement was true when made but has subsequently become untrue (e.g. in *With* v. *O'Flanagan* (9) 1936, the vendor of a doctor's practice failed to disclose the fall in the receipts of the practice since the original valuation).

Remedies	Where there has been a misrepresentation, which has been acted upon, the nature of the remedy will depend on whether it was made innocently or fraudulently. *An innocent misrepresentation is one made honestly in the belief that it was true. A fraudulent misrepresentation is one 'made knowingly or without belief in its truth or recklessly, careless whether it be true or false'. (Derry* v. *Peek* (10) 1889).

Where the misrepresentation is proved to have been made *fraudulently* the plaintiff may:

1. Avoid or repudiate the contract for fraud; and
2. Claim damages in the tort of deceit, the measure of damages will be the amount of the plaintiff's loss as a result.

Where the misrepresentation is innocent the remedy will depend on whether it was made negligently or not. If it was made negligently the innocent party has the right:

1. To claim damages for the loss incurred under s.2(1) Misrepresentation Act 1967.
   N.B. Under that Act the onus of proving negligence is *not* on the plaintiff as usual, but on the defendant who must disprove negligence;
2. To rescind the contract, i.e. to end the contract and restore the parties to their pre-contract position.

Where the misrepresentation is innocent and the defendant disproves negligence, the plaintiff's primary remedy is rescission. The court has a discretion under s.2(2) Misrepresentation Act 1967 to award damages instead which is particularly useful when rescission is not available. It should be remembered, whenever rescission is sought, that it is an *equitable* remedy. It is not available as of right, and must be sought within a reasonable time (*Leaf* v. *International Galleries* (11) 1950). When it is impossible to return the parties to their pre-contract position, rescission is in any case not possible.

MISTAKE

Given that a contract is an *agreement*, there is always a problem when the parties have reached their apparent agreement by mistake.
   N.B. The agreement required is not subjective, the law looks at what the parties have done rather than what they meant – see Ch. 5. As a general rule *when there is an agreement the fact that it has been made on the basis of a mistake will not affect the validity of the contract.* It may be that the mistake is so fundamental that there is no agreement at all, but these cases are rare.
   Examiners frequently ask questions on the effect of mistake. The

most important thing is again to analyse the problem carefully and then to apply quite simple rules. There are three kinds of mistake, each of which has different consequences. Start by looking at the facts and deciding with which kind of mistake you are dealing.

Common mistake

A common mistake is a mistake common to both parties. It has nothing to do with a frequent occurrence! *Where there is a common mistake as to the existence of the subject matter, the contract will be void* (*Couturier* v. *Hastie* (12) 1856). *Where the common mistake is as to the quality of the subject matter, the mistake does not affect the contract.* The rule is 'caveat emptor', let the buyer beware. In *Bell* v. *Lever Bros* (13) 1932, the company were held unable to recover compensation payments paid out under a contract which both parties thought was binding but which in fact could have been repudiated by them.

However, when there is a valid contract at common law, made on the basis of a common mistake, equity may grant relief where it would be inequitable to allow one party to obtain the benefit of the mistake. For example, in *Solle* v. *Butcher* (14) 1950, a tenant was not allowed to take advantage of a common mistake as to the effect of the Rent Acts to remain in possession at a controlled rent, but had either to give up the tenancy or allow the landlord to apply for an increase in the statutorily allowed rent.

Mutual mistake

Mutual mistake occurs where the parties are literally at cross purposes. *Each party is mistaken without the knowledge of the other.* Neither knows what the other is thinking and neither is aware that there is a problem. The only test to be applied here is, *is there an agreement at all?* If there is an agreement which a third party could clearly identify, the fact that there was a muddle will not affect the validity of the contract, e.g. in *Tamplin* v. *James* (15) 1880, where the bidder for a property thought that more land was included in the sale than was in fact the case, the vendor was held entitled to specific performance on the grounds there was a clear agreement. Where it is not possible to find any complete agreement, the contract will be held void. In this case it may be more sensible to say there was *no* agreement rather than that the agreement was void, e.g. in *Raffles* v. *Wichelhaus* (16) 1864 an agreement for the sale of a cargo of cotton on board SS Peerless in Bombay Harbour was held void when it was discovered there were two ships of the same name both in Bombay Harbour. The buyer had in mind one and the seller the other!

Unilateral mistake

This occurs where one party is mistaken to the knowledge of the other. In principle where a party knows that an agreement has been made by the other party as a result of a mistake, it is undesirable that he should be allowed to take advantage of such a mistake. In an action for enforcement equity may grant a defence. For example, in *Webster* v. *Cecil* (17) 1861, a purchaser tried to take advantage of a slip of the pen. However, where third parties are concerned, different issues are involved. In most cases of unilateral mistake there has been fraud, i.e. the mistake has been induced by one of the contracting parties. In accordance with normal principles such a contract is voidable. But, unless and until it *is* avoided, it will be valid and a third party will obtain a valid title to goods sold to him (see Ch. 8).

Identity

In exceptional circumstances it may be possible to prove there was no valid contract because there was no intention to contract on the apparent terms or with the particular party. This is difficult to prove and you should learn the criteria carefully. The effect of holding there is no valid contract is to protect the original contracting party at the expense of a subsequent innocent third party. The cases where this has occurred have almost all concerned mistaken identity. In *Phillips* v. *Brooks* (18) 1919 the original contract was held voidable rather than void. A rogue entered a jeweller's shop and gave a false name in order to obtain credit. The goods the rogue acquired were subsequently passed to an innocent third party. In deciding whether the original contract with the jeweller was void or voidable on the grounds of the mistake the court held that in order to prove a contract void for mistake of this kind a plaintiff would have to prove:

1. The identity of the contracting party is material to the contract – usually this means there is an intention to deal only with one particular person;
2. The other side knows that;
3. The other side is not that person.

This is, of course, a question of fact. It will be quite difficult in a personal transaction when the parties are present for one party to say he had no intention of dealing with the man in front of him (*Lewis* v. *Averay* (19) 1971). It may be easier where the transaction is by letter and the rogue has misrepresented himself as an established bona fide customer (*Cundy* v. *Lindsay & Co* (20) 1878).

Documents

In the case of a document, where the document does not accurately express the parties' true intention, equity may grant a *decree of rectification*. It is up to the parties to prove that there was a complete and valid agreement and that the mistake arose simply in its reduction into writing e.g. in *Craddock* v. *Hunt* (21) 1923, a conveyance accidentally included land not originally part of the contract for sale. Where a contract is signed the general rule is a party is bound by his signature. However, where there is a mistake as to the essential nature of a document, the signatory may be able to avoid it by the technical defence of *non est factum*. Literally this means 'not my deed'. As a matter of policy it is undesirable to allow people to deny the effect of their own signatures. Such a defence will only be permitted where the signatory is able to prove:

1. The document which he signed was totally different in nature from the one he thought he was signing, and
2. He was not negligent in signing.

It is extremely difficult to prove that the signatory was not negligent in signing something without knowing what it was. The defence succeeded in *Foster* v. *McKinnon* (22) 1869, where an old man of poor sight was induced to sign a bill of exchange in the belief that it was a guarantee, but not in *Saunders* v. *Anglia Building Society* (23) 1970 where an elderly widow signed a conveyance without reading it thinking it to be a gift to her nephew, when in fact it was an assignment to X.

ILLEGALITY, DURESS AND UNDUE INFLUENCE

There are some factors which affect the validity of a contract on the ground of public policy. Sometimes the effect is that the law holds the contract completely void, in other cases the contract is merely voidable.

Illegal contracts

Contracts to commit a crime, to trade with the enemy or *to defraud the revenue, are all void at common law.* As a matter of public policy, money or other property which has changed hands under such an illegal agreement is not normally recoverable (contrary to the usual rule that where an agreement is void and there has been a total failure of consideration, property is recoverable). In exceptional cases some recovery may be possible, e.g. where one party has repented of the illegal transaction before it has been carried out.

Additionally, *certain contracts are declared illegal by statute.* Such contracts are not necessarily criminal but will not be enforced by the courts, e.g. contracts of gaming and wagering. *Contracts in restraint of trade which are intended to restrict competition are prima facie void as illegal at common law*, and are also subject to the Restrictive Trade Practices Act 1976. Such agreements will only be enforced if they can be shown to be reasonable both in the interests of the parties and the public. Where the offending clause is only one part of a large whole, the court may sever the illegal clause and enforce the balance.

Such clauses are often inserted in contracts of employment and contracts for the sale of a business. In each case the test of reasonableness relates to what restrictions are necessary to protect the legitimate interests of the employer or purchaser in relation to:

1. Content of the restrictions imposed;
2. Length of time of the restrictions and
3. Area of the restraint imposed.

Duress

Duress means actual or threatened physical violence to a contracting party or his immediate family. Where a contract has been induced under such a threat the consent has clearly not been freely given. Such a contract is voidable at common law. In recent years the courts have extended the principle to purely economic pressure, as in *Universe Tankships* v. *ITF* (24) 1982, where a union refused to allow a ship to depart until her owners had made a payment into a welfare fund. The court held the agreement voidable and allowed the shipowners to recover the money paid.

Undue influence

Whereas it used to require threats of actual violence to the person to render an agreement voidable at common law, equity would grant relief by avoiding the contract where there had been no force but more than acceptable persuasion, or undue influence. If there is no special relationship between the parties, the one who alleges undue influence must prove it; where there is a fiduciary or special relationship of trust between the parties undue influence is presumed, and the defendant must rebut it. Independent advice is the surest protection. Relief in cases of undue influence is equitable and therefore subject to the normal limitations, e.g. relief must be sought within a reasonable time (*Allcard* v. *Skinner* (25) 1887).

USEFUL APPLIED MATERIALS

1

The Moorcock 1889
The court will imply terms into a contract where this is necessary
    In the case of a contract to use a wharf for unloading a ship, the court held there must be an implied term on the part of the owners of the wharf that the river bed next to the wharf would not damage ships using the wharf. The tide went out stranding a boat on the rocky bottom of the river. There was no term expressed in the contract as to the condition of the river bed. The court was prepared to imply a term that the river bed would not damage vessels using the wharf in order to give the contract 'business efficacy'. Presumably no shipowner would have used the wharf if it were not safe!

2

Parker v. *S E Railway Co* 1877
An exclusion clause will not be enforced unless reasonable notice of it has been given.
    A notice to 'see back' on the front of a left luggage ticket was held sufficient notice to the plaintiff of terms limiting the company's liability.

3

Olley v. *Marlborough Court* 1949
Notice of an exclusion clause given after the contract has been made is not binding.
    In this case the Olleys booked into a hotel. On arriving in their room they found a notice on the back of the door excluding the hotel's liability for theft of guests' property from their rooms. Mrs Olley subsequently had two fur coats taken from her room. The court held the hotel was not covered by its exclusion clause.

4

Chapelton v. *Barry UDC* 1940
An exclusion clause printed on a receipt which is not a contractual document is not binding.
    Barry UDC were held not protected by an exclusion clause contained in a receipt for a deck chair, which collapsed injuring C.

5
    Curtis v. *Chemical Cleaning and Dyeing Co* 1951
Where an exclusion clause has been misrepresented, it is binding only as represented.
    In this case an assistant at the cleaners misrepresented the effect of their standard form exclusion clause. Despite the fact that the misrepresentation was oral and the original exclusion clause in writing, and signed by the plaintiff, the court held the misrepresentation limited the effect of the original clause.

6
    L'Estrange v. *Graucob* 1934
Where a party has signed a contract its terms are binding, whether they have been read or not.
    In this case an automatic vending machine was sold on terms which excluded any conditions or warranties. The plaintiff signed the agreement and was later held bound by it despite pleading she had not read it, some of it being in very small print.

7
    Suisse Atlantique Case 1966
There is no rule of law which prevents a carefully drafted exclusion clause from covering even a fundamental breach of contract.
    In this case a clause fixing the damages payable in the event of delay was held to be a liquidated damages clause rather than an exemption clause.

8
    Dimmock v. *Hallett* 1866
As a general rule silence does not amount to a misrepresentation. However, where silence distorts a positive representation, it will amount to misrepresentation. In this case the vendor said that certain farms were let without saying that the tenants had given notice.

9
    With v. *O'Flanagan* 1936
Silence amounts to a misrepresentation where a statement, true when made, subsequently becomes untrue and is not corrected.
    In this case a doctor failed to disclose a drop in the value of the receipts of his practice to the prospective purchaser.

10
    Derry v. *Peek* 1889
A fraudulent misrepresentation is a false statement 'made knowingly or without belief in its truth or recklessly, careless whether it be true or false'. Where there is an honest belief in the truth of the statement there is no fraud.
    In this case the directors of a company were held not liable for fraud for publishing untrue statements in their company prospectus.

11
    Leaf v. *International Galleries* 1950
The principal remedy for innocent misrepresentation is rescission. This is an equitable remedy and relief will not be granted in cases of delay.
    In this case a picture innocently attributed to Constable was bought. Five years later the purchaser sought to rescind the contract

on the ground of innocent misrepresentation since the picture was not by Constable. The court held the action must fail on the grounds of delay.

---

12   *Couturier* v. *Hastie* 1856
A common mistake as to the existence of goods at the time the contract is made avoids the contract.

In this case there was a contract for sale of corn. Unknown to both parties the corn had already been sold at sea. The court held the contract void. (This is now s.6 of Sale of Goods Act 1979).

---

13   *Bell* v. *Lever Bros* 1932
A common mistake as to the *quality* of the subject matter will not affect the validity of the contract.

Here Lever Bros tried to set aside a contract under which they had paid a large sum of compensation to a former employee on the grounds that they could have terminated his contract unilaterally because of his breach. The House of Lords held such a mistake was only as to the quality of the contract not its existence and held the contract valid.

---

14   *Solle* v. *Butcher* 1950
Where a contract is not void at common law for common mistake, equity may set the contract aside on terms fair to both parties. In this case a tenancy agreement was made on the mistaken assumption by both parties that the Rent Acts did not apply. When the tenant discovered the mistake he sought a reduction in rent. The court held the contract valid at common law, since the mistake was only as to quality, but allowed the agreement to be set aside on terms either that the tenant gave up the tenancy, or allowed the landlord to apply for a statutory increase in rent.

---

15   *Tamplin* v. *James* 1880
In the case of mutual mistake the court will enforce the agreement in an objective sense.

There was a contract for sale of property at auction. The extent of the property was accurately displayed on plans. The purchaser sought to have the sale set aside on the grounds of his mistake as to the extent of the property. The court refused, holding that there was a valid sale and ordered specific performance.

---

16   *Raffles* v. *Wichelhaus* 1864
In the case of mutual mistake where there is no complete agreement, the contract will be held void.

There was a contract for the sale of a cargo of cotton on board SS Peerless in Bombay Harbour. In fact there were two ships with the same name both in Bombay Harbour and both carrying cotton. The court held the contract void on the ground there was no clear agreement.

17

Webster v. *Cecil* 1861

In the case of unilateral mistake equity will not allow a contract to be enforced against the party who was known to be mistaken.

In this case there was an apparent slip of the pen, after rejection of an offer of £2000, a counter-offer of £1250 was held to be a clear mistake when £2250 was meant.

18

Phillips v. *Brooks* 1919

Where one person is mistaken as to the identity of the other this will not affect the validity of the contract unless the identity is vital. Where there has been impersonation, the contract will be voidable for fraud.

Here a rogue went into a jeweller's shop and obtained goods by giving a false name. The rogue subsequently passed the goods to an innocent third party, T. The jeweller was held unable to recover the goods from T. Because the original contract was voidable for fraud not void for mistake, the identity of the contracting party was not essential.

19

Lewis v. *Averay* 1971

Where one party contracts face to face with another it will be very difficult to prove the identity of the contracting party was vital so as to avoid the contract.

This was the ruling in a case where a rogue obtained a car by giving a false name. (Presumably if *identity* is vital, as opposed to creditworthiness, where the rogue is standing in front of the plaintiff it will be very hard for the plaintiff to plead he did not know with whom he was dealing).

20

Cundy v. *Lindsay* 1878

Where identity is vital, a mistake as to identity will avoid the contract.

The plaintiffs were able to prove they intended to deal only with a particular firm. The rogue knew that, and he was not part of that firm. The rogue ordered goods by post on credit pretending to be the firm well known to the plaintiff. The goods were sent, but no money was recovered. The rogue sold the goods to an innocent third party who was sued for their return by the plaintiffs in the tort of conversion. The plaintiffs were able to recover from the defendants on the grounds that the defendants had no valid title since the original contract was void for mistake.

21

Craddock Bros v. *Hunt* 1923

Where the mistake consists of the incorrect reduction of an oral agreement into writing, equity may grant rectification.

In this case the parties orally agreed for the sale of a house without an adjoining yard. By mistake the yard was included in the conveyance. The court rectified the conveyance to accord with the parties' intentions.

22

Foster v. *McKinnon* 1869

Although it is the general rule that a party is bound by his signature, where the signature is not his act he may escape liability. This technical defence of 'non est factum' is difficult to establish.

In this case M was induced to sign a bill of exchange thinking it was a guarantee. M was held not liable on the bill on the ground that he believed it was a totally different kind of document from the one he had signed.

23

Saunders v. *Anglia Building Society* 1970
Where a signature is given negligently, the defence of non est factum is not available.

In this case an old lady who signed a deed thinking it was a deed of gift when in fact it was an assignment of a lease was held bound by the deed and unable to plead 'non est factum'. The court found there was no mistake as to her intention to effect a conveyance, the character of the document signed was not fundamentally different from that which she thought she was signing, and her negligence in not reading the document was no defence.

24

Universe Tankships v. *ITF* 1982
Economic pressure may render a contract voidable.

As part of an industrial campaign members of a union prevented a ship from leaving port until her owners paid a substantial sum into the union's welfare fund. The court held the money had been paid under duress and allowed the owners to recover it.

25

Allcard v. *Skinner* 1887
An action to recover money paid under undue influence must be brought promptly.

In the course of eight years as a member of a religious order, 'A' gave a substantial sum of money to the head of the order. Six years after leaving the order, 'A' sought to recover the money on the grounds that it had been paid under undue influence. The court held that undue influence would be presumed in the circumstances but refused the plaintiff relief on the grounds that delay defeats the equity – six years was too long a time after which to claim.

26

British Crane Hire Corporation v. *Ipswich Plant Hire Ltd* 1974
Terms will be implied into a contract where it is the custom of the trade or industry.

Here the customary written terms for hiring a crane were incorporated into an oral contract.

RECENT EXAMINATION QUESTIONS

It may be helpful to spend around ten minutes planning an answer to each question before turning to the outline answers.

Question 1.

In many contracts the parties omit some of the terms which govern the agreement and certain terms must be implied. Explain, with illustrations, when these terms may be implied (a) at common law, and (b) by statute. Explain briefly, in each illustration, whether the parties could expressly exclude such an implied term.   (ICMA 1982)

Question 2.	(a) What is misrepresentation? Distinguish between the following kinds of misrepresentation and explain the legal effects of each:
	    (i) innocent misrepresentation;
	    (ii) negligent misrepresentation;
	    (iii) fraudulent misrepresentation.
	(b) Peter, an antique dealer, sold Jane an objet d'art which both parties wrongly but honestly believed to be the work of Fabergé, a famous artist. Three years later Jane discovers that the objet d'art is not the work of Fabergé but of a less well-known craftsman. Jane now wonders what action she can take, if any, against Peter. Advise Jane. (ACCA 1981)

Question 3.	Distinguish between duress and undue influence in the law of contract. What is the effect on a contract of one party entering into it, under either duress or undue influence? (ACCA 1981)
Question 4.	(a) You are employed by the Commercial Company. They have sold to Watson a thousand bales of nylon material believed by him and them to be stored in a certain warehouse. Unknown to either party the entire consignment had been destroyed by fire at the time of the sale. The truth now being known you are asked by your chairman whether the company can recover the agreed price for the goods. Advise him. (b) Badman came to the offices of Thompson & Co and offered to buy from them a quantity of goods. Thompson & Co's manager asked Badman to establish his credit. Badman said, 'That's simple, my good Sir,' and he produced a personalised cheque book with the name 'Robert Henry Richweiser' on it. As the manager knows, Robert Henry Richweiser was a substantial figure in the city. He therefore agreed to sell the goods which were duly delivered to Badman. Badman has now sold them to Clueless and absconded. Advise Thompson & Co. (ICSA 1983)
OUTLINE ANSWERS	The above examples of recent past questions have been chosen to cover the material covered in this chapter and to give an indication of the range of questions you can expect. In general, students find it easier to answer the more straightforward questions, which require the ability to present the applicable rules simply and straightforwardly. I shall therefore present possible outline answers to the first three questions and give a fuller answer to the last question, which is perhaps a little more intimidating.
Answer 1.	There are really four parts to this question when it is broken down. A brief introduction explaining the difference between express and implied terms; a consideration of (a) and (b) and the rules on exclusion of implied terms.

Implied terms are the terms the parties are presumed to have intended in the absence of any express provision in their agreement. Like express terms they may be either conditions or warranties.

(a) Such terms will be implied at common law:
  (i)   to give the contract business efficacy. *The Moorcock* 1889.
  (ii)   where it is the custom of the trade or industry *British Crane Hire Corporation* v. *Ipswich Plant Hire Ltd* (26) 1974. (Examples might be the implied terms governing the duties of employers and employees, and principals and agents).
(b) There are many examples where statutes imply terms, e.g. the Sale of Goods Act 1979 and the Supply of Goods and Services Act 1982, and the Partnership Act 1890, which sets out the implied rights and duties of partners inter se and in relation to third parties.

In principle an implied term is overruled by an express term which may vary or exclude it. However, certain terms implied by statute may not be varied or excluded except within narrow limits e.g. the Unfair Contract Terms Act 1977 prevents the exclusion of the Sale of Goods Act terms in consumer sales and restricts their exclusion in other sales, and the obligations of partners to third parties under the Partnership Act may not be varied or excluded.

Answer 2.

(a) This requires a straightforward explanation of the meaning and effect of the different forms of misrepresentation.
(b) Requires you to apply the rules to a problem. This is probably the most usual form of question.
(a) A misrepresentation is a false statement of fact made by one contracting party to another which induces the other to enter the contract.
  (i)   an innocent misrepresentation is a statement made innocently without negligence or fraud. The principal remedy is rescission, but the Misrepresentation Act 1967 gives the court a discretion to award damages instead where rescission is not available.
  (ii)   negligent misrepresentation is a false statement made without fraud, but where the maker is unable to disprove negligence, this is presumed on his part by the Misrepresentation Act 1967. The remedy is to claim damages.
  (iii) a fraudulent misrepresentation is one made knowingly, or without belief in its truth, or carelessly reckless whether it be true or false, *Derry* v. *Peek* 1889. The innocent party may avoid the contract for fraud and claim damages in the tort of deceit.
(b) There is a common mistake as to the value of the object. This does not affect the validity of the contract at common law, *Bell* v. *Lever Bros.* There may have been a misrepresentation at the time the contract was made. On the facts this would seem to have

been an honest mistake. If P is able to prove he was not negligent in making the statement, J's only remedy is to ask the court for rescission. This is an equitable remedy, however, and the court might feel that she had delayed too long in bringing her claim, *Leaf* v. *International Galleries*.

If P is not able to disprove negligence, J will be able to claim for damages under the Misrepresentation Act 1967.

If there were a term of the contract, express or implied, that the object *was* made by Fabergé, J has a claim at common law for damages for breach of contract. She will be unable to reject the object after she has accepted it, but she will be able to claim damages.

Answer 3.

This is part of a question inviting candidates to explain a number of separate legal points. A simple answer is called for.

Duress is force, or the threat of force, applied by one contracting party to another to induce him to enter the contract. Economic pressure has recently also been held to amount to duress, *Universe Tankships* v. *ITF* 1982. Undue influence is an equitable extension of the common law doctrine of duress. Relief may be granted in equity where one party has taken undue advantage of the other due to some influence over him. Sometimes such influence is presumed, at other times it must be specifically pleaded. The effect of duress is to make the contract voidable at common law. The effect of undue influence is to make the contract voidable in equity, subject to the usual equitable defences. *Allcard* v. *Skinner* 1887.

A TUTOR'S NOTES AND ANSWER

Notes

Question **4** is quite a long one. Students are often intimidated by a long set of facts so this question has been chosen to give you practice in breaking a problem down and learning how to pick out the key points. An examiner is looking for the same information as if he had set the question out in a more straightforward way. He is here testing the student's ability not only to remember what the law is on a particular point, but to apply it.

In (a) what are you actually being asked to do? You are being asked essentially, is the contract a valid contract or not? What is the effect of the fire? Be careful not to say 'This is *Couturier* v. *Hastie*'; the case is similar and you may wish to quote *C* v. *H* but you must establish clearly the facts in front of you.

Answer 4(a)

The chairman should be advised that the company's right to recover the agreed price depends on the precise terms of the contract of sale. There seem to be three possibilities:

1. The contract was for the sale of a *specific* thousand bales of nylon. The fact that the bales had perished unknown to either party at the time the contract was made will render the contract void for common mistake as to the existence of the subject

matter, *Couturier* v. *Hastie* and s.6 Sale of Goods Act 1979.

2. The contract was for the sale of any thousand bales rather than specific goods. If there was an implied term that the goods were all stored in the warehouse where both parties thought they were stored, there is again a common mistake as to their existence rendering the contract void. In neither of these cases will the company recover the price.

3. The contract is simply for the sale of a thousand bales of nylon and their whereabouts is neither an express nor implied term of the contract. The chairman should be advised the company remains liable to deliver the agreed quantity of nylon bales and will *then* be able to recover the purchase price. Unless and until the company deliver, however, they will be unable to recover the price, and may be sued for non-delivery.

Notes

In (b) again start by analysing what you are actually being asked to find out. In this case, can the company recover the goods from Clueless? (Since Badman has absconded there is really no point in advising the company to sue him). Whether the company can recover the goods from Clueless depends on whether C's title to the goods is valid or void. That will depend on the title C got from B. So the crux of this question is, what is the effect of B's deception on T & Co? Or when will unilateral mistake as to identity avoid a contract?

Answer 4(b)

T & Co should be advised there is no point in their suing B since he has absconded. In order to recover the goods from C they must prove that the initial contract between T & Co and B was void for mistake. In order to do this they must prove

1. That they intended to contract only with RHR and no-one else;
2. That B knew this,
3. That B was not RHR (*Phillips* v. *Brooks*).

On the facts it will be difficult for them to establish that the *identity* (as opposed to the creditworthiness) of RHR was vital. The court in *Lewis* v. *Averay* held that it would be very difficult to establish a vital mistake as to identity where a contract was made eyeball to eyeball, as in this case.

If T & Co fail to establish a mistake as to identity which is sufficient to make the contract void, it will still be voidable for B's fraud. However, in this case B has already disposed of the goods. Provided C acquired in good faith without notice of the fraud, C will have a valid title. In this case T & Co should be advised they cannot recover the goods from C.

A STEP FURTHER

You might usefully look at the terms on a standard travel brochure. Try to identify the various conditions and warranties. Are there any exclusion clauses?

A guide to further reading on this topic is presented at the end of Chapter 7.

Chapter 7	# Discharge of Contract

GETTING STARTED

Most contracts are discharged by performance, i.e. by each party fulfilling their contractual obligations, without posing any legal problem at all. However, where there is a dispute about what the contract required or whether it was adequately carried out, the law becomes involved. In some cases there is no performance at all, either through fault on the part of one of the parties or sometimes due to events outside the parties' control. In some cases the contract may have made provision for fixing the compensation payable for defective performance. In the event of outright breach there are a series of rules governing the measure of damages and some alternative remedies to be considered.

ESSENTIAL PRINCIPLES

Traditionally there are four ways in which a contract may come to an end:

1. Performance;
2. Agreement;
3. Frustration;
4. Breach.

BY PERFORMANCE

The basic rule is that performance must be precise and exact, i.e. the parties must perform their agreement to the letter (*Cutter* v. *Powell* (1) 1795). However, *there are a number of exceptions to this rule* on practical grounds.

Exceptions

Where the contract is substantially performed

Where a party's performance is not precise and exact he cannot claim his contracted remuneration. However, the courts may sometimes be willing to allow such a claim and then to reduce the amount recoverable on account of the defective performance. It is a question of degree whether the performance is no performance or merely defective performance. Compare *Hoenig* v. *Isaacs* (2) 1952 with *Bolton* v. *Mahadeva* (3) 1972. In *H* v. *I* the plaintiff was allowed to recover the contract price less a deduction for faulty workmanship, in *B* v. *M* no money was recoverable because the performance was regarded as no performance at all.

Where partial performance has been voluntarily accepted by the other party	Emphasis should be placed on the *voluntary* nature of the acceptance. Where work has been asked for, and *accepted*, although incomplete, it is clearly unfair that a technical rule of law should prevent the recovery of any payment. In this case the performing party is not entitled to his contracted sum, since he has not performed his side of the contract, but he *is* entitled to a reasonable sum for the work done. This is recoverable on a *quantum meruit*. Literally this means 'what it is worth'. Such a claim will not lie where work is simply abandoned leaving the original client no alternative whether to accept or not (*Sumpter* v. *Hedges* (4) 1898).
Where payment is due on an instalment basis	A contract will not be presumed to be divisible into instalment payments unless there is a clear intention that this should be so. In the case of delivery of goods in batches, where each batch is at a fixed price, it may be possible to infer such an intention. Many long-term service or construction contracts incorporate stage payments for practical reasons, such as cash-flow.
Where performance is incomplete because one party has prevented the other from completing his part	It is clearly unfair for one party to prevent the other from completing his part and thereby earning his money. In this case a claim for expenses on a quantum meruit will lie, *Planche* v. *Colburn* (5) 1831.

BY AGREEMENT

Just as a contract is made by agreement, so in principle it may be ended by agreement. An agreement to end a contract is itself a contract the usual rules on consideration apply, i.e. the agreement must be supported by consideration or be under seal.

Where the contract is wholly or partly executory on both sides, there is no problem; each side gives up the right to performance from the other side. When one party has performed and the other has not, there will be no valid discharge without fresh consideration. This new agreement is then called 'accord and satisfaction'.

BY FRUSTRATION

A contract is said to be discharged by frustration when its performance becomes impossible due to some unforeseen change in circumstances arising from events outside the control of the parties.

The following are some examples of frustrating events:

1. The destruction of the subject-matter of the contract or a thing essential to the performance of the contract (*Taylor* v. *Caldwell* (6) 1863).

2. Death or serious illness of a party to a contract for personal services (*Robinson* v. *Davison* (7) 1871).
3. The removal of the whole basis of the contract – it is a question of fact what this basis is, compare *Krell* v. *Henry* (8) 1903, and *Herne Bay Steam Boat Co* v. *Hutton* (9) 1903. Both these cases involved the postponement of the coronation of Edward VII due to illness in 1902. In the first case, a contract to lease a room 'to view the coronation procession' was held frustrated by the postponement, in the second a contract for a trip round Spithead and to view the naval review was held not frustrated.
4. Supervening illegality, or outbreak or war (*Avery* v. *Bowden* (10) 1855).
5. Government interference radically altering the performance of the contract (*Metropolitan Water Board* v. *Dick, Kerr & Co* (11) 1918).

N.B. The mere fact that performance is more expensive than originally envisaged or that performance is delayed will not amount to frustration unless the whole basis of the contract has been destroyed. (*Davis Contractors* v. *Fareham UDC* (12) 1956 and *Tsakiroglou Ltd Case* 1962).

The effect of frustration

The contract is avoided from the moment of the frustrating event. The Law Reform (Frustrated Contracts) Act 1943 provides that:

1. All sums paid before the frustrating event are prima facie recoverable;
2. All sums payable before the frustrating event prima facie cease to be payable.
3. Where a party has incurred expenses in performing the contract, he may be allowed to recover all or part of these costs out of the money paid or payable at the time of the frustrating event;
4. Where one party has received a benefit, he may be allowed to recover such sum as the court thinks just.

N.B. These rules will not apply where the parties have made their own provision for frustrating events. Such a clause, called a 'force majeure' clause is very common in commercial agreements.

BY BREACH

Breach may occur in a number of ways: e.g. by non-performance at the agreed time; by defective performance; or by express refusal to perform. This may occur at the time performance is due or earlier. In the latter case it is known as anticipatory breach.

Whatever the type of breach the injured party will have the right to claim *damages*. Where the breach amounts to a **breach of condition** the injured party may choose additionally to treat the contract as at an end and repudiate it, i.e. decline to complete his own part of the bargain. Whether the breach amounts to a breach of condition or a breach of warranty is a question of construction.

Where the breach is an anticipatory breach, the innocent party has a choice either to take action at once, or to wait until the date performance was due.

Remedies for Breach

Damages

The purpose of damages in contract is to compensate, to put the plaintiff into the position in which he would have been had the contract been carried out.

However, this is subject to the *rules on remoteness of damage* which govern the kind of loss for which a plaintiff ought to be compensated. The rule was laid down for contract in *Hadley* v. *Baxendale* (14) 1854.

A plaintiff may recover:

1. Such damage as may fairly and reasonably be considered as arising naturally from the breach; and
2. Such loss as may reasonably be supposed to be in the contemplation of the parties when they made the agreement.

These rules are illustrated by the decision of the House of Lords in *Victoria Laundry (Windsor) Ltd* v. *Newman Industries Ltd* (15) 1949.

Here the plaintiffs had a contract with the defendants for the supply of a new boiler. The boiler was delivered late. The plaintiffs claimed damages for the loss of profit from the lost use of the boiler. The loss of profits included their normal profit plus the additional loss incurred through their inability to undertake an exceptionally lucrative dyeing contract. The House of Lords held their normal loss of profit was recoverable under the first head of *Hadley* v. *Baxendale* (14), but not the extra losses as these were outside the parties' contemplation.

A party is required to mitigate or reduce his loss, e.g. where a seller has failed to deliver goods, the buyer should take steps to purchase similar goods elsewhere reasonably quickly. The duty is only to take *reasonable* steps. This is really a question of causation, i.e. if the losses were attributable to the plaintiff they should not be recoverable from the defendant.

In line with the overall intention of the law to compensate, the plaintiff's liability to taxation is taken into account, e.g. in a claim for loss of earnings, net wages rather than gross wages are calculated.

Liquidated damages

Frequently the parties to a contract will attempt to foresee in advance the effect of possible breach and make provision for it. A fixed sum agreed in advance as the sum payable in the event of breach is called 'liquidated damages'. Where such a sum has been agreed in advance this is the sum the court will award in accordance with the contract provided it is a '*genuine pre-estimate of loss*' and not a penalty. A penalty is essentially what it says it is, an arbitrary sum not related to the actual damage suffered and designed to put pressure on the other party. Where the court finds a sum is in the nature of a penalty it will not award the sum, and will itself consider the proper measure of damages. *Dunlop Ltd* v. *New Garage Ltd* (16) 1915. In deciding for Dunlop, the House of Lords laid down useful guidelines for assessing whether a fixed sum clause would be considered a penalty. See p. 77.

Specific performance	Where damages would not be an adequate remedy equity may grant *specific performance*, an order requiring the defendant actually to carry out his agreement. As an equitable remedy it is not available as of right and is subject to the usual equitable rules. It is particularly useful in relation to contracts for the sale of land. It *may* be granted to enforce the sale of unique objects, though this is rare as most goods have a money value for which damages would be adequate compensation. It will not be granted in a contract for personal services, or a contract of continuing obligation as the court cannot supervise such an agreement.
Injunction	This is another equitable remedy. **It is an order requiring a person not to break his contract**. It may be used to prevent a threatened breach or to enforce a negative stipulation in a contract of personal services (e.g. *Warner Bros* v. *Nelson* (17) 1937).
Quantum meruit	*This is really a quasi-contractual remedy for expenses for work carried out*. It is a useful remedy where one party has repudiated after the other has carried out work, or where work has been done under a void contract (*Planche* v. *Colburn* (5) 1831; *Craven-Ellis* v. *Canons Ltd* (18) 1936). It may also be used where one party has failed to perform the contract completely, but the other side is willing to accept less than full and complete performance (*Sumpter* v. *Hedges* (4) 1898).

USEFUL APPLIED MATERIALS	Like the other areas of contract already covered, the rules on discharge of contracts are almost all based on mercantile custom and practice. This section collects together brief summaries of the cases referred to earlier in the section. Remember a case is only authority for the rule of law which was the reason for the decision. There are many cases which could be used to illustrate the points, the cases cited here are necessarily only a small number. In addition to the cases named, the Law Reform (Frustrated Contracts) Act 1943 should be referred to.
1	*Cutter* v. *Powell* 1795 Performance of a contract must be complete and exact. C was contracted to work for P as second mate on a voyage from Jamaica to Liverpool. C died shortly before the ship arrived. His widow claimed for a proportion of the agreed reward. The court held no money was due as the performance was incomplete.
2	*Hoenig* v. *Isaacs* 1952 Where a lump sum contract is substantially performed the plaintiff is entitled to the contract price less a deduction for defects.

Here H agreed to carry out interior decorating work for I for an agreed sum. When the work was completed, I complained it was faulty and paid only just over half the agreed price. The court held the full contract sum was payable less an abatement for defects.

3

Bolton v. *Mahadeva* 1972
It is a question of fact in a lump sum contract whether the work has been carried out although defectively, or whether there has been no real performance at all.

In this case a central heating contractor was held not to have performed his part of the contract at all when the system he installed failed to work.

4

Sumpter v. *Hedges* 1898
Where a contract is for a lump sum for a complete performance and the work is incomplete but the client is willing to accept what has been done, a claim on a quantum meruit will lie for the value of the work done.

Here S, a builder, abandoned building work giving H no option whether to accept or reject. House of Lords refused S's claim for a quantum meruit on the grounds that H had not 'accepted' work done.

5

Planche v. *Colburn* 1831
Where performance is incomplete because it is prevented by one party, a quantum meruit will lie to recover the value of work already carried out.

Here P had a contract to write a volume in a series to be published by C. C subsequently abandoned the series. P had already written part of the book. The court held P entitled to recover for expenses incurred.

6

Taylor v. *Caldwell* 1863
A contract will be held frustrated where its performance depends on the existence of a specific thing and that thing is destroyed without the fault or either side.

In this case C had let a music hall to T for a series of concerts. The hall was accidentally burnt down before the date of performance. The contract was held frustrated.

7

Robinson v. *Davison* 1871
The death or illness of a party to a contract for personal services will frustrate the contract where the disability is sufficiently serious to prevent the execution of the main part of the contract.

Here a pianist was contracted to play in a concert on a particular day. His illness was held to frustrate the contract.

8

Krell v. *Henry* 1903
The non occurrence of an essential event will frustrate the performance of a contract.

Here H had agreed to hire K's flat to view the coronation

procession of King Edward VII. The coronation had to be postponed owing to the king's illness; the agreement to rent the room was held to be frustrated.

9	*Herne Bay Steam Boat Co* v. *Hutton* 1903
	It is a question of fact in each case whether the happening of an event is an essential element in a contract.
	In this case H agreed to hire a boat from the Co to view the naval review at Spithead and to cruise round the fleet. Due to the postponement of the coronation the review was cancelled, but the fleet was still in the bay and a cruise would have been possible; the court found the contract not frustrated.

10	*Avery* v. *Bowden* 1855
	The outbreak of war may render a contract illegal and therefore frustrate it.
	In this case a contract to charter a ship from Odessa was held to be frustrated by the outbreak of the Crimean war.

11	*Metropolitan Water Board* v. *Dick, Kerr & Co* 1918
	A vital change in circumstances rendering performance substantially different from that contracted for will frustrate a contract.
	In this case a construction contract entered into before the First World War and subsequently suspended at government direction was held to be frustrated at the end of the war, for performance would be radically different from that contracted for.

12	*Davis Contractors Ltd* v. *Fareham UDC* 1956
	The mere fact that a contract is more onerous to carry out than originally envisaged will not amount to frustration.
	Here a firm of building contractors entered into a fixed price contract to build a number of houses. Due to circumstances beyond their control delays were incurred and costs rose beyond the agreed price. The court held performance was still possible, there were no frustrating circumstances, and refused a claim for a quantum meruit for the increased cost.

13	*The Tsakiroglou Case* 1962
	A contract will not be held frustrated where performance is still possible even though changed circumstances make performance more expensive.
	Here a contract for the shipment of ground nuts from the Sudan to Germany was affected by the sudden closure of the Suez Canal in 1956. The contract was held not frustrated because shipment via the Cape of Good Hope would still have been possible.

14	*Hadley* v. *Baxendale* 1854
	A plaintiff may not recover in damages for all loss he suffers as a result of breach but only that loss which is:

1. Fairly and reasonably to be considered as arising naturally; or
2. Reasonably to be supposed to have been in the contemplation of both parties at the time they made the agreement.

In this case the plaintiff sued for damages for loss of profit due to the total shutdown of his mill. The court held it was neither inevitable nor expressly foreseen that this would be the result of delay by the defendant carrier and refused to award damages for loss of profit.

---

15   *Victoria Laundry (Windsor) Ltd* v. *Newman Industries Ltd* 1949
N contracted to deliver to V L a second-hand boiler for use in their laundry. The boiler was late being delivered and V L sued:

1. For the loss of ordinary profits arising from the lack of the new boiler and,
2. For the additional profit lost through their inability to undertake a specially lucrative dyeing contract without the new boiler.

The court applied the rules in *Hadley* v. *Baxendale* 1854 (above) and gave damages under the first head as being the natural loss, but gave no damages under the second head on the grounds these losses were not foreseen.

---

16   *Dunlop Ltd* v. *New Garage Ltd* 1915
Where the parties have agreed in advance a sum to be payable on breach the court will award such sum if it is a genuine pre-estimate of the plaintiff's loss but not if it is in the nature of a penalty.
In this case D sued N G for breach of a price maintenance agreement. The court upheld the pre-agreed sum as liquidated damages. The court laid down the following guidelines:

1. The sum will be regarded as a penalty if it is extravagant or unreasonable,
2. Where a payment of a smaller sum is secured by payment of a larger sum, and
3. Where a single sum is payable for a range of breaches of differing degrees of severity, there is a presumption that such a sum is a penalty.

---

17   *Warner Bros* v. *Nelson* 1937
An injunction may be granted to enforce a negative stipulation in a contract for personal services.
Here N agreed to give her services exclusively to W B and to work for no-one else. W B were allowed an injunction to prevent her working for a rival company.

---

18   *Craven-Ellis* v. *Canons Ltd* 1936
C E was employed under a void contract of employment. Held he could recover under a quantum meruit for work rendered.

It may be helpful to spend around ten minutes planning an answer to each question before turning to the outline answers.

Question 1.

Outline the ways in which a contract may be discharged. Illustrate your answer with examples. (DPA 1983)

Question 2.

(a) In what circumstances will a contract be discharged through frustration?

(b) (i) Bill books a room in an hotel in London in order to visit a Jazz Festival which is to be held in Hyde Park. The Festival is cancelled and Bill wishes to cancel his reservation. Advise Bill.

(ii) Peter accepts an engagement to play the piano at the OK Club in Newtown for two weeks commencing 1 June 1981. On 30 May, he is arrested by the police for being in possession of drugs and is held in custody by them until 3 June. The OK Club now refuses to engage Peter. Advise Peter. (ACCA 1981)

Question 3.

A builder agrees to erect a factory within one year. Discuss the validity of the following defences if he has failed to complete the work on time and is being sued for breach of contract.

(a) The Government imposed building restrictions which prevented him from continuing with the work.

(b) The cost of building materials increased, obliging him to buy in smaller quantities because of a shortage of working capital.

(c) An influenza epidemic led to the illness of a number of his specialist workers.

(d) Some building materials on the site were damaged by fire. (ICMA 1981)

Question 4.

Better Builders contracts to reconstruct a laundry and to complete the work within eight weeks. The work in fact takes ten weeks and the laundry is now claiming damages for the loss of normal profits during the two additional weeks and also for the loss of a particularly valuable contract which it could not accept because its plant was out of action.

(a) Advise Better Builders.

(b) To what extent would your advice differ if the contract had contained a clause under which Better Builders agreed to pay £200 by way of penalty for each week late in completing the work? (ICMA 1982)

OUTLINE ANSWERS

Answer 1.

This is a very straightforward question requiring a summary of the four ways in which a contract may be discharged plus examples. A contract may be discharged in four ways, by performance, by agreement, by frustration and by breach.

The normal rule is that performance must be complete and exact, *Cutter* v. *Powell*. However there are a number of exceptions to this rule. These include substantial performance, *Hoenig* v. *Isaacs*; partial performance if accepted by the party, *Sumpter* v. *Hedges*; and incomplete performance due to the act of the other party, *Planche* v. *Colburn*.

A contract may be discharged by agreement without formality. Where it is executory on both sides there is mutual consideration. Where one side has performed, consideration for the discharge will be needed from the other. This is called accord and satisfaction.

A contract is discharged by frustration when performance of its main purpose becomes impossible without the fault of either party. It will be a question of fact whether performance is impossible. Compare *Krell* v. *Henry* and *Herne Bay Steam Boat Co* v. *Hutton*.

A contract is discharged by breach amounting to breach of condition. It will be a question of fact whether the breach is a breach of condition or merely a breach of warranty entitling the innocent party only to claim damages.

Answer 2.

(a) A contract will be discharged by frustration where it has become impossible to carry out the main purpose of the contract without fault on either side. It is a question of fact whether performance is impossible. Consider some examples, perhaps, *Taylor* v. *Caldwell*, *Robinson* v. *Davison*, *Krell* v. *Henry*. A contract will not be frustrated where performance is merely more difficult or more expensive. *Davis Contractors* v. *Fareham UDC* or where the main purpose of the contract can still be performed, *Herne Bay Steam Boat Co* v. *Hutton*.

(b) (i) Consider what is the main purpose of the contract. Was it an express term that the room was only wanted for the Festival? If so, contract probably frustrated and Bill need not pay. If no express term, the contract to rent room is still possible and therefore the contract is not frustrated, Bill must pay.

(ii) A contract for personal services may be discharged through the illness of one of the parties or other sufficient disability. It will be a question of fact whether Peter's inability to play for the first three days of his contract is sufficient to frustrate the whole purpose of the contract.

Answer 3.

(a) The builder may plead the defence of frustration where the Government restrictions have made performance of the contract impossible in the sense originally agreed, *Metropolitan Water Board* v. *Dick, Kerr & Co.*

(b) An increase in cost is not enough to frustrate a contract, *Davis Contractors* v. *Fareham UDC*. So no defence here unless contract contains express provisions.

(c) If the specialist workers were an identified part of the contract, i.e. their labour was an essential element of the contract, the contract may be held frustrated if they are absent for so long as to prevent the performance of the contract. Influenza is not a long term illness, however unpleasant, therefore very unlikely to frustrate the building of a factory. Builder has no defence.

(d) The performance is not made impossible by this fire, the builder could obtain other supplies. No frustration. See *Tsakiroglou Case*. No defence.

A TUTOR'S ANSWER

Here I present a full answer to question 4.

Answer 4.

(a) It was an express term of the contract that the work would be completed in eight weeks. The work in fact took ten weeks. There is therefore clear evidence of breach of contract by Better Builders. Better Builders should be advised they will be liable to pay damages to their client. The measure of damages in contract is governed by the rule in *Hadley* v. *Baxendale*, damages are recoverable for the loss which is the direct and inevitable result of the breach, or such loss as must be taken to be within the parties' contemplation at the time the contract was made. Applying this to the facts, a delay of two weeks in completion is clearly going to involve the company in two weeks' loss of normal profit. The loss of a particularly valuable contract is not an inevitable loss, however. Better Builders will only be responsible for this if they knew of it. This is a question of fact, *Victoria Laundry* v. *Newman Industries Ltd*. Better Builders should be advised accordingly.

(b) Where a sum is fixed in advance by the parties to be paid in the event of breach, the court will award this sum if it is by way of liquidated damages but not if it is in the nature of a penalty. The House of Lords in *Dunlop* v. *New Garage* laid down that a sum would be regarded as liquidated damages if it were a genuine pre-estimate of loss but not if it were out of proportion to the likely effect of breach.

In this case the sum of £200 per week may be regarded as a genuine attempt to anticipate the loss. The sum is on a pro rata basis, i.e. it increases in proportion to the length of the delay. If it is a liquidated damages clause the court will enforce it and Better Builders should be advised to pay.

A STEP FURTHER

An Introduction to the Law of Contract (3rd edn) P. S. Atiyah, OUP, 1981.

BASIC READING

Contract (4th edn) F. R. Davies, Sweet and Maxwell, 1981.
An Outline of the Law of Contract (3rd edn) Treitel, Butterworths, 1984.

FURTHER READING

The Law of Contract (10th edn) Cheshire and Fifoot, Butterworths, 1981.
Chitty on Contracts (25th edn) Sweet and Maxwell, 1983.
A Casebook on Contract (7th edn) Smith and Thomas, Sweet and Maxwell, 1982.

Look at some standard form contracts, e.g. those used by travel agents and identify the liquidated damages/penalty clauses. Which are they and why?

Chapter 8

Sale of Goods

GETTING STARTED

Buying and selling are perhaps the simplest examples of commercial activity. The framework of obligations arising from a sale was established by mercantile custom and practice. (The sale of goods is a useful example of the role of custom as a source of law.) However, having been established by commercial custom the rules have since been codified, collected together in one statute, and subsequently amended in further statutes. Today any study of the sale of goods is based on statute. The current act is the Sale of Goods Act 1979. This in large measure reproduces the original Sale of Goods Act 1893, with amendments.

N.B. When discussing a statute it is important always to give the date of the Act to which you are referring, its date is part of its name.

It is an advantage to be able to refer to the rules by reference to their section numbers. There is no great virtue in learning the sections like a parrot, in a practical situation direct reference to the Act should always be made, but you should be familiar with the content of the most important sections and the general framework of the Act.

Various technical expressions are used in the Act, their meanings will be explained as necessary. The advantage of using a technical expression is that it is a kind of shorthand. There is no need to give a lengthy explanation in the examination of a particular term. Provided that you have used the term correctly an examiner will see that you know and understand its meaning.

Although this area of the law is now governed by statute, the common law principles underlie the statute. On any point where there are no specific rules the common law applies. Thus the basic contract rules on offer and acceptance, form, consideration and damages all apply. Additionally there are a number of cases which illustrate the working of the SGA or the common law on which the Act was based. You will need to quote both section numbers and cases.

ESSENTIAL PRINCIPLES

DEFINITION

Section 2(1) SGA 1979 defines a contract of sale as:

'*a contract whereby the seller transfers or agrees to transfer the property in goods to the buyer for a money consideration called the price.*'

Clearly the Sale of Goods Act applies only to *sales*! Before applying any of the Act's rules you must firmly establish that the contract you are considering is a contract of sale and not, for example, a contract of hire or barter. In a contract of hire there is no intention that the ownership shall pass. In a contract of barter goods are exchanged for goods rather than money. 'Goods' is defined by s.61, to include all moveable, tangible property – except money – plus things attached to the land or forming part of the land which are to be separated from the land under the contract of sale, for example growing crops. The principal exclusions from the definition, apart from money, are land (including everything attached to it) and intangible property, that is things you cannot touch, for example, stocks and shares, or copyright. These forms of property *can* of course be bought and sold, they are simply not covered by the SGA.

There are four main areas which examiners regularly choose as the topics for their questions:

1. The obligations of the parties;
2. Risk and passing of property;
3. The nemo dat rule;
4. Remedies.

THE OBLIGATIONS OF THE PARTIES

A. The seller's obligation

'. . . *it is the duty of the seller to deliver the goods . . . in accordance with the contract of sale*': s.27.

Variations in quantity or quality of the goods, or the time or place of delivery may all amount to breach.

The contract of sale includes not only the express terms agreed by the parties but implied terms, implied in the usual way by custom, by necessity, or by law. The SGA 1979 implies a number of very important terms. Originally these were the terms implied by custom and incorporated into the codifying Act of 1893. In principle implied terms may be excluded by the express agreement of the parties, however, this is now impossible in some cases and limited in others.

The following **implied terms** in relation to the goods are laid down in ss.12–15. You should learn them carefully; they are frequently the subject of examination questions.

Implied terms

1

Section 12 provides an implied condition that the seller has a right to sell.

Where the seller sells without such right, the buyer has the normal remedies for breach of condition, i.e. he can repudiate the contract and recover the full price which he paid. This is so even if the breach comes to light sometime after the sale and the buyer has had some use of the goods (*Rowland* v. *Divall* (1) 1923).

There is no implied term that the seller is the 'owner' of the goods

– a number of people other than the owner may have a *right* to sell. Where the seller makes clear that he has only a putative title, or a possibly defective title, the implied condition as to title is replaced by a warranty that all known defects have been disclosed, the buyer buys the risk.

2

Section 13 provides that in a contract for the sale of goods by description there is an implied condition that the goods shall correspond with the description.

Obviously where goods are ordered unseen, for example from a catalogue or newspaper, there must be a sale by description. But even where a buyer chooses goods in person there may be a sale by description – e.g. the goods may be packaged in descriptive material, or the buyer will ask for what he wants by describing the product.

The courts have been very strict in requiring compliance with the most detailed parts of the description including quantity, weight, ingredients, place of origin and even packing (*Re Moore & Co and Landauer & Co* (2) 1921). Even a very small deviation may amount to breach. (*Arcos* v. *Ronaasen* (3) 1933).

3

Section 14 imposes obligations as to the quality of goods sold. Unlike the other sections imposing implied terms *it only applies to a seller in the course of business.*

Section 14 (2) provides that the goods supplied shall be of merchantable quality.

There are many old cases on the meaning of merchantable quality; it is not easy to be specific and efforts are being made to improve the definition. Section 62 defines 'merchantable' as 'as fit for the purpose or purposes for which goods of that kind are commonly bought as it is reasonable to expect having regard to the description applied to them, the price (if relevant) and all the other circumstances'. Although this is a statutory definition whether the goods are of merchantable quality is still a question of fact and common sense. The definition has not really added anything to the common law. 'You get what you pay for' may sum it up! e.g. where goods are sold as secondhand or with a clearly marked defect, it would be unreasonable to expect such goods to have the same qualities as new goods of similar type. There are two important exceptions where s.14 (2) does not apply:

(a) Where a defect has been specifically drawn to the buyer's attention before the contract was made – this is very common practice in shops where defective goods may be sold off at a discount; or:

(b) If the buyer has examined the goods before he bought them there is no implied condition as regards those defects which a reasonable examination ought to have revealed.

N.B. It is not enough that the buyer could have discovered the defects *if* he had looked, he must actually have examined the goods.

Section 14 (3) provides that where the buyer expressly or by implication makes known to the seller any particular purpose for which the goods are being bought, there is an implied condition that the goods supplied are reasonably fit for that purpose, whether or not that is a purpose for which such goods are commonly supplied, except where the circumstances show that the buyer does not rely, or that it is unreasonable for him to rely on the seller's skill or judgment.

It will be assumed that goods are wanted for their normal purpose, thus underpants are for wearing (*Grant* v. *Australian Knitting Mills* (4) 1936); a hot water bottle is for filling (*Priest* v. *Last* (5) 1903); and milk is for drinking (*Frost* v. *Aylesbury Dairies* (6) 1905). The obligation is only to supply goods which are *reasonably* fit for normal use; a plaintiff with a particular problem undisclosed to the seller has no ground for complaint if the goods were reasonably fit for a 'normal' buyer (*Griffiths* v. *Peter Conway Ltd* (6) 1939). Where a buyer discloses the particular purpose he has in mind the seller must supply goods fit for that particular purpose (*Baldry* v. *Marshall* (8) 1925). However, if the buyer does *not* rely on the seller's advice, the seller has no obligation if the goods prove unsuitable, e.g. a buyer asks a seller in a DIY shop for paint suitable for outside use, the seller recommends brand X, but the buyer instead chooses brand Z.

4 *Section 15 provides that where goods are sold by sample there are implied conditions (i) that the bulk will correspond with the sample, (ii) that the buyer shall have a reasonable opportunity of comparing bulk with the sample and (iii) that the goods shall be free from any defect rendering them unmerchantable which would not be apparent on reasonable examination of the sample.*

Any goods may be sold by sample, e.g. it is usual in the case of cosmetics, carpets, fabric, wallpaper, paint etc. and most bulk supplies.

Exclusion of implied terms

Although the normal contract rule is that implied terms may be varied or excluded by consent of the parties, this is now subject to the Unfair Contract Terms Act 1977. Section 6 of UCTA applies to any clause claiming to exempt the seller from his liability under ss.12–15 SGA. *It provides that in a consumer sale the seller may not exempt himself from any of his implied liability. In a non-consumer sale the seller may not exempt himself from liability under s.12 (title) but he may exempt himself from liability under ss.13–15 SGA provided the exemption was fair and reasonable.* A consumer sale is a sale, other than by auction or by tender:

1. By a seller in the course of business;
2. Of goods of a type ordinarily bought for private consumption.
3. To a person who does not buy or hold himself out as buying in the course of business.

It is a question of fact whether it is a consumer sale or not. It is up to the person who contends the sale is not a consumer sale to prove it.

In an examination question it will usually be fairly easy to apply the test. It is very important to make the distinction because of the different rules on exclusion of the implied terms.

Where it is a non-consumer sale an exemption of ss.13–15 is permitted provided it is fair and reasonable. This is also a question of fact. The court will take into account the position of the parties, their previous dealing, the notice given of the term, alternative sources of supply, the price and other relevant terms.

B. The buyer's obligations

'To accept the goods and to pay for them in accordance with the contract': s.27.

The buyer must accept goods which conform to the contract specification. He is entitled to a reasonable opportunity to examine the goods to check that they conform: s.34. He may only validly reject goods where there is a breach of condition. He loses the right to reject goods once he has accepted them. Rules as to the measure of damages are the ordinary common law rules.

Details as to prices, i.e. how much, when and where it is payable, are usually fixed in the contract. The amount of the price may be fixed later by the parties or fixed by a valuer. Where no price is fixed a reasonable price is due. The time for payment is on delivery of the goods unless an earlier date has been agreed or credit allowed.

RISK AND THE PASSING OF PROPERTY

The purpose of a contract for the sale of goods is to transfer the ownership of the goods from S to B. The legal expression for ownership of goods is 'property in the goods'. The rules in the SGA governing the passing of property are concerned not with the physical delivery of the goods but with the passing of title. It is important to define the moment when the legal right to the goods passes for a number of reasons:

1. S can only sue B for the price after the property (ownership or title) has been transferred (unless the parties have otherwise agreed).
2. As a normal rule B cannot transfer to another person any better title to the goods than he himself has, the nemo dat rule.
3. The risk of accidental damage is normally borne by the owner.
4. In the event of either B or S becoming bankrupt, the rights of the other party will depend on whether the property has passed to the buyer.

The rules for determining the time when property passes differ according to whether the contract is for the sale of *specific goods* or *unascertained* goods. This distinction is crucial. Examiners frequently include a question involving both specific and unascertained goods. Learn the definition carefully. *Specific goods* are *defined in s.61* as **'goods identified and agreed upon at the time a contract of sale is made'**, e.g. in a self-service shop B is offering to buy the specific item in his basket rather than asking for items from stock.

Any goods which are not specifically identified at the moment of contract are non-specific or unascertained goods, e.g. 'a' bottle of wine, 'a' packet of soap powder.

Specific goods

Section 17 provides that property in specific goods passes when the parties intend it to pass. This is a question of fact to be determined from what the parties said or did at the moment of contracting. Sometimes it is clear that title is not to pass until payment has been made even though the goods have been delivered, at other times it may be very difficult to find any express or implied intention. In this case s.18 lays down a series of rules.

Rule 1 *provides that 'where there is an unconditional contract for the sale of specific goods in a deliverable state the property in the goods passes to the buyer when the contract is made and it is immaterial whether the time of payment or the time of delivery or both be postponed',* i.e. in this case the property passes on agreement.

Rule 2 *provides that if the specific goods are not in a deliverable state property will not pass until the seller has taken the necessary steps and informed the buyer.* Goods will not be in a deliverable state where the seller has agreed to do something to them under the contract and has not yet done it, e.g. a minor repair or alteration.

Rule 3 *provides that where the seller must first test, weight, or measure specific goods to determine the price, property does not pass until that has been done and the buyer notified.*

Rule 4 *lays down the rules for the passing of property in a 'sale or return' contract.* By definition such goods are specific. Property passes:

1. On acceptance by the buyer expressly or impliedly;
2. On retention by the buyer of the goods beyond the specified time or a reasonable time.

N.B. Where B does an act inconsistent with S's ownership, e.g. sells the goods, this normally amounts to appropriation and acceptance: the property passes and S's rights are against B for the price not the goods. Until the property passes the goods remain at S, the owner's risk. Therefore B is not liable for accidental damage to the goods while on approval, unless otherwise agreed.

Unascertained goods

Rule 5 *provides that property in unascertained goods passes when goods in a deliverable state are unconditionally appropriated to the contract by either party with the consent of the other.*

'Unconditionally appropriated' does not merely mean a setting apart or selection by the seller, but an intention by both parties to attach the contract irrevocably to those goods. Assent may be implied where the seller gives notice to the buyer and the buyer makes no objection within a reasonable time.

Risk

Unless otherwise agreed risk passes with property: s.20, i.e. the owner bears the loss. If goods are damaged or stolen before the property passes, the loss falls on the seller, if after, it falls on the buyer. This is irrespective of who was in possession of the goods at the time. For example, in a contract for the sale of specific goods in a deliverable state, property will pass to the buyer on agreement even though the goods have not been delivered (the party who bears the risk may insure himself). The risk carried is that of accidental damage. Any party in possession of goods of another owes the normal duty of a bailee to take care of the goods bailed. Where goods are lost or damaged through the *fault* of the party in possession, he will be liable in the ordinary way.

Where either party has been guilty of delay in delivery or collection the goods are at the risk of the party at fault as regards any loss which might not have occurred but for such fault.

Goods perishing before the contract is made

The owner bears the risk of loss but what is the effect of such loss or damage on the parties' liability to perform the contract? Are they relieved of their obligations?

Section 6 provides 'where there is a contract of the sale of specific goods, and the goods without the knowledge of the seller have perished at the time the contract is made, the contract is void' (*Couturier* v. *Hastie* (9) 1856 held such a contract void at common law as being impossible when made).

Whether goods have 'perished' or not is a question of commercial sense. Slight deterioration is clearly not enough but damage or loss making goods commercially useless has been held to amount to perishing.

Goods perishing after the contract is made

Section 7 provides 'where there is an agreement to sell specific goods, and subsequently the goods, without any fault on the part of the seller or buyer, perish before the risk passes to the buyer, the agreement is avoided'.

In cases of unascertained goods the common law doctrine of frustration may apply. It will be a question of fact whether the contract has become impossible to perform. The Law Reform (Frustrated Contracts) Act 1943 will apply if it has.

Once the property *has* passed, there can be no question of frustration or avoidance.

The effect of the contract being frustrated or avoided is that both parties are excused further performance of the contract, S need not deliver and B need not pay. Where the contract is not frustrated or avoided both parties must fulfil their original obligations or pay damages in lieu.

THE NEMO DAT RULE

As a general rule only the owner of goods can validly sell them. *'Nemo dat quod non habat'*, i.e. 'no-one can give what he has not got' – a non-owner has no title to pass. Accordingly, s.21 provides that where goods are sold by an unauthorised person the buyer acquires no better title to the goods than the seller had. The innocent purchaser must return the goods to the true owner, if asked, and may claim damages from the seller for breach of s.12. But a seller in such a case will frequently have disappeared or have no funds.

For commercial convenience a number of exceptions to the nemo dat rule have been developed.

The most important exceptions are:

1. *Sale by an agent* – with authority, actual, implied or apparent (see Ch. 9). Sales by a factor (mercantile agent) are governed by the Factors Act 1889. A factor can pass a good title to a buyer in good faith to goods entrusted to the factor in the normal course of business by the owner: s.9 Factors Act 1889.
2. *Estoppel: s.21.* This provides an exception where the owner is prevented by his words or conduct from denying the seller's right to sell (*Eastern Distributors Ltd* v. *Goldring* (10) 1957).
3. *Sale in Market Overt: s.22.* A market overt is a market privileged by Act of Parliament, by charter or by custom plus all the shops in the City of London. A buyer in good faith will obtain a good title if he buys goods in market overt of a type normally sold in the market, during normal market trading hours, and in the open and public part of the stall or shop.
4. *Sale under a voidable title*: s.23. Allowing a buyer in good faith to obtain a good title where he buys from a seller whose title is voidable, e.g. for fraud.
5. *Resale by a seller in possession: s.24.* Where a seller remains in possession of goods after he has sold them, and resells them, the second or subsequent buyer obtains a good title on taking delivery of the goods.
6. *Resale by the buyer in possession with the consent of the seller: s.25.* This provides that a purchaser in good faith from such a buyer will obtain a good title on delivery provided the buyer in possession acted in the normal course of business as a mercantile agent.
7. *A private purchase of a motor vehicle sold by a person who is hiring the vehicle under an HP agreement* obtains a good title provided he buys in good faith under the 1964 HP Act.
8. There are a number of other specific occasions when there is a power of sale at common law or by statute, e.g. sale by a pawnbroker of his security when the loan is unpaid, or sale of uncollected goods under the Torts (Interference with Goods) Act 1977.

REMEDIES

1.Buyer's remedies

(a) If the seller's breach amounts to a breach of condition the buyer may:
    (i) Reject the goods,
        or
    (ii) Accept the goods,
        and in either case, claim damages.

Choices (i) and (ii) are alternatives, the buyer cannot both accept and reject the same goods. Once the goods have been accepted, the right to reject is lost. The measure of damages is assessed according to the rules in *Hadley* v. *Baxendale* 1854, i.e. according to normal contractual principles.

(b) If the breach does not amount to breach of condition, the buyer has a claim for damages for breach of warranty.
(c) Where there has been a total failure of consideration the buyer may recover the purchase price, even where he has had some use of the goods (*Rowland* v. *Divall* (1) 1923).
(d) If the contract was for the sale of specific goods, which are not obtainable elsewhere, the court may grant an order of specific performance. However this is an equitable order, not available as of right, and only granted where damages would not be an adequate remedy.

2. Seller's remedies

This is a very common area for examination questions. You should be sufficiently familiar with the rules to be able to give positive practical advice to a client.

(a) *Personal actions against the buyer*
  (i) *For the price*, when this is due and has been wrongfully withheld by the buyer.
  (ii) *For damages for non-acceptance of goods*, provided this is unjustified.
  N.B. Where the buyer has no money or cannot be found these remedies are very little help. In that case remedies against the goods are of greater value.

(b) *Remedies against the goods*
  (i) *A right of lien*, i.e. a right to hold onto the goods until the seller is paid.
  (ii) *A right of stoppage in transit* where the buyer becomes insolvent. 'Insolvent' means, for this purpose, unable to pay his debts as they fall due; it is *not* the same as bankrupt. Having stopped the goods, the seller may then keep them as under (i).
  (iii) *The right of resale.* This arises: where the goods are perishable; where the unpaid seller gives notice of his intention to resell and the buyer fails to pay within a reasonable time; or where the contract expressly provides for a right of resale in the event of non payment.

USEFUL APPLIED MATERIALS

The sale of goods is now predominantly a statute based area of law so the most important source is the Sale of Goods Act 1979 itself.

HMSO publishes all the statutes. It may be helpful to use an annotated copy, giving not only the text of the Act but explanatory notes, e.g. Current Law Statutes Annotated.

The Unfair Contract Terms Act 1977 has played an important part in the sale of goods. You may find it easier to understand just how it applies from an annotated copy of the Sale of Goods Act or textbooks rather than the UCTA itself, if only because the 1979 SGA was passed *after* the UCTA and the section incorporating it is quite complicated.

CASES

In addition to the Act there are a number of cases which may be helpful in illustrating particular points. The cases given here are the cases referred to in the text. They are not intended to be exhaustive or exclusive. For further references please see textbooks. Be careful when citing them to remember that the Act is the principal source of law and the cases are merely illustrations.

1

Rowland v. *Divall* 1923
This case illustrates the essence of a contract of sale.

After three months use the buyer of a car discovered the seller was not the true owner and had no right to sell. He returned the car to the original owner, and sued the seller for breach of s.12. The court allowed him to recover the total purchase price for a complete failure of consideration, holding that the purpose of a contract of sale is to pass title, where this had not occurred the buyer had got nothing.

2

Re Moore & Co and Landauer & Co 1921
The fact that goods were not packed in accordance with contract specification was held to be a breach of s.13 (goods must correspond with description) and the buyer was allowed to reject the consignment even though total quantity of goods was correct.

3

Arcos v. *Ronaasen* 1933
Contract for the supply of wooden stakes half-an-inch thick was broken by the supply of stakes nine-sixteenths of an inch thick.

4

Grant v. *Australian Knitting Mills* 1936
Purchaser bought underpants which when worn caused dermatitis because of a chemical substance remaining in the wool. The court held the underpants were not of merchantable quality, and not fit for their purpose, which was impliedly to be worn!

5

Priest v. *Last* 1903
The sale of a hot water bottle which burst was held to be a breach of s.14(3) (fitness for a particular purpose) even though the buyer had not expressly said he was going to put hot water into the bottle. The 'normal' purpose will readily be regarded as the particular purpose.

6

Frost v. *Aylesbury Dairies* 1905
Milk contaminated with typhoid was held unfit to drink. The seller's defence that he had taken reasonable care was held irrelevant to an absolute obligation.

7	*Griffiths* v. *Peter Conway Ltd* 1939
	A good example of goods being of merchantable quality but not fit for their particular purpose. A lady with sensitive skin bought a Harris Tweed coat from the defendants. The coat was found to be of merchantable quality and reasonable fitness for most people to wear. The sellers were not in breach of s.14(3) because the purchaser had not made known her particular purpose, i.e. a coat suitable for her particular skin problem. Contrast with *Baldry* v. *Marshall*, below.

8	*Baldry* v. *Marshall* 1925
	Buyer asked for a car suitable for touring. Seller supplied a Bugatti, a large racing car. The court held the goods were not fit for their particular purpose, which the buyer had disclosed, and relied on the seller to supply.

9	*Couturier* v. *Hastie* 1856
	Here is a good example of an old common law rule being translated into statute. Section 6 SGA 1979 reproduces.
	The sale of a cargo of corn was held void when it was discovered that at the time of sale, unknown to either party, the ship's master had already sold the cargo, and therefore the corn no longer existed.

10	*Eastern Distributors Ltd* v. *Goldring* 1957
	An interesting example of estoppel, as an exception to the nemo dat rule. A car owner gave a dealer his documents of title intending to make the dealer appear to be the owner. The dealer subsequently sold the car in breach of his agreement with the owner. The court held the owner was estopped from denying the dealer's authority to sell and was therefore unable to recover the car from an innocent third party.

RECENT EXAMINATION QUESTIONS	It may be helpful to spend around ten minutes planning an answer to each question before turning to the outline answers.

Question 1.	What are the remedies of an unpaid seller in a contract for the sale of goods? (DPA 1981)

Question 2.	(a) In what circumstances, if at all, can a person who is not the owner of goods confer a valid title upon another person?
	(b) Stevens sold a quantity of canned meat to Roberts for £5000. Roberts left the cans at Steven's warehouse intending to fetch them in due course. Stevens later received an offer of £6000 for the goods from Webster and sold them to Webster who collected them.
	Advise Roberts. (ICSA 1981)

Question 3.	(a) When does the property in goods pass to the buyer under the Sale of Goods Act 1979?

(b) (i) John sells Barbara fifty tons of wheat, his entire stock, which he is holding in Silo no. 2 in his warehouse; Barbara to take delivery and pay for the goods within a week from the date of the sale. The next day John's warehouse (which is not insured) is burnt down. Barbara is concerned as to who will have to bear the loss of the wheat.
Advise her.

(ii) Would your advice be any different if the wheat had formed part of a quantity of 1000 tons of wheat lying in John's warehouse and at the time of the fire no wheat had been set aside to meet Barbara's order? (ACCA 1981)

Question 4.

Julie buys a set of casseroles in a sale from her local hardware store. The casseroles are in a box on which is written: 'Oven to Tableware. Made in Britain. Suitable for all types of cooking. Do not wash in a dishwasher.' Give advice to Julie as to whether she has a claim against the store in each of the following situations.

(a) The first time she uses one of the casseroles, while she is removing it from the oven, it cracks and she scalds her hand.

(b) After two months' use, another of the casseroles becomes porous, and starts to leak.

(c) On the bottom of one of the casseroles, she finds a label which indicates it was made in Hong Kong.

(d) She puts a casserole in the dishwasher by mistake and the pattern comes off. (DPA 1983)

Question 5.

(a) What terms as to quality of fitness for purpose are implied by law in a contract for the sale of goods?
To what extent, if at all, is it possible for a seller to exclude liability for the breach of such terms?

(b) In the course of his employment with the Radon Co, Watkins was sent to take delivery of a machine which the company was buying from the Metalwork Co. Watkins examined the machine superficially and failed to notice that an important part was defective. He took delivery and, due to the faulty part, the machine did not work. The Radon Co wish to know their rights (if any) against the Metalwork Co.
Advise them. (ICSA 1983)

OUTLINE ANSWERS

These outlines are intended as a guide to the sort of material you should include and the method of approach to be taken in tackling the question. More detailed rules will be found either earlier in the chapter or in standard texts on the Sale of Goods.

Answer 1.

This is a short compulsory question, one of ten which must be answered in a suggested time of one hour. A very brief summary will do.

An unpaid seller has a personal action against the buyer for the price when this is due; a right to keep goods still in his possession until the price is paid (a lien); a right to stop goods in transit where the buyer is insolvent; and in certain cases a right of resale.

(You can list the occasions when a right of resale will arise if you have time at the end of the paper. Beware of spending too long writing all you know about a relatively simple question, you may be short of time for a more complex question later).

Answer 2.

Explain the normal rule that no one can pass a better title that he himself has, *nemo dat quod habet*, and then list the exceptions with a brief explanation:

•	Agents	(see Ch. 9)
•	Estoppel	s.21
•	Sale in market overt	s.22
•	Sale by a seller with a voidable title	s.23
•	Sale by a seller in possession	s.24
•	Sale by a buyer in possession	s.25

and specific examples at common law or under other statutes.

(b) S is a seller in possession of goods he has sold to R. Under s.24 SGA 1979 a buyer in good faith will obtain a good title on taking delivery of the goods. R should be advised that provided W bought in good faith, the goods belong to W. R cannot reclaim the goods from W but may sue S for conversion.

Answer 3.

(a) The rules for determining when the property in goods passes to the buyer are set out in the SGA 1979 in ss.17, 18.

Section 17 provides the property passes when the parties intend it to pass. Section 18 lays down rules when the parties have made no express or implied arrangements. In the case of specific goods in a deliverable state, property passes on agreement. Where the goods are not in a deliverable state, or something remains to be done to the goods by the seller, property passes when this has been done and the buyer notified.

In the case of unascertained goods, no property can pass until goods conforming to the contract have been unequivocally set aside for the contract with the knowledge of both parties.

(b) (i) The goods here are specific, J's entire stock. The contract is unconditional and the goods are in a deliverable state. Therefore, unless the parties specifically agreed that the property was not to pass, the property will have passed to B on agreement. Goods are at the owner's risk unless otherwise agreed. B is the owner, therefore she will have to bear the loss of the wheat. (Perhaps the fact that J's warehouse is uninsured may be a clue that he was not prepared to accept the risk of B's goods.)

(ii) If the wheat is only part of N's stock the goods are unascertained and no property can pass until the goods are picked out. Until this has been done the wheat remains J's and at J's risk.

Answer 4.

When you get a question with lots of small parts, usually variations on a theme, it may be easier to set out the basic rules first and then apply them to the problem. All these cases seem to relate to the implied terms as to quality of goods.

You might therefore start by setting out the basic rules.
The SGA 1979 provides certain implied terms as to the quality and fitness of purpose of goods. Section 13 provides that goods shall correspond with their description. Section 14(2) that where a seller sells goods in the course of business, the goods shall be of merchantable quality, and s.14(3) that the goods shall be fit for their particular purpose.

(a) This appears to be a breach of ss.14(2), (3): *Priest* v. *Last* (5) 1903. This would be a breach of condition. J is entitled to repudiate the contract, claim her money back and claim damages for the scald.

(b) This may be a breach of s.14(2). Discuss what is meant by merchantable quality, consider the effect of sale goods. Two months' use seems very little, suggesting breach.

(c) Breach of s.13. Goods must correspond with their description. J has the usual right to repudiate or treat as a breach of warranty, and claim damages.
    N.B. No marks for mentioning Trade Descriptions Act – not relevant to the question.

(d) Nothing to suggest breach by the seller here. J has not used the casserole in accordance with the maker's instructions and it is her own fault the pattern comes off. No claim.

A TUTOR'S ANSWER

Answer 5.

This is a very common type of question, both in content and format, and a full answer is therefore provided to this question. It is a help to break it down:

(a) *What terms as to quality and fitness for purpose are implied by law in a contract for the sale of goods?*

This is a very straight question calling for a very straight answer. It is almost impossible to quote accurately in an examination but give section numbers and a brief résumé of the content.

The Sale of Goods Act 1979 implies terms as to quality and fitness for purposes into contracts for the sale of goods. Section 13 implies a condition in all sales that the goods shall correspond with their description, s.14 applies to sales by a seller in the course of business. Section 14(2) provides that goods shall be of merchantable quality. 'Merchantable quality' means as fit for their purpose as it is reasonable to expect having regard to the price, any description applied to the goods and all other relevant factors.

Section 14(3) provides that where the buyer makes known to the seller the particular purpose for which he requires the goods, the goods shall be fit for that purpose provided the buyer relied on the seller's skill or judgment (*Baldry* v. *Marshall* (8) 1925).

(You may wish to give further examples but be careful, there are a lot of parts to this question. Most examiners in law are looking for an ability to get to the heart of the matter; there is no need to write all you know!).

To what extent, if at all, is it possible for a seller to exclude liability for the breach of such terms?

This is a good clue that liability can be excluded, but not always. This kind of question can often be quite helpful in reminding the examinee of distinctions.

Sections 13 and 14 SGA 1979, may not be excluded in consumer sales. A consumer sale is a sale where the seller deals in the course of business, and the buyer deals as a private person buying goods normally bought for private purposes. In a non-consumer sale the implied terms may be excluded subject to the Unfair Contract Terms Act 1977. This provides that an exclusion is valid so far as it is fair and reasonable. This is a question of fact taking into consideration all the circumstances.

(I have not considered s.15 (sale by sample) because of its very precise application, but if you had time you could include its provisions. No marks will be gained for including s.12, this deals with title, not quality or fitness of purpose.)

(b) *In the course of his employment with the Radon Co Watkins was sent to take delivery of a machine which the company was buying from the Metalwork Co. Watkins examined the machine superficially and failed to notice that an important working part was defective. He took delivery and, due to the faulty part, the machine did not work. The Radon Co wish to know their rights (if any) against the Metalwork Co. Advise them.*

Here we have a problem involving the principles asked for above.

The question itself gives clues: W was sent *in the course of his work* he *examined* the machine.

N.B. Specific exceptions to s.14.

This is a sale in the course of business between one company and another. Section 14 SGA 1979 applies, i.e. there is an implied condition that the goods sold shall be of merchantable quality. In this context it seems reasonable to suppose that this would mean the machine worked. Section 14 may be excluded by the parties as this is not a consumer sale, as long as this is fair and reasonable. Section 14 is also specifically excluded, by its own words, where the defect is drawn to the attention of the buyer at the time of sale, or where the buyer examined the goods before the sale and the defect is one which ought to have been discovered on a reasonable examination. On the facts there has been no obvious express exclusion, but W did examine the machine, albeit superficially. This examination, if it should have revealed the defect, is sufficient to exclude the implied terms under s.14 and the Radon Co should be advised they have no legal right against the Metalwork Co.

A STEP FURTHER

This is predominantly a statute-based area. Perhaps the first place to look is the Sale of Goods Act 1979 itself. HMSO publishes all the statutes and Halsbury provides an annotated edition which is most helpful since the 1979 Act is a consolidating Act and reference to other Acts is frequently needed.

Most standard textbooks on commercial or business law contain chapters on the sale of goods. There are also some detailed texts devoted solely to this area.

BASIC READING

Sale of Goods and Consumer Credit (3rd edn) A. P. Dobson, Sweet and Maxwell, 1984.
Sale of Goods (6th edn) P. S. Atiyah, Pitman 1980.
Charlesworth's Mercantile Law (14th edn), Stevens [Part 3], 1984.

FURTHER READING OR REFERENCE

Consumers and the Law (2nd edn) R. Cranston, Weidenfeld, 1984.
The Consumer, Society and the Law (4th edn) Borrie & Diamond, Penguin, 1981.
Benjamin's Sale of Goods (2nd edn), Sweet and Maxwell, 1981.

For a simple explanation the Department of Fair Trading publishes leaflets, many of them free, setting out the basic rules on the sale of goods designed to help consumers to know their rights. These explain in a very straightforward way what the law is. Most public libraries and citizens' advice bureaux stock these leaflets.

USEFUL ADDRESSES

National Consumer Council, 18 Queen Anne's Gate, London SW1H 9AA.

British Standards Institute, 2 Park Street, London W1A 2BS.

National Association of Citizens' Advice Bureaux, 26 Bedford Square, London W2.

National Union of Small Shopkeepers, Westminster Buildings, Theatre Square, Nottingham NG1 6LH.

Chapter 9   **Agency**

Agency is a relationship we are so familiar with it is easy to take it for granted. Whenever one person acts on behalf of another there is a possible agency. The essence of agency is that the agent, A, is able to make contracts with third parties, X, which are binding on his principal, P, while he, A, incurs no personal liability.

Individuals may use an agent for a specific purpose, e.g. to buy or sell a house or book a holiday; sole traders use agents to conduct their business as full or part-time employees or on a freelance basis; and companies, who by definition are not natural persons, can *only* act through their agents. Partners are agents of each other and of the firm while acting in the course of partnership business: Partnership Act 1890 s.5.

Because agency is so central to the running of business, it is an area which is frequently examined. In a problem question concerning agency, begin by establishing the relationship in your opening sentence, e.g. Smith is the agent of Jones. In some cases the problem will specify, F is the agent of R, and in other cases the names of the parties may help you, e.g. Albert and Percy – whom you may identify as agent and principal. For clarity, and brevity, once you have established the agency relationship it is quite legitimate to use initials only. A and P for agent and principal, and X or T for any third party. Until you have established the initial agency relationship, it will be meaningless to use these terms. You can now go on to consider which duties arise under the contract and what the consequences of the parties' conduct are.

ESSENTIAL PRINCIPLES

A CLEAR UNDERSTANDNG OF THE NATURE AND PURPOSE OF AGENCY

A contract of agency is a contract between principal (P) and agent (A) under which A is employed to make contracts with third parties on behalf of his P. The effect of such contracts is that A brings his P into privity of contract (i.e. direct contractual relations) with X (the third party) and A drops out, acquiring neither rights nor obligations to X. P and A are bound by the separate contract of agency between themselves.

HOW AGENCY IS CREATED

Agency may arise in a number of ways. Sometimes it is the deliberate act of the parties, sometimes it arises almost incidentally. You should be able to explain the usual ways in which agency arises and be able to identify the existence and effect of agency in a problem question.

Agency may arise in any of the following ways:

Express authorisation of the agent by the principal

There are no special rules on the formation of the agency contract; the instructions may be given orally or in writing or by deed. Where the agent is to execute a deed the agent must himself be appointed by deed. Very few contracts in English law are required to be made by deed (See Ch. 5); a conveyance of land would be a good example – if P wishes to authorise his agent to transfer land in his absence, authority must be given by deed. Express authorisation is the most common and the most straightforward situation. The basic principle applies, there is privity of contract between P and X, and A drops out.

Implication

An agent is taken to have the authority necessary to realise his task. At a practical level it is impossible for P to give detailed instructions for every possible eventuality. The law therefore implies such authority as is requisite or usual for someone in the position the agent has been asked to fill. This is so even if P has expressly limited or restricted A's authority, unless X knew of such restriction. This is sometimes called 'usual authority' because it involves A doing things usually done by a person in his position. For example in *Watteau* v. *Fenwick* (1) 1893, A was the manager and licensee of a pub. He ordered cigars from X, a salesman. Unknown to X, P had expressly forbidden A to purchase cigars. Nevertheless the court held that P was bound to pay for the cigars because A had made the contract on P's behalf, and it was within the usual authority of pub managers to order cigars.

Sometimes the implication of agency arises by statute, e.g. the Partnership Act 1890 s.5, specifies that all partners are agents of each other and of the firm while acting on partnership business (see Ch. 10).

Apparent or ostensible authority

In certain cases where A has no authority, express *or* implied, P will be liable as if he had. This arises where P has previously held A out as having authority, so that he appears to X to be authorised. P will now be estopped or prevented from denying A's authority, unless X knows of A's lack of authority through express notice or some other source.

This apparent or ostensible agency arising from estoppel, may be distinguished quite simply from implied authority. An estoppel cannot arise unless there has been a previous course of conduct involving the parties. The essence of the rule is that P cannot mislead X by holding out A as having authority and then deny it. Where there has been no previous conduct this cannot arise.

Apparent or ostensible authority may arise in two situations:

1. Where an unauthorised person is treated by P as having authority.
2. Where a duly appointed agent exceeds his actual authority, express or implied, but P nevertheless treats himself as bound.

In each case X is entitled to treat A at face value – in the former case as P's agent, in the latter as an A acting within his authority.

In *Freeman and Lockyer* v. *Buckhurst Park Properties Ltd* (3) 1964, BPP had allowed one of their directors to assume the powers of managing director although he had not been expressly appointed to the post. They were held liable to F and L on the basis that they were estopped from denying A's authority as managing director since they had allowed him to appear as if he were duly appointed, and the contract he had made with F and L was within the usual authority of a managing director.

Ratification

Where an agent has acted without initial authority or has exceeded the authority he was given, his P is not bound. However, P may subsequently agree to and adopt the agent's transaction; this is known as ratification. It is often the subject of examination questions, either of an 'explain what is meant by . . .' type, or inherent in a problem. The conditions necessary for ratification should be carefully learnt, together with its effect.

The following is a *brief summary of the conditions necessary for ratification*, together with supporting authorities.

1. The agent must have acted as an agent and not in his own name (*Keighley, Maxted & Co* v. *Durant & Co* (4) 1901).
2. P must have existed and had contractual capacity when the agent made the contract (*Kelner* v. *Baxter* (5) 1866).
3. P must have known all material facts before ratifying (*Marsh* v. *Joseph* (6) 1897).
4. The act to be ratified must have been legal, e.g. not a forgery and not ultra vires (*Ashbury Railway Carriage Co* v. *Riche* (7) 1875).

The effect of the ratification dates back to the time the agent made the original contract. Thus even if X has sought to change his mind between the agent making the contract and P agreeing to it, where P does ratify the contract it is valid from the moment the agent made it and not only from the moment of P's agreement (*Bolton Partners* v. *Lambert* 1889).

Necessity

In practice this is not very common, but it is an easy target for an examiner. You should be familiar with *the conditions needed* for it to arise. Briefly these are:

1. A must have control of P's property.
2. There must be a *genuine* emergency – a matter of convenience is not enough.
3. It must be impossible to obtain P's instructions.
4. A must act in good faith to protect the property.

In most cases where an agency of necessity has been successfully pleaded, the property was perishable and immediate action was needed to preserve it. For example in *Gt Northern Railway Co* v. *Swaffield* (8) 1874 the company were held to be agents of necessity when they arranged for emergency keep of a horse consigned to their care which was uncollected.

N.B. It is important to remember that an agent's primary duty is to consult his P; only when this is impossible is there the chance of agency by necessity arising.

DUTIES OF A AND P TO EACH OTHER

This is another favourite topic for examiners, either as a 'list . . .' type question or implied in a problem. In a problem question there is no need to write out the complete list, merely identify the duties which are in issue, apply them to the facts, and then conclude.

The main duties of A to P

1. A must obey P's instructions.
2. A must perform his services personally.
3. A must use reasonable care and skill.
4. A must act in good faith, i.e. not allow his interests to conflict with those of his P. This, being a common law duty, is not closely defined. It includes the following:
   (a) A must not buy or sell from his own P without full disclosure (*Armstrong* v. *Jackson* (9) 1917).
   (b) A must not act for both sides without full disclosure (*Fulwood* v. *Hurley* (10) 1928).
   (c) A must disclose all relevant information to his P and must not disclose confidential matters to others (*Keppel* v. *Wheeler* (11) 1927).
   (d) A must account to his P for money or property received, and must not mix P's property with his own (*Lyell* v. *Kennedy* (12) 1889).
   (e) A must not make a secret profit or receive a bribe (*Salford Corporation* v. *Lever* (13) *1891*).

   For breach of any of these duties P may seek compensation from A, recover any secret profits and, in the event of a *serious* breach, terminate A's contract without notice or compensation. If A acted fraudulently, P may avoid any contracts made by A.

The main duties of P to A

1. To pay A according to their agreement. Be careful to establish precisely what A has to do before the payment is earned.
2. To indemnify A for expenses properly incurred.

THE EFFECT OF AGENCY

The general rule is that A brings his P into privity of contract with X and himself incurs no personal liability. He can neither sue nor be sued on the contract with X. An A has been likened to a conduit pipe, a mere channel of communication. It is this ability of A to negotiate on behalf of his P without in any way incurring liabilities himself, and conversely allowing P to benefit from his deals, which makes agency so fundamental to the functioning of companies and all other business. Legally, when A acts within his authority, and as an agent, there are no problems and the general rule applies. Examiners, of course, look for problems and the following situations, which are exceptions to the general rule, should be learnt. *A may incur personal liability* on the contracts he makes with X:

1. When it is customary for a person in A's position to incur personal liability, e.g. A is a stockbroker.
2. If A expressly agrees with X that he, A, should be personally liable. This may occur where P is either unknown to X, or P is abroad.
3. If A signs a document in his own name without indicating that he signs as an agent.
4. If the *identity* of P is not disclosed.
5. If the *existence* of P is not disclosed. In this case A is primarily liable as he is the contracting party with whom X intended to deal, *but*, if X discovers P's existence, X may choose whether to sue A or P. He cannot sue both. Conversely, P may sue X directly, provided this is not inconsistent with A's contract. For example X made it clear he would only deal with A personally.

A's WARRANTY OF AUTHORITY

Whenever A tells X that he, A, is acting *as* an agent, A is impliedly telling X that he, A, has the necessary authority. In reliance on this X enters into the contract with P via A. If A does *not* have the necessary authority and P either cannot or will not ratify A's act, P is not bound by A's act because A was unauthorised. A is not personally liable on the contract because he acted as an agent and X had no intention to contract with A personally. In these circumstances A will be held liable to X for *breach of warranty of authority*. X may recover from A his losses incurred through there being no contract between himself (X) and P.

Thus in every case where A has acted as an agent, X will be able to sue either P, where the agency has been effective, or A under this head where it was not. Where A has not disclosed the agency, A will in any case be personally liable as the contracting party. The liability of A for breach of warranty of authority is strict. It is immaterial that A did not know of his lack of authority (*Yonge* v. *Toynbee* (14) 1910.

TERMINATION OF AGENCY

Agency ends either by law or by act of the parties. You may be asked a 'straight' question on this, or it may be the root of a problem. In brief here are the points to remember.

Agency ends by operation of law	1. On the death of either party. 2. On the bankruptcy of P or of A, if it makes him unfit for his duties. 3. On the insanity of either party. 4. By frustration, i.e. subsequent impossibility (see Ch. 7). 5. By performance, e.g. A has carried out the agreed services, perhaps found a buyer for a house. 6. By lapse of time, i.e. the agreed time period of the agency has expired.

Agency ends by act of the parties	1. By agreement between the parties.
	2. By P withdrawing his authority. In principle he can do this at any time subject to payment of damages to A for breach of contract, if this occurred. In two circumstances, however, P cannot revoke A's authority:
	  (a) Where A was appointed by deed and has a power of attorney irrevocable under the Powers of Attorney Act 1971;
	  (b) Where A's authority is coupled with an interest, as when A has authority to collect and keep P's debts to repay P's debt to him.
	3. By A resigning or giving notice to terminate the contract with P subject to liability in damages to P if the withdrawal is in breach of their agreement.
	
	As between P and A termination as to the future takes effect immediately, but their existing obligations are unaffected. As between P and X where the termination is by act of parties, termination does not affect X unless and until he hears of it. P will be estopped from denying A's authority if he has previously held A out to X as having authority, until X is notified (*Drew* v. *Nunn* (15) 1879).
	
	Where the agency is terminated by operation of law, e.g. P dies or becomes insane, the agency normally ceases immediately. X's remedy is to sue A for breach of warranty of authority (*Yonge* v. *Toynbee* (14) 1910).

USEFUL APPLIED MATERIALS	Chapter 2 gives advice on how to use authorities. In principle each time you give a rule you should try to quote the case in which the rule was either applied or laid down. Agency is essentially based on case law, there are almost no statutory rules. The principles have been expounded by the judges in applying commercial custom. Where the custom itself is very clear there may be a case you can cite as an illustration of the principle in practice. The following cases have been cited in the text. There are many others equally appropriate.
1	*Watteau* v. *Fenwick* 1893 This is a good illustration of the working of implied authority and the effect of P's limitation on A's authority. X is entitled to rely on the implied authority of A.

A, a pub manager/licensee, ordered cigars from X for sale in the bar. Unknown to X, P, the pub's owner, had forbidden A to order cigars. X was held entitled to recover the price from P because ordering cigars was within the implied or usual authority of a pub manager.

2   *Kinahan and Co Ltd* v. *Parry* 1910

This makes a good contrast with 1. above. In this case the agent acted beyond his authority and P was held not bound on the grounds that X knew or ought to have known of the limitation on A's authority.

A, the manager of a *tied* pub, ordered drink from X, who knew it was for a tied pub. X was held not entitled to recover the price from P, because X must have known A was acting outside his authority.

3   *Freeman and Lockyer* v. *Buckhurst Park Properties Ltd* 1964

This is a classic example of agency by estoppel, and is again an illustration of implied or usual authority.

BPP were held liable on a contract made by A whom they had previously held out as their managing director, although he had never been officially appointed. The contract A made was one within the usual authority of a managing director.

4   *Keighley, Maxted and Co* v. *Durant and Co* 1901

This is authority for the proposition that where P wishes to ratify a contract, A must have acted *as* an agent.

A contracted in his *own* name intending the contract to be on behalf of P. P ratified, but later refused to accept the goods. P was held not liable to pay, his ratification was held to be ineffective because A had not disclosed the agency.

5   *Kelner* v. *Baxter* 1866

This is authority for the requirement that in order to ratify an unauthorised contract P must have existed and had capacity to contract at the time A made the contract.

Three promoters of a company bought goods for the company before incorporation. After incorporation the company sought to ratify the deal. It was held that ratification was ineffective because the company was not in existence at the time the contract was made.

6   *Marsh* v. *Joseph* 1897

A good authority for the proposition that in order to ratify, P must have known all the material facts at the time.

P was held not bound by A's contract which he had ratified without knowing that A had concealed the whole truth.

7   *Ashbury Railway Carriage Co* v. *Riche* 1875

A good illustration of an attempt to ratify an ultra vires act.

The attempt by shareholders to ratify an ultra vires contract made by the company was held ineffective.

8	*Great Northern Railway Co* v. *Swaffield* 1874
	This is a good example of agency by necessity. GNR stabled a horse which had been consigned to them for transit, having been unable to contact the horse's owner when it was uncollected. The company was held entitled to recover livery costs as agents of necessity.

Loyalty and good faith

	The following group of cases are illustrations of the agent's common law duty of loyalty and good faith to his P.
9	*Armstrong* v. *Jackson* 1917
	A was held to be in breach of duty by selling some of his own shares to his P without disclosing their source.

10	*Fulwood* v. *Hurley* 1928
	An estate agent was held to be in breach of duty by claiming commission from both sides without disclosing his dual role.

11	*Keppel* v. *Wheeler* 1927
	An estate agent who failed to disclose a bid to his P was held liable to account for the loss incurred.

12	*Lyell* v. *Kennedy* 1889
	An A who was entrusted with money on his P's behalf was held to be in the same position as a trustee and bound to keep P's property separate from his own.

13	*Salford Corporation* v. *Lever* 1891
	A was held liable to P for making a secret profit. Salford Corporation was allowed to recover not only the profit from A but also the increased price from X, which X had charged them.

14	*Yonge* v. *Toynbee* 1910
	A was held liable to X for breach of warranty of authority where A's P had become insane, thereby automatically revoking A's authority.
	Where A acts without authority, whether he is aware or not, he will be liable to X for breach of warranty of authority.

15	*Drew* v. *Nunn* 1879
	Where P holds A out as having authority, P remains liable to X until X is notified of the withdrawal of authority.
	Here a husband who had always paid his wife's bills became insane. His wife continued to buy goods on credit. Tradesmen who were unaware of N's condition were held able to recover debts from him during a sane interlude.

It may be useful to spend around ten minutes planning an answer to each question before turning to the outline answers.

Question 1.

(a) Outline the ways in which an agent may acquire authority to enter into contracts on behalf of his principal.

(b) Arthur is a partner in a firm of wholefood distributors. It is agreed by the partners that all must consent to any contract in excess of $5000. Arthur enters into three contracts in the firm's name above this amount to purchase (a) a consignment of tinned fruit, (b) office equipment and (c) an expensive car. To what extent are the other partners liable on these contracts?

(ICMA 1982)

Question 2.

(a) Explain the ways in which an agent's authority may come to an end.

(b) Albert is an agent who sells paint on behalf of Peter, and wallpaper on behalf of William. He agrees to sell a quantity of both products to Thomas. At the time of sale, unknown to both Albert and Thomas, Peter had withdrawn Albert's agency and William had died. In consequence Albert is unable to deliver the goods. Advise Thomas on his rights to bring an action for breach of contract.

(ICMA 1983)

Question 3.

(a) In what ways may the authority of an agent arise?

(b) Paul engages Arthur as his agent to sell 1000 sacks of dried beans. Arthur entrusts the beans to Stan for storage until he can find a buyer. After a few days Stan notices that the beans are beginning to go rotten and are likely to contaminate other goods in the warehouse. He decides to get rid of the beans quickly, and sells them to Terry, a farmer, at a low price for use as pig food. Advise Paul.

(ACCA 1982)

Question 4.

(a) What duties are owed by an agent to his principal?

(b) Henry and George were once partners in a firm manufacturing furniture. Three years ago the partnership was dissolved and Henry carried on the business. Henry received supplies of raw material from suppliers, having led them to believe George was still a partner. Henry has not paid for the raw materials and the suppliers want to sue George.

Advise George.

(ACCA 1982)

Question 5.

(a) Explain the scope and limitations of the doctrine of 'ostensible authority' in the law of agency.

(b) The Granary Co Ltd were corn merchants. Thompson was accustomed to act as their agent in the buying of corn. In his own name he ordered a consignment of corn from the Wheat Co Ltd without informing the Granary Co Ltd of the transaction. He later informed the latter and they agreed to adopt it. When the Wheat Co Ltd presses the Granary Co Ltd to take delivery of the consignment they refused to do so.

Advise the Wheat Co Ltd.

(ICSA 1981)

OUTLINE ANSWERS

The following answers refer briefly to principles and cases considered more fully in the earlier part of this chapter, or in standard texts on agency.

Answer 1.

(a) Agency may arise in any one of five ways, namely, by express authorisation, where no special rules apply; by implication, where the agent is held authorised to carry out acts incidental to his express task; by estoppel, where P has previously held A out to X, as having authority; by necessity; or by ratification, where P accepts and adopts A's previously unauthorised act.

(b) All partners are impliedly agents of each other and of the firm in the course of the partnership business: s.5 Partnership Act 1890. In addition, a partner has express authority as given to him.

(i) Appears to be within the normal business of the partnership, therefore the partners would be bound by it, even though the amount is above the agreed level.

(ii) This might be in the ordinary course of partnership business. The partners will then be liable as under (i) above.
Additionally the partners will be liable if they have expressly authorised the purchase or have previously held A out as having their authority to buy similar equipment.

(iii) This is not apparently within the course of partnership business. The other partners will not therefore be liable unless A was expressly authorised.

Answer 2.

(a) An agent's authority comes to an end either by law or by act of parties. It will end by operation of law where either party dies; on the bankruptcy of P or A, if this affects his ability to execute his task; on the insanity of either party; by frustration; by performance; or by lapse of time. The agency will end by act of the parties either by agreement or by withdrawal by either side.

(b) Where P voluntarily terminates A's authority this does not as a rule affect X unless and until X hears of it. Peter will therefore be estopped from denying A's authority to Thomas and T should be advised to sue P. In the case of William's death the agency is terminated at once. T should be advised to sue A for breach of warranty of authority (*Yonge* v. *Toynbee* 1910).

Answer 3.

(a) Agency arises in five ways; by express authorisation, no special rules apply; by implication; by estoppel; by necessity; by ratification.

(b) Discuss whether this is an illustration of agency arising by necessity. A must be in control of P's goods; there must be a genuine emergency; it must be impossible for A to contact P; A must act in good faith on behalf of P. Consider *GNR Co* v. *Swaffield* 1874.

Stan may be able to prove he was acting as agent of necessity for A. An A must exercise his duties personally. If A was not authorised expressly or impliedly to entrust the beans to S, then A may be liable to P for breach of this duty.

Answer 4.

(a) In addition to the express duties in the contract of agency, an A owes common law duties to his P. These include: a duty to perform his services personally; to use reasonable care and skill in the performance of his duties; duties of loyalty and good faith; duty to render accounts to his P.

(b) Partners are agents of each other and of the firm in the course of the partnership business. (Partnership Act 1890 s.5). Although the partnership has been dissolved, G will be estopped from denying its continued existence to clients with whom he had previously dealt until he gives them express notice. G should be advised to advertise his retirement from the partnership and meanwhile he will be liable jointly with H for the raw materials H ordered, apparently in the course of partnership business.

A TUTOR'S ANSWER

I have chosen to give a fuller answer to question 5 because many students find this area particularly difficult. The answer deals with most of the points an examiner would be looking for. A degree of brevity is acceptable in law examinations as long as the points are clearly made.

Answer 5.

(a) An agent acting within the scope of his actual authority, express or implied, binds his P in all contracts made with X on P's behalf. Where A has no such authority, in principle his acts, even if purportedly done on behalf of P, do not bind P. However, where A *appears* to have authority, P will be bound by A's acts. This is known as the doctrine of 'ostensible authority'.

'Ostensible authority' is no *real* authority but the authority A appears to X to have. If P, by his words or conduct, represents to X either that a person who is not his agent *is* his agent, or that his agent has greater authority than in fact is the case, P will be estopped or prevented from denying his representation. The basis for this rule is that it is clearly inequitable for P to generate a mistaken understanding on the part of X, and then to seek to rely on the true state of affairs.

For instance, in *Freeman and Lockyer* v. *Buckhurst Park Properties Ltd* 1964, BPP Ltd allowed one of their directors, K, to act as managing director without formal appointment. The company honoured contracts made by K on the company's behalf in his apparent capacity as MD. In an action by F & L against BPP for breach of contract, made by K on behalf of BPP, the company was held bound by K's 'ostensible authority'. Having held K out as having authority as managing director, and honouring his contracts made as such, they were estopped from denying the truth of their representation, i.e. that K had the authority he appeared to have.

Where X *knows* the true position, i.e. that the purported agent is in fact *not* P's agent, or that the agent has exceeded his authority, then he cannot rely on P's representation and the doctrine will not apply.

(b) An agent binds his P when he has authority, express or implied; or where P is estopped from denying A's authority owing to a previous course of dealing. In this problem, T has no authority express or implied and since he acts in his *own* name rather than as agent for G Company there can be no question of estoppel.

Where an agent acts without authority, his P may still be liable on the contract if he, P, accepts and ratifies A's unauthorised act when he hears of it. In order for P's ratification to be effective, certain conditions must be met. These include the rule that the agent must have acted as an agent and not in his own name (*Keighley, Maxted & Co* v. *Durant* 1901).

In this problem T has acted in his *own* name, therefore even though G Co purport to ratify A's unauthorised transaction, the ratification is ineffective. W Co should be advised they may sue T for non-acceptance of the order. The contract was made with T personally, so that T is personally liable on it. W. Co have no liability.

A STEP FURTHER

Most standard textbooks on commercial law contain a chapter on agency. Students taking 'A' Level or professional examinations, would probably find such textbooks give adequate coverage. Those taking degree examinations or specialising in the area might prefer one of the more detailed texts devoted solely to agency (see below).

BASIC READING

An Outline of the Law of Agency, Markesinis and Munday, Butterworths, 1979.
Agency in Commerce, M. Kay, Sweet and Maxwell, 1979.
Charlesworth's Mercantile Law (14th edn) Stevens [Part 2], 1984.

FURTHER READING OR REFERENCE

Law of Agency (5th edn) Fridman, Sweet and Maxwell, 1985.
Law of Agency (15th edn) Bowstead, Sweet and Maxwell, 1985

USEFUL ADDRESSES

British Importer's Confederation, 69 Cannon Street, London EC4N 5AB.

CBI, 103 New Oxford Street, London WC1A 1DV.

London Chamber of Commerce and Industry, 69 Cannon Street, London EC4N 5AB.

Chapter 10

Partnerships and Companies

GETTING STARTED

Apart from the sole trader there are two very common forms of business association, the partnership and the company. This chapter will set out the main rules covering the legal requirements for the formation of each, consider their differences and conclude with some thoughts on the criteria for choosing one form rather than another.

Many people trade or work as sole traders or in some form of co-operative enterprise, but partnerships and companies are the most common trading units. It is an advantage to a business to have the combination of skills and capital which they are able to offer. The law on partnerships is largely contained in the Partnership Act 1890 which codified the then common law. Most of the rules had previously been established by custom and practice. In the absence of specific provision in the Act it is still the common law which governs. By contrast the law on companies is almost all to be found in statutes, notably the series of Companies Acts culminating in the Companies Act 1985. This is an area where UK membership of the EEC is very clearly responsible for the introduction of changes in the law required to bring our own internal system into line with that of Europe. The harmonisation of company law has been one of the Commission's first tasks.

ESSENTIAL PRINCIPLES

A. PARTNERSHIPS

Definition

Section 1 Partnership Act 1890 defines a partnership as '*the relation which subsists between persons carrying on a business in common with a view to profit*'.

Note carefully what the definition requires:

1. There must be a *business* carried on, the mere fact that property is owned jointly, or that profits are shared is not enough. There may be other reasons, quite apart from partnership, for these arrangements.

2. There must also be a view to *profit*, a combination for charitable purposes or mutual help is thus not within the legal rules.

Formation

There are no specific legal rules governing the formation of a partnership other than those governing the formation of any contract (see Ch. 5). In practice it is common, certainly in professional partnerships, to make the agreement by deed – this is then known as the 'articles of partnership'. Such a deed is not required and there are many partnerships made quite informally without anything in writing. Where there is *no* written record it will be a question of fact whether there is a partnership or not. This is a question of the parties' intention to be discovered in the normal way from what they did.

The maximum number of partners is limited to 20 by the Companies Acts except for professional partnerships such as solicitors and accountants who cannot practise as companies. The partners may trade collectively under a group or firm name. In principle they may choose any name they wish subject to the provisions of the Companies Act 1985. This requires that names are not misleading e.g. suggesting connections the firm does not have, nor too similar to another firm's name. Whenever the firm wishes to use a name consisting of names other than the surnames of all the partners, the true surnames of all the partners must be displayed on letter headings and other office stationery, and displayed prominently at the firm's place of business. The word 'company' may be included in the firm name but not the words 'limited company' or 'PLC'.

Obligations between the partners and outsiders

It is of the essence of a partnership that the partners remain independent individuals, although they may combine to work together and use a joint, or firm name. Their relations to outsiders are governed by the Partnership Act 1890, these cannot be changed by internal agreement. Once a partnership is established, these rules will apply.

The liability of the firm for its partners.

1. *Every partner, acting on behalf of the firm, acts as agent for the firm and the other partners*: s.5 Partnership Act 1890. Partners bind the firm when they are acting with express authority and when they are acting within the normal course of partnership business. What is the normal course of partnership business is a question of fact. The rules of ostensible or apparent authority arising from estoppel also apply (see Ch. 9). It is what a reasonable third party would assume which is the key factor rather than the actual purpose of the partnership, e.g. a partner in a garage letting and car repair business was held liable for his partner's sale of a car to which he had no title on the ground that his partner 'was doing an act of a like kind to the business carried on by persons trading as a garage', (*Mercantile Credit Ltd* v. *Garrod* (1) 1962). Where the third party *knows* a partner is acting without authority the firm is not liable.
2. *Liability in contract, where a partner has contracted on behalf of the firm, is joint*: s.9. The plaintiff may choose to sue the firm

collectively under the agency principle, or one or some of the partners. However, he has only *one* course of action which is extinguished by the judgment, i.e. he cannot later bring a second cause of action if the judgment is unsatisfied against other partners not named in the first action.

3. *Liability in tort arises according to the ordinary principles of vicarious liability* (see Ch. 14), i.e. the firm will be liable where the tort was expressly authorised, or where the wrong was committed in the course of the partnership business, (*Hamlyn* v. *Houston & Co* (3) 1903).

   Liability in tort is joint and several: s.10, i.e. the plaintiff in a tort action has several causes of action which he may bring jointly, suing the partners collectively, or severally, suing first one and then, if unsatisfied, another (*Kendall* v. *Hamilton* (2) 1879).

4. *In principle each partner is wholly liable for the full amount of the firm's liability*. In practice a plaintiff will normally sue the firm collectively rather than any one individual, but he is entitled to claim from a single partner, or having obtained a judgment against the firm to enforce it against any partner. Contribution will then be a matter of internal account between the partners.

5. *The* **partnership property** *is primarily liable to satisfy the firm's debts owed to outsiders and to account to the partners for expenses incurred*. Partnership property consists of all the property specifically brought into the partnership stock, acquired with partnership money, or otherwise acquired on behalf of the firm. Where the partnership property is insufficient to meet the firm's debts, recourse may be had to the assets of the individual partners – unlike a company a partnership has no separate existence and the partners have unlimited personal liability.

Relations of the partners to each other

Unlike the partners' obligations to third parties which are governed by law, the partners' *internal* relations are a matter for agreement between themselves. Where there is no specific agreement, or the agreement is silent, s.24 Partnership Act lays down the following rules:

1. All partners are entitled to an equal share in the profits and must contribute equally to the losses.
2. The firm must indemnify partners against liability properly incurred in the ordinary course of business or in anything necessarily done for the preservation of the business.
3. A partner is entitled to interest on loans made to the firm beyond his agreed capital input.

   N.B. He is not entitled to interest on his capital before the calculation of profit.
4. Every partner is entitled to participate in the management of the firm.
5. No partner is entitled to remuneration for his services unless expressly agreed (for practical purposes partners will usually need some regular income, and this may be provided in the form of an

agreed salary to be taken into account before assessment of profits).

6. No new partner may be introduced without the consent of all the existing partners.

7. Disputes as to ordinary matters may be settled by majority, but any change in the nature of the business requires unanimous agreement.

8. Partnership books (records and accounts) must be kept at the firm's principal place of business and be available for inspection and copying by any partner or his agent at any time.

9. A partner can only be expelled from the firm if an express power has been conferred by agreement between the partners: s.25.

In addition to these specific duties there are also general duties of good faith based on the old common law duties. These are:

1. To render true accounts and full information on all things affecting the partnership to any partner or his legal representative: s.28.

2. To account to the firm for any benefit derived by him without the consent of the other partners from any transaction concerning the partnership property, name or business connection: s.29.

3. Not to compete with the firm by carrying on a rival business. Section 30 requires any profit made from such rival business to be paid over to the partnership.

Dissolution of partnership

A partnership may end automatically by law or by act of the parties.

1. **By law** on:
   (a) The death or bankruptcy of any of the partners (however, provision is commonly made for the continuation of the business as a new partnership with the remaining partners continuing on the same terms).
   (b) Any event making the carrying on of the business illegal, e.g. government regulation.
   (c) The expiry of a fixed term or the completion of the venture.

2. **By agreement.** Any partner may retire from the partnership on giving the agreed notice to the others. Where the original agreement was by deed, notice must be given in writing, otherwise oral notice is sufficient.

3. **By order of the court.** Any partner may apply to the court for a dissolution order on a number of specified grounds, including the insanity of a partner or circumstances rendering it just and equitable to dissolve the partnership.

Settlement of accounts

Section 44 lays down the rules which apply to the distribution of assets on a dissolution in the absence of contrary agreement. Very often partners will vary these provisions and make their own arrangements, particularly where there is the intention that the firm shall continue after the death or retirement of a partner.

B. COMPANIES

Introduction

In addition to natural (human) persons the law recognises certain groups as having collective rights or duties. For example, a partnership is recognised as a unit to the extent that the partners may trade under a firm name, sue and be sued collectively and hold partnership property which is primarily liable for the partnership debts – but this liability is *in addition to*, rather than instead of, the liability of the individuals who make up the partnership. The partners always remain personally and individually legally responsible for their firm's debts. A trade union, or a sports club, may also be regarded as a unit for certain purposes, but again the individual members retain separate liability. However, it is possible, by incorporation, for a group of individuals to create a new artificial legal person, a corporation, which exists independently from them and for whose debts they are not automatically responsible.

There are various forms of corporation depending on their purpose and method of creation.

Corporations generally

Corporations may be created in three ways:

1. Royal Charter;
2. An individual Act of Parliament; or
3. Incorporation under the Companies Acts.

Cities and Boroughs have been incorporated by Royal Charter from Norman times. Trading corporations were first created by Royal Charter in the sixteenth and seventeenth centuries; the Hudson's Bay Co, and the East India Co are early examples. Today a Royal Charter is only likely to be issued to an educational or charitable foundation e.g. a new college.

During the eighteenth and nineteenth centuries with the expansion of trade and the increasing demands of industry, both for capital and resources, corporations were created by individual Acts of Parliament. Most of the early public utility companies, gas, water, electricity and railway, were formed in this way. Today our nationalised industries, or privatised national industries, such as British Telecom are created in this way.

The Companies Act 1844 provided for the first time a method of incorporating *any* company *by registration* according to the rules it set down. This Act was the forerunner of a whole series of Acts which have modified and adapted the rules.

Under this legislation a company may be:

1. *Limited by shares.* This is the usual for a trading company and is the model discussed in this chapter.
2. *Limited by guarantee.* This is often used for educational purposes or arts festivals. The liability of the individual members for the debts of the company is limited to the amount of their guarantees.
3. *Unlimited.* This is unusual because although it has the advantage of a separate legal identity, its members are in the same position

as partners with unlimited liability, but without the rights of partners to participate in the management of the company.

Characteristics of corporations	*All* corporations share the following characteristics:

1. They are a separate legal entity;
2. They cannot die;
3. They are subject to control on formation and running;
4. Their legal capacity is limited by their documents of creation.

A limited liability company

This is by far the commonest form of trading association. Like all corporations a *limited liability company is an artificial legal person with a separate and distinct existence apart from its members (Salomon* v. *Salomon & Co Ltd* (4) 1897). In the event of the business failing and being unable to meet its debts the liability of its members for the company's debts is limited to the amount remaining unpaid, if any, on their shares. It should be noted carefully that, although the company is called a limited liability company, it is not the *company's* liability which is limited, only that of its members. The company remains liable for its own debts in the same way as an individual.

A limited liability company may be either a *private limited company* or a *public limited company.* A public company may sell its shares to the public and for this reason is subject to greater control than a private company. A company will be a private company unless it specifically asks for registration as a public company. In practice the majority of companies are private companies. A private company may apply to 'go public' and a public company may less commonly convert to a private company.

Formation of a limited liability company

A company may be registered under the Companies Acts by its promoters or founders filing the relevant documents with the Registrar of Companies. These documents are:

The Memorandum of Association

This is a formal request to form the company signed by at least two subscribers who are the firm's first shareholders. The document must contain the following information:

1. *The company's name.* In principle the subscribers may choose any name they wish with the same limitations as applied to a partnership's choice of name, i.e. it must not be misleading or too similar to another company. The name should end 'limited company' or 'PLC' if a public company.
2. *A statement that the company is to be a public company, if this is the case.*
3. *Whether the registered office is to be in England and Wales or Scotland.* The actual address of the registered office has to be given separately. This may be at any fixed address, not necessarily at a place of business.
4. *The objects clause.* This sets out the purposes for which the company is being incorporated. It is one of the most important clauses since the company's ability to trade is limited to its

registered objects. Any contract made outside these objects is *ultra vires* and void, (*Ashbury Railway Carriage Co* v. *Riche* (5) 1875). However, an outsider dealing with the company in good faith and not knowing the transaction is outside the company's power is now protected by s.9 European Communities Act 1972 which permits him to enforce the transaction.

In addition to s.9 the effect of the *ultra vires* rule is mitigated in two ways:

(a) It is the practice to draft the objects clause widely to give the directors maximum scope; but potential investors may be wary of too unlimited power being given!

(b) There is power to amend a company's articles by special resolution given in s.4 Companies Act 1985.

5. *A clause stating that the members have limited liability,* if this is the case.

6. *A statement of nominal capital and its division into shares.* The nominal capital is the face value of the total number of shares which the company is authorised to issue, e.g. £50,000 divided into 50,000 shares at £1 each. Some of the shares must be issued immediately, others may be issued later when the company needs more capital.

The Articles of Association	These are the rules which provide for the internal organisation of the company. Every company is free to draft its own rules. If they do not, the model set of Articles provided in the Companies Regulations 1984 will be implied. The Articles must provide for such matters as, company meetings; the rights of shareholders, the appointment, retirement, removal and powers of directors, and the declaration of dividends. Alteration to the Articles is possible under s.9 1985 Act.
Statement of the nominal capital	This is the nominal value of the shares the company is authorised to issue – the shares will of course, be bought or sold at their current *market* value, which may be more or less than the nominal value.
Particulars of first directors/ secretary – and address	With their signed consent to act and the proposed address of the registered office.
A statutory declaration	This declares that all the requirements of the Companies Acts have been complied with.

The running of a limited liability company

Directors

Since it is an artificial legal person, a company can only act through its agent, the board of directors, which is responsible for the management of the company's affairs. The directors' rights and duties are laid down in the articles of association. Directors of the company are not, as such, employees of the company and will not be entitled to any remuneration unless express provision is made. Notice of loans and payments made to directors must be published annually.

In addition to the specific rights and duties laid down in the articles, directors owe common law duties of loyalty and good faith to the company similar to those owed by agents to their principal (see Ch. 7) *Regal (Hastings) Ltd* v. *Gulliver* (6) 1967.

Individual directors acting without express authority, have no power to bind the company. They are not agents of the company.

N.B. Where a company has held an individual director out on a previous occasion as having authority, it may be estopped or prevented from denying the authority on a subsequent occasion (*Freeman and Lockyer* v. *Buckhurst Park Properties Ltd* (7) 1964, see Ch. 7).

Control	Companies are closely controlled by law. There are a large number of statutory requirements with which they must comply, e.g. all companies are required to submit annual returns to the Registrar of Companies including their audited accounts, directors' statements and current particulars of members. The Department of Trade has wide powers to conduct investigations into a company's affairs. Internally companies are required to have a company secretary who is responsible for the administration of meetings, notices, resolutions and accounts.
Meetings	All companies are required to hold an annual general meeting which all shareholders have the right to attend. The directors are answerable at such meetings to the shareholders who usually have the power to vote a director out of office. An extraordinary meeting may be called at any time by the directors or at the request of the holders of one tenth of the paid up shares. The articles provide for the periods of notice required and the majority needed for the resolutions. Normally ordinary resolutions are passed by simple majority and special or extraordinary resolutions (e.g. to alter the objects clause) require a three-quarters majority.
The winding up of a limited company	Since a company is an artificial entity it cannot die. It will only cease to exist if it is legally brought to an end, this is known as a winding up. A winding up may be either voluntary, or by court order. The shareholders may resolve at any time that the company should stop trading. This may be for *any* reason, not merely financial pressure. If the company is in financial difficulty and the shareholders do not agree to a winding up, one of its creditors may petition the court for a winding-up order. In this case the court will appoint a receiver or liquidator to realise the assets and preside over their distribution in the statutory way. A specific order for the payment of debts is laid down with the shareholders and other unsecured creditors being postponed to the claims of the preferred creditors.
Choice of Form	There are many factors which will influence the choice of legal form in which a business is run. The following points of contrast and comparison between a company and a partnership may help.
1	*A company is a separate legal person distinct from its members, and cannot die.* Its members or directors may change but the company goes on. This avoids the problems which may arise for partners when one partner dies or retires.

2	*A company is able to raise money by selling its shares.* A partnership has a normal maximum of 20 partners contributing capital.
3	*The shareholders in a limited company enjoy limited liability.* The company is a separate legal entity, its debts are its own and are not recoverable from its members. Partners are liable wholly for the firm's debts. (It is *possible* to have a partnership where some of the partners have their liability limited under the Limited Partnership Act 1907 but this is very uncommon.)
4	*A company is able to borrow money against the security of a floating charge* (a charge over current movable assets which crystallizes if the company is unable to repay, giving the creditor a real security). This is not available to partners.
5	*Both companies and partnerships may hold property and sue and be sued in the firm's name as a unit.* In the case of partnerships, the partnership property is primarily answerable for the firm's debts.
6	*A company separates management and capital, all partners have the right to manage.* The shareholders in a company, as such, have no rights of management other than to participate in the annual general meeting and other extraordinary meetings. It is the directors of the company who have the power to manage. *N.B.* In fact most companies require their directors to hold some 'qualifying' shares, so directors will also be shareholders.
7	*In a company an investor may hold as many shares as he can afford and may sell all or any of them whenever he wishes.* In a partnership, there is usually a substantial minimum input and once invested this can only be recovered on dissolution of the partnership. A partner cannot sell his share in whole or in part. Thus there is much more liquidity for the investor in a company.
8	*There is no necessary formality in the setting up of a partnership and no outside control over its running; its accounts are private, and there is no limit to the changes in the business the partners may make.* A company must be incorporated under the provisions of the relevant Companies Acts, and throughout its life is strictly controlled by them. Its accounts must be published annually, its shares may be bought by people over whom it has no control, and its objects clause limits its power to contract.
9	*Partners are taxed as individuals, company profits are taxed at corporation tax rates.* At the point where it is cheaper for the business to pay corporation tax rather than for its members to be taxed individually the business should consider incorporation. The size and turnover of the business is thus a very key element.

10

Emotional Factors. If the choice is not made on economic grounds, e.g. to raise money, or to maximise income by minimising tax liability, emotional factors may be relevant. Some people may prefer to remain as individuals with personal responsibility rather than shelter behind the facade of incorporation. The advantages of freedom from outside control may be seen as outweighing the costs.

USEFUL APPLIED MATERIALS

This area of law is based on statute, the most useful materials are very often the relevant Acts themselves. However, there are a number of old common law decisions illustrating the working of particular sections, or principles. Only a few cases have been cited in this section, preference having been given to concentrating on the basic issues involved. The following cases are very well known and illustrate the most basic points.

1

Mercantile Credit Ltd v. *Garrod* 1962
All partners are agents of the partnership while acting in the course of partnership business.

G was held liable as a partner in a car repairing and garage letting business for the default of his partner in selling a car to which he had no title. G was held liable despite the fact that the partners had expressly agreed *not* to sell cars on the ordinary principles of implied authority of an agent. It appeared to X that the firm would be likely to sell cars, and X was unaware of the internal agreement of the partners.

2

Kendall v. *Hamilton* 1879
The liability of the partners in a firm for their contractual obligations is joint. Once the action has been brought a second action will not lie on the same cause. (This is now s.9 Partnership Act 1890). X sued some partners in the firm for the return of a loan. They were insolvent and the judgment was unsatisfied. X then started a second action against the remaining partner. The court dismissed the action.

3

Hamlyn v. *Houston & Co* 1903
Following the normal principles of vicarious liability a firm will be liable for the torts of the partners committed in the course of partnership business. This is always a question of fact. In this case the firm was held liable for the act of a partner in bribing the clerk of a rival form to disclose information!

4

Salomon v. *Salomon & Co Ltd* 1897
This is the classic case which is the authority for the proposition that a company is a separate legal entity distinct from its members.

S was a successful boot manufacturer and leather merchant. He formed a limited company and sold his business to the company. The company issued paid up shares for two thirds of the value of the business which were held by S, his wife, and their five children, and issued debentures for the remaining third to S. (Debentures are secured loan stock giving their holders preference in any liquidation.) Subsequently the business declined and the company went into liquidation. Its assets were insufficient to meet its debts. S, as the debenture holder, was paid before the unsecured creditors. They complained that S and the company were in reality the same person and that it was a fraud on them that he should be paid first. The House of Lords held the company was an entirely separate entity, there had been no fraud since the company had been solvent when properly incorporated, and S was entitled to payment.

The collapse in the UK of Sir Freddie Laker's 'Laker Airways.' is a recent example of a 'one man company' being separate from its founder/members.

5

Ashbury Railway Carriage Co v. *Riche* 1875
A company has limited legal powers, these are contained in the objects clause of its memorandum of association. Any act outside these powers is ultra vires and void.

In this case the company was authorised to make railway carriages. It undertook to finance the building of a railway line in Belgium. This agreement was held void as outside its powers and subsequent ratification by the shareholders was therefore invalid.

6

Regal (Hastings) Ltd v. *Gulliver* 1967
Directors of a company must not make secret profits from confidential information acquired through their position.

The company successfully bought and sold some cinemas. Some of the directors, using their knowledge of the project, invested some of their own money and made a personal profit. The court held the directors were liable to account to the shareholders for this secret profit.

7

Freeman and Lockyer v. *Buckhurst Park Properties Ltd* 1964
A company may be bound by unauthorised acts according to the ordinary rules of estoppel.

B Ltd were held estopped from denying the managing director's authority they had previously held out one of their members as having, even though he had no formal appointment (see Ch. 7 for fuller details).

RECENT EXAMINATION QUESTIONS

It may be useful to spend around ten minutes planning an answer to each question before turning to the outline answers.

Question 1.	What is a corporation? How is it created? How are its powers affected by the ultra vires rule? (ICSA 1983)
Question 2.	(a) What is a corporation? How may corporations be created? (b) What are the main consequences which follow from the incorporation of a company? (ACCA 1981)
Question 3.	(a) Explain what is meant by a partnership and illustrate your answer with examples. (b) Lucy and Jane are in partnership to run a hairdressing business. Without consulting Jane, Lucy places an order for six new hair dryers; the business does not have enough money in the bank to pay for them. Jane uses the wrong solution on a customer's hair which turns green. Discuss their liability. (DPA 1981)
Question 4.	Harriet and two of her friends are considering opening a small factory to manufacture soft toys. They seek your advice on whether they should form a partnership or a small company. Explain to them: (a) What is meant by and how to form: (i) a partnership (ii) a company; (b) Whether there are any advantages in forming a company rather than a partnership. (DPA 1983)
Question 5.	Pam, May, Kath and Sally are partners in a small business which produces hand-knitted garments. The business grew out of part-time work they had previously done together and no formal documents such as articles of partnership have ever been signed. Each partner is dissatisfied with the business and feels she has a cause for complaint. (a) Pam, who is unmarried, believes that she works much harder than the other partners but receives only the same amount of money from the business as the other three. (b) May wants her sister Doris to join the business since she has recently studied textile design at college, but the other partners will not agree. (c) Kath wishes the business to use some of the firm's profits to buy a yarn factory. The other partners believe the capital outlay is too great. (d) Sally wants to take up part-time work with a firm which produces shetland sweaters by machine. The sweaters are similar to the ones produced by her own firm, so the other partners object to her proposal. Advise each partner on the legal implications of her separate complaints. (DPA 1982)

OUTLINE ANSWERS

Answer 1.

(A very straightforward question but one which is frequently asked with variations on the theme). A corporation is an artificial legal person recognised by the law, having capacity to own property and sue and be sued in its own name.

Corporations may be created in a variety of ways:

(i)   By Royal Charter,
(ii) By special Act of Parliament,
(iii) By incorporation under the Companies Act 1985.

Explain briefly the differences and give some examples known to you.

The ultra vires rule means that any act which a company commits which is outside the objects in memorandum of association is void, *Ashbury Railway Carriage Co* v. *Riche* 1875. In practice this rule is mitigated; the objects clause is always drafted widely to give the directors maximum flexibility; an outsider dealing in good faith with the company, not knowing of the restriction, is not affected by it – the company's act is valid as far as he is concerned: s.9 European Communities Act 1972, i.e. he may enforce it although the company may not; and the company may change its objects clause by special resolution.

Answer 2.

(a) Give the same points as for 1. above.
(b) Look at the section comparing companies and partnerships for some discussion of this. The following points could be listed with elaboration as required, including the advantages gained.
   (i)   A company is a separate legal entity distinct from its members, *Salomon* v. *Salomon & Co Ltd* 1897.
   (ii)   The members of a company may have limited liability.
   (iii) The company cannot die.
   (iv)   The running of the company will be governed by the company legislation. Annual accounts must be presented to the Registrar of Companies.
   (v)   The company may raise money on the security of a floating charge over its assets.
   (vi)   The company may be taken over if enough of its shares are bought.
   (vii) The company will only cease trading if officially wound up in accordance with the procedures.
   (viii) The company must have a secretary who is responsible for its administration and the keeping of the statutorily required records.

Answer 3.

(a) A partnership is defined in s.1 Partnership Act 1890 as 'the relation which subsists between persons carrying on a business in common with a view to profit.' Common examples are firms of accountants or solicitors. (You could expand on the definition if you have time.)

(b) This is a favourite topic for examination questions, either asking what is the difference between joint, and joint and several liability? or in the form of a problem question involving a contractual duty or a tort by a partner. Ask first, was the act committed in the course of partnership business, expressly or impliedly? Then consider the nature of the liability, contract or tort? and then the liability of the parties concerned.

L and J are partners. All partners are agents of each other and of the partnership when acting in the course of the partnership business: s.5 Partnership Act 1890. L's placing an order for six new hair dryers appears to be within the ordinary business of a hairdresser, therefore the partnership is bound. The partnership is primarily liable for the debts of the firm but if the firm's assets are insufficient the partners individually are liable to pay for them. L and J should be advised that they are jointly liable for the cost of the hair dryers.

J's using the wrong solution on a customer's hair appears to be negligence, a tort, committed in the course of partnership business. The partnership will therefore be liable for the damage to the customer, according to the ordinary principles of vicarious liability. Partners' liability in tort is joint and several: s.10 Partnership Act 1890.

Answer 4.

(a) (i) give definition of partnership as above (3.(a)). No special form is needed, it is a question of intention.
(ii) explain what a corporation is and the consequences of incorporation (see 2. above), distinguishing public and private companies.
(b) This will depend in large measure on the size and needs of the business. Consider points made in the section on choice of form. The consequences of incorporation may be an advantage or not.

A TUTOR'S ANSWER

Here I present a full answer to question 5.

Some examinees are rather overawed by this sort of long and involved question. Really there is no need to be alarmed. When the problem is broken down it becomes a series of individual points which are quite straightforward to answer. Always follow the same technique, analyse what is the difficulty, state the applicable law, apply to the facts and conclude.

Answer 5.

Where a partnership has been formed without any firm agreement, the provisions of the Partnership Act 1890 apply. In the problem given there is no formal agreement, therefore the Partnership Act applies to the various problems experienced by the partners.

(a) Under s.24 all partners are entitled to an equal share in the capital and profits of the business if there is no agreement to the contrary. This is so even if the amount of work put in is not equal.

Pam should therefore be advised she has no right to any greater share of profits than her partners even if she does work harder.

(b) Section 24 provides that in the absence of express intention to the contrary a new partner may only be introduced into a partnership with the consent of all the existing partners. May should be advised that the decision whether or not to take in her sister, Doris, as a partner rests with *all* the partners and she, May, has no right unilaterally to introduce Doris.

(c) In principle all partners have implied authority to act on behalf of the firm in the course of the firm's business: s.5 Partnership Act 1890. The purchase of a weaving factory is quite different from the business of producing hand-knitted garments. This would therefore seem to be outside any such implied authority. Where a change of business is contemplated, the change must be agreed by all the parties unanimously: s.24. Since the other partners will not agree, Kath should be advised the firm cannot be committed to the purchase of the factory.

(d) All partners owe a duty of loyalty and good faith to each other and to the firm. This duty includes the duty to account for benefits derived from the partnership property or business without the consent of the other partners, i.e. not to make secret profits: s.29, and not to compete with the firm without the consent of the other partners: s.30. Sally should be advised that her working part-time for a firm producing a product similar to that produced by her partners, and being marketed in competition with them, would certainly amount to breach of these obligations. As the other partners do not consent to Sally taking this part-time job, she should be advised not to take the job, or if she does, that she will be answerable to her partners for any profit she might make.

A STEP FURTHER

Companies and partnerships are very much part of everyday commercial life. A close look at the financial pages in the national press, or the more specialist *Financial Times* will keep you up to date with City news. By their very nature, partnerships are private and less is published about their internal workings. You could make a survey of firms and see which ones operate as partnerships and which have chosen to incorporate. Architects have recently been given permission by their professional body, RIBA to incorporate, perhaps you could enquire how many local firms have taken advantage of this new freedom, and consider why they have made the change. Your local small business centre will have some literature on setting up in business giving advice and guidelines on the pitfalls to be avoided. This should contain useful information on the comparative advantages of the different forms of business, and checklists for a new entrepreneur to consider.

Banks, unit trust funds, and the Stock Exchange, all produce promotional material on their services which will give you an insight into the world of financial markets from the investors viewpoint. The Stock Exchange also has its own internal regulations. The Exchange has a visitors gallery and provides guides to explain the nature and purpose of its operation. Most public libraries contain collections of the annual reports of some of the larger companies, such reports are usually also available on request to the companies directly.

BASIC READING

Charlesworth & Cain on Company Law (12th edn), Sweet and Maxwell, 1983.
Cases and Materials in Company Law (3rd edn) Sealy, Butterworths, 1985.
Law of Partnership (3rd edn) C. D. Drake, Sweet and Maxwell, 1983.

FURTHER READING OR REFERENCE

Company Law, Farrar, Butterworths, 1985.
Guidebook to British Company Law, J. Lowe, CCH Eds, 1983.
Partnership Law and Practice, Burgess & Morse, Sweet and Maxwell, 1980.
The Law of Partnership (15th edn) Ld. Lindley, Sweet and Maxwell, 1984.

USEFUL ADDRESSES

Companies House, 55–71 City Road, London E.C.1.

Stock Exchange, Tower Building, Old Broad Street, London E.C.1.

Chapter 11

Employment – Creation and Content of Contract

A contract of employment is a contract made by agreement of the parties like any other contract, but in recent years Parliament has laid down a great many rights and duties on the part of both employer and employee which are implied automatically. It is now one of the more technical branches of the law. Because of its great practical importance it is an area examiners often choose.

Where one person wishes to hire the services or labour of another, there are various ways in which he can do it, not all resulting in a contract of employment. For example if I hire a taxi-driver to drive me home after a late-night party, he does not become my employee. For political and economic reasons there has recently been a shift away from councils employing direct labour towards 'privatising' services. This means that instead of the council employing its workers directly they have contracted out their needs to independent firms. The relationship between the council and the contractors is similar to my relationship with the taxi-driver, in each case a firm or an individual has been hired to do a particular job rather than join the organisation.

Legally there are great differences in the rights and duties incurred according to the nature of the contract made. In this chapter consideration will be given to defining who is an employee under a contract of service, and the method of creating the contract of employment. Additionally the main terms and obligations arising under such a contract will be summarised.

ESSENTIAL PRINCIPLES

A contract of employment is a contract of service, a contract for the work of an independent contractor is a contract for services.

WHO IS AN EMPLOYEE?

There is no clearcut definition of the distinction between a contract of service and a contract for services. If there is doubt or the matter is in issue the court or tribunal must decide. The following tests may be used:

1. *What does the contract say? Does it read like a contract of service?* Where there is a written contract this should always be referred to first. If the contract states clearly whether a man is an employee or an independent contractor that is likely to be conclusive. However the courts will always consider the reality of the relationship and will not allow something to be dressed up as something which it is not. Where there is no express statement but the contract makes provision for holiday pay or sick pay, it will probably be read as a contract of service.

2. *Who pays National Insurance Contributions?* Where an employer is paying employer's NI contributions on behalf of a worker, the contract is likely to be construed as one of employment. On the other hand, the fact that an employer is *not* paying, or that a man is paying his own contributions, is not conclusive that there is no contract of employment – many 'employers' are quite happy to try to opt out of their statutory obligations by presenting their labour as self-employed.

3. *How much control is exercised over the way the work is done?* Traditionally the common law test to establish the liability of a master for the torts of his servants rested on the control the master exercised over the way in which work was done (see Ch. 14). In an increasingly technical age people are often employed for their particular skill and it is quite unrealistic to suppose that their employer would be in a position to influence how their work should be done. This control test has therefore rather fallen into disuse but the general idea it conveys of the relationship of an employer and his worker remains helpful.

4. *Is the man an integral part of the business or is he working on his own account for his own profit?* This is one of the more recent attempts to formulate a coherent test. It asks the commonsense question, is the man an integral part of the team? or brought in from outside to do a specific job? If the former he is an employee, if the latter he is an independent contractor.

    N.B. No single test is conclusive – when the distinction is in issue the court or tribunal will take into account all the relevant factors. This is known as the *multiple test.*

| **Consequences of the distinction** | In principle it is entirely up to the parties whether they contract for service or services, subject only to the overriding rule that an agreement must not be illegal or designed to defraud. However the following differences may influence their choice: |

1. An employer is liable for the torts of his employees committed in the course of their employment. He is not normally so liable for the torts of his independent contractors (see Ch. 14).
2. An employee is taxed under Schedule E (PAYE), an independent contractor is taxed under Schedule D.
3. The employment protection legislation applies, by definition, only to employees.

MAKING THE CONTRACT OF EMPLOYMENT

No special rules apply. A contract of employment (other than one of apprenticeship which must be in writing) may be made orally or in writing, or where feasible, by conduct. However the Employment Protection (Consolidation) Act 1978 (EPCA) provides that a written statement of the main terms of the employment must be given to all full-time (16 hours plus per week) employees within 13 weeks from the start of the employment and to all part-time (eight hours plus per week) employees who have been continuously employed for five years or more. This written statement may be incorporated in an employer's written contract.

In practice many employers use standard form contracts which may be given to employees on recruitment. The statutory written statement of main terms is regarded as written *evidence* of the terms rather than the contract itself. In addition to the express terms there will be unwritten implied terms. Thus no written agreement is ever the whole contract.

The EPCA 1978 ss.1–7 and s.11 provides that the statutory notice of terms should contain the following information:

1. The names of the parties.
2. The date the employment began.
3. Whether employment with a previous employer is to count as part of the employee's continuing period of employment, and if so, when such employment began. (Many of the statutory rights are based on the length of continuous service, so the date the employment began is important.)
4. The scale or rate of remuneration, or the method of calculating it (in a great many cases the employee will be paid according to a national scale or at a union agreed rate – reference to this scale is sufficient, with the point on the scale at which the employee is to start).
5. The intervals at which remuneration is paid.
6. Any terms and conditions relating to hours of work.
7. Any terms and conditions relating to entitlement to holidays, including holiday pay.
8. Any terms and conditions relating to incapacity for work due to sickness or injury, including provision for sick pay.

9. Any terms and conditions relating to pensions and pension schemes.
10. The length of notice which the employee is obliged to give and entitled to receive to determine his contract.
11. The title and description of the job which the employee is employed to do.

At the same time the EPCA requires that notice of any disciplinary and grievance procedures operated by the employer should be given to the employee.

There is no specific formula for these though the Advisory Conciliation and Advisory Service, ACAS, has a model code which many employers find useful. Whereas there is no statutory obligation to have such a code, in the event of a dismissal involving disciplinary matters the existence of, and adherence to, such a code may be of great importance (see Ch. 12). The required information need not all be provided in one document, for example, detailed information on pension schemes, sickpay schemes and holiday entitlement may be provided in separate documents. The employee must know that the schemes exists and where he needs to go to find out more.

Express terms

Information on the points listed above is required by the EPCA, additionally an employer will spell out those terms which he feels are important. These might include, for example, some specific directions on security, safety, or hygiene. Covenants in restraint of trade limiting the employee's right to work at the end of the employment are often inserted. Such a clause will only be upheld if reasonable (see Ch. 6).

An employee may only legally be required to do what is in his contract. Where it is possible that an employee might be required to move, either in the course of his existing job, or because the firm as a whole might relocate, this should be expressly stated.

It is helpful to be specific on the precise nature of the job the employee is employed to do. Employers often prefer a fairly loose job description encompassing a range of duties. This provides flexibility but may lead to difficulty where an employer is seeking to slim his workforce on the grounds of redundancy. Technically it is not the individual who is redundant but the job, the wider the job the more difficult it is to prove it is redundant (see Ch. 12).

Implied terms

The express terms are not the whole contract, a whole series of unspoken terms are implied into contracts of employment by common law and statute.

The common law implied duties of an employee

1. *To conduct himself properly at work and elsewhere.* What amounts to misconduct is a question of fact. Guidance may be given in the terms of the contract itself, and in the disciplinary procedures. In principle lateness, absenteeism, being under the influence of drink or drugs, dishonesty, insolence or immorality would all qualify as misconduct. The requirement of proper conduct is not limited to working hours or to the workplace, any

conduct of the employee at any time and anywhere which could prejudice the employer is covered. This may seem a hard rule but any overt display of unseemly conduct may have the effect of reducing the public's confidence in an employee and hence his usefulness to his employer.

2. *To be loyal.* In the same way that an agent owes his principal duties of loyalty and good faith (see Ch. 9), so an employee owes similar duties to his employer. In particular he must not accept bribes or make secret profits. He must not disclose confidential information, even when his conscience suggests that he should. He must not compete with his employer, for example by working for a rival establishment in his spare time.

3. *To perform his services personally.* Again, like agency, employment is a personal contract, it cannot be discharged by delegation except by the employer's express consent.

4. *To be obedient.* In principle an employee must do what he is told to do, but this obligation is limited to tasks which lie within his contractual duties. Hence it is important to be precise over the job specification. For example, an employee would be entitled to refuse to obey an order to move from London to Hull unless his contract specified that he might be required to move. Where an order is to carry out an *illegal* act, or one which is totally unreasonable, the employee is released from this obligation.

5. *To take reasonable care in the exercise of his duties.* The duty extends to taking care of his employer's property and other staff or customers with whom he is in contact. The degree of care which must be exercised varies with the circumstances as in negligence (see Ch. 15). Where he breaks this duty the employee is liable to compensate his employer in the normal way, *Lister* v. *Romford Ice and Cold Storage Co Ltd* (1) 1957.

The common law implied duties of an employer	1. *To pay the agreed wages or what is reasonable.* Normally the amount and time of payment are expressly agreed. Where there is no such agreement a reasonable sum is due. What is reasonable is a question of fact to be decided by taking into account the custom of the particular trade or industry and local conditions. Where an employee is not at work because of illness it seems there is a common law obligation on the employer to pay him anyway. For this reason many employers make explicit rules as to when, and for how long, they will pay wages during sickness. Frequently entitlement to benefit is related to length of service.

     N.B. Such provisions are unrelated to the Statutory Sick Pay Scheme.

2. *To provide work.* Curiously the obligation on the employer to provide work, as opposed to paying the agreed wages, arises in only two cases:

(a) Where payment depends on work being available; for example, payment as commission on sales presupposes goods to sell even if not customers to buy.

(b)   Where work is necessary to maintain a reputation; for example, a media image is quickly lost if no opportunity of public appearance is given.

In other cases as long as the employer pays the contracted wages an employee has no cause for complaint.

3.   *To behave reasonably to their employees.* This is a very good example of the creative role of the courts in implying terms into a contract. In a number of recent cases the employer has been held to be in breach of an implied duty to treat his employees reasonably, notably where he has varied the conditions of service unilaterally or put undue pressure to conform to unreasonable work practices, *Cox* v. *Philips Industries Ltd* (2) 1976.

Statutory terms

In addition to the terms expressly agreed between the parties and the terms implied by common law, there are many terms implied into contracts of employment by the employment protection legislation. Most of the individual rights of employees are given by the Employment Protection (Consolidation) Act 1978 (EPCA) as amended by the Employment Acts 1980–82 (EA), but there are also rights arising under the Equal Pay Act 1970 (EPA), the Sex Discrimination Act 1975 (SDA), The Race Relations Act 1976, (RRA), and the Health and Safety at Work etc Act 1974 (HSWA).

Because these rights are given by statute rather than by agreement or by custom, they are extremely precise, depending on the words of the individual sections. Any detailed study would require a close analysis of the statutory provisions. Such an analysis is beyond the scope of this guide. Instead it may be useful to provide a summary of the main statutory rights given to those employees who qualify – these are the right to:

1.   Written statement of main terms of employment.   (EPCA)
2.   An itemised pay statement identifying pay and deductions.
                                                            (EPCA)
3.   Equal pay   (EPA)
4.   Guarantee of lay-off pay when work is not available.   (EPCA)
5.   Benefit when suspended from work on medical grounds. (EPCA)
6.   To be treated without discrimination on grounds of sex, race, or trade union involvement. (SDA/RRA/EPA/EPCA)
7.   Reasonable time off work to participate in union activities, with pay for union officials.   (EPCA)
8.   Time off work to carry out public duties, e.g. to sit as a magistrate,   (EPCA)
9.   Maternity pay and the right to return to work   (EPCA)
     following a pregnancy.   (EPCA)
10.· A minimum period of notice where the employer terminates the contract.   (EPCA)

11. Not to be unfairly dismissed and to ask for written reasons for dismissal. (EPCA) (RRA/SDA)
12. Redundancy pay in the event of dismissal due to redundancy. (EPCA)
13. Some payment of wages in the event of the employer's insolvency. (EPCA)
14. Protection on the transfer of an undertaking. (EPCA)

The rights which are given by statute are minimum, or floor rights, an employer may not give less and he may by agreement give more. This is frequently done in relation, for example, to a minimum notice period and to the number of days within a given period for which employees will qualify for lay-off pay. Disputes over most employment rights are heard in the industrial tribunals rather than in the common law courts.

SAFETY

Safety is governed by all three types of term; contractual, implied by common law and statutory. It is a topic of great importance and one of which examiners are very fond. At common law an employer is liable to take reasonable care for the safety of his employees. The rules are essentially those of negligence (see Ch. 15). In the event of breach the employee has the right to sue for damages in the normal way.

By contract the parties may impose whatever duties they please. According to the nature of the workplace, additional specific obligations may be agreed; breach of any of these may lead to an action for breach of contract or result in disciplinary proceedings.

The Health and Safety at Work Act 1974 provides a single statutory standard of workplace safety. It applies to all places of work, as well as any specific statutory regulations which relate to particular industries only. The HSW Act provides the following duties:

1. Every employer must ensure so far as is reasonably practicable the health, safety and welfare at work of all his employees.
   This is a very general duty. Subject in each case to the limitation of *as far as is reasonably practicable, the employer must*:
   (a) Provide and maintain plant and systems of work that are safe and without risks to health.
   (b) Arrange for the safe use, handling, storage and transport of articles and substances.
   (c) Provide adequate information and training, instruction and supervision.
   (d) Maintain any place of work under the employer's control in a safe condition.
   (e) Provide a safe working environment with adequate facilities for the welfare of employees at work.
2. Every employer owes a duty to persons other than his employees not to expose them to risk to their health or safety by reason of his operations.

3. Every person who has control over premises where people work owes a duty to the workers to see that the premises are safe and without risk to health.
4. Manufacturers, designers, suppliers and importers of things for use at work must ensure the article is so designed and constructed as to be safe and without risk to health when properly used.
5. Every employee must take reasonable care for his own health and safety at work and of those who may be affected by his work.
6. Every employee must co-operate with his employer or others to carry out the statutory duties.

In order to implement the general policy of the Act all employers are required to have a safety policy and to make this known to their employees. There is provision for the setting up of safety committees to monitor safety matters and for union members to be elected as safety representatives. Time off work with pay is given to carry out approved safety functions. Breach of any of the Act's provisions is a criminal offence punishable on first offence by a fine in the magistrates' court. The Act does not give any individual an additional right to damages. Enforcement is in the hands of the Health and Safety Executive which operates through teams of regional inspectors.

The HSW Act imposes duties to take care not just on employers with regard to their employees, but also on the *employees* themselves in respect of their own safety and that of others whom they may affect. The duties imposed are in all cases only to take such care as in all the circumstances of the case is reasonable, liability is *not* strict as it may be under the Factories Acts, e.g. for failure to fence dangerous parts of machinery. What is reasonably practicable will always be a question of fact, taking into account all the relevant circumstances as in negligence (see Ch. 15).

Where an injury at work occurs it may be necessary to consider:

1. The employer's personal liability in tort, usually for negligence.
2. The employer's vicarious liability for the tort of one of his employees committed in the course of employment.
3. Breach of contract – of an express or implied term.
4. Breach of any statutory duty. Some statutes are for the protection of a specific class, e.g. the Factories Acts, and their breach gives an individual victim a private action in tort. The HSWA gives no such private action, but breach is a criminal offence.

USEFUL APPLIED MATERIALS

The most important materials are the various statutes. There are a number of guides to employment legislation collectively, in addition to annotated editions of the actual Acts. The Department of Employment publishes very simple guides to different areas of the law, each one covering specific statutory provisions. These are obtainable free of charge from job centres and clearly outline the basic rules and how they apply.

Decisions in almost all employment cases are made by industrial tribunals rather than courts. These decisions are interesting but are not binding as precedents in the same way as decisions by the courts. It may be interesting to refer to the published cases in, for example, the Industrial Relations Law Reports. However, the courts have recently reiterated that these tribunal decisions are *not* to be treated as binding.

For this reason extensive reference has not been made by name to particular tribunal decisions, the facts and ratio of the few cases mentioned are given below.

1

Lister v. *Romford Ice and Cold Storage Co Ltd* 1957.
(This was a House of Lords decision.) An employee owes his employer a duty of care to carry out his duties carefully. Where this duty is broken the employee is liable to indemnify his employer for the loss he has caused.

L, a lorry driver, employed by the Co, drove his lorry negligently and injured his father who was also employed by the company. The father recovered damages from the Co who were held vicariously liable for the tort of their servant committed in the course of his employment. The Co was then allowed to recover the loss they had thus suffered from L.

2

Cox v. *Philips Industries Ltd* 1976
An employer has an implied duty to treat his employees reasonably. Altering the conditions of service unilaterally may amount to breach of such duty.

C was demoted after asking for an improvement to his salary. His new duties were unclear and he was given no defined role. As a result he became ill. The court allowed him to recover damages for breach of his employer's duty to behave reasonably.

RECENT EXAMINATION QUESTIONS

It may be useful to spend around ten minutes planning an answer to each question before turning to the outline answers.

Question 1.

(a) There are certain requirements essential for the validity of all contracts. Explain, with examples, how these apply to the formation of contracts of employment.

(b) When Eric is engaged as a machine operator he does not disclose that he has defective eyesight. He is injured when part of the machine breaks away because it has not been properly maintained. A person with good eyesight might have seen the forthcoming danger in time to take avoiding action.
Discuss Eric's claim for damages against his employer.

(ICMA 1982)

Question 2.

(a) Explain the distinction between an employee and an independent contractor.

(b) Your company has recently bought an old warehouse and wishes to convert this into a factory. This will involve a considerable amount of electrical installation which will take about eight months to complete. Consider the advantages and disadvantages from a legal point of view of employing electricians to carry out the work compared with engaging an electrical contractor to do it. (ICMA 1982)

Question 3.

Compare and discuss the common law duties that are owed between employer and employee and the statutory obligations owed by employers and employees under the Health and Safety at Work etc Act 1974. (DPA 1980)

Question 4.

(a) It is said that an employee owes implied duties of loyal and faithful service to his employer.
Explain the meaning of this expression and give examples of situations in which it would apply.

(b) X and Y are employed to repair television sets. Their employer has discovered that X is repairing television sets for friends at weekends whilst Y is working several nights a week as a barman in a local hotel.
On what grounds, if any, may the employer object to these spare-time activities. (ICMA 1983)

OUTLINE ANSWERS

Answer 1.

(a) Outline the normal requirements for the formation of all contracts, i.e. agreement, intention and consideration. These all apply to contracts of employment. Discuss the normal rules on the form required to make a contract, i.e. usually no special rules. In relation to contracts of employment explain the statutory rules on giving a written statement of the main contractual terms. Mention the rules on capacity, normal rules apply but remember infants are only bound by contracts of continuing obligation where the contract is substantially for their benefit. Perhaps mention that any contract which has an illegal purpose is void, covenants in restraint of trade are valid only so far as is reasonable.

(b) Outline the nature of an employer's common law and statutory obligations to his employees in respect of their safety. This problem looks like a clear breach. E's right to damages may be affected, however, because the employer's duty is only to take *reasonable* care. Since E had not disclosed his defective eyesight the employer would owe him no greater a duty of care than he would owe a sighted man. It will be a question of fact whether there was a breach in respect of *any* employee, in which case E will recover in full, or whether there was no breach in respect of a sighted man, perhaps because the risk was too slight, in which case E will not recover. Explain what is meant by reasonable care and 'as far as is reasonably practicable' in relation to the likelihood of the risk, the degree of danger and the cost of remedying the defect.

Answer 2.

(a) An employee is said to have a contract of service, while an independent contractor has a contract for services. The former is an integral part of his employer's business and under his employer's control. The latter is self-employed, and working for his own profit.

(b) An employer owes legal rights and duties to his employees which are far more extensive than those he owes to his independent contractors. He will normally be vicariously liable for the torts of his employees committed in the course of their employment, but not for the torts of his independent contractors. Perhaps most importantly an employer will be subject to the duties imposed by the Employment Protection (Consolidation) Act 1978 in respect of his employees. However, many of these rights are not earned until an employee has spent a minimum period of continuous employment with one employer. Since the company expects to finish the job in eight months, they would be free from many of the statutory obligations. In respect of safety, obligations are owed to both employees and independent contractors by those who have control over the workplace. An employer has more control over his employees and therefore owes them a slightly greater degree of care.

An employer has to pay employer's NI contributions for his employees.

Answer 3.

Outline the common law obligation to take reasonable care, usually broken down into a three-fold duty to provide adequate materials, a safe system of work and proper supervision. The statutory duties are imposed not only on employers but also on employees, manufacturers, designers, and importers. The range and effect of the statutory and common law duties are very similar. In each case an employer must take such care as in all the circumstances is reasonably practicable. Explain what factors should be taken into account here. At common law an employee injured by a breach has an action in contract or tort for damages. Breach of the statutory duty under the Health and Safety at Work etc Act 1974, is a criminal offence punishable with a fine, but does not give an individual any right of action. Breach of statutory duty under the Factories Acts gives an individual a cause of action where appropriate.

A TUTOR'S ANSWER

Answer 4.

Here I present a full answer to Question **4.**

(a) An employee's duty to render loyal and faithful service is a duty implied into all contracts of employment by the common law. Because the duty is a common law duty rather than a statutory one, it is not closely defined. It has been held to cover the following types of conduct; setting up in competition with an employer; borrowing or taking money from an employer without permission; disclosing trade secrets; exploiting customer contacts to his own advantage; taking a bribe; doing his own work in the employer's time or otherwise allowing his own interest to compete with that of his employer.

(b) In principle what an employee does in his own time is his own affair but this is subject to his overriding duty of loyalty to his employer. Any conduct which might be prejudicial to his employer should be avoided. In each of these two cases it will be a question of fact whether the conduct complained of is sufficient to amount to breach of the employee's implied duty of loyalty and good faith.

As far as X is concerned it would seem that his employer could legitimately object to X's weekend activities for X is taking potential business away from his employer. Where he is paid by his friends he is setting himself up in competition with his employer. Where he is not being paid, he may be damaging his employer by reducing the demand for his services.

In relation to Y, Y owes the same duties of loyalty and good faith but it is not so obvious that his activities are damaging his employer. The fact that Y works as a barman in a local hotel several nights a week will only entitle Y's employer to complain if he can show that Y was less able to perform his duties, perhaps through tiredness, or that in some other way he was causing him loss – e.g. where potential clients lost confidence in Y because of the nature of the job Y was doing. On the facts it seems that Y would be in a position to talk to prospective clients and even generate business for his employer. In this case the employer has no ground for complaint against Y.

A STEP FURTHER

The industrial tribunals, like the courts, are open to the public; it might be interesting to see your local one at work. The Health and Safety Executive publish publicity material about what they do and also reports on their work which illustrate problems they have had to deal with. The local Health and Safety Inspectors can be contacted for advice or help, you will find their address in the local telephone directory. The Equal Opportunities Commission deal with matters arising under the Sex Discrimination Act and Equal Pay Act. They also publish annual reports.

BASIC READING

Selwyn's Law of Employment (5th edn), Butterworths, 1985.
Butterworth's Employment Law Handbook (3rd edn) Peter Wallington, Butterworths, 1984.
Titles in Law at Work Series, Sweet and Maxwell.

FURTHER READING OR REFERENCE	*Kahn–Freund's Labour and the Law* (3rd edn), Sweet and Maxwell, 1983.
	Hamlyn Lectures Honoré, Stevens, 1982.
	Trade Union Law (2nd edn) R. Kidner, Sweet and Maxwell, 1983.
	Encyclopaedia of Health and Safety at Work, Sweet and Maxwell.
	Articles on employment law may be found in many journals including:
	Industrial Law Journal; Employment Gazette; New Law Journal.

USEFUL ADDRESSES	Commission for Racial Equality, Elliot House, 10–12 Allington Street, London SW1.
	Equal Opportunities Commission, Overseas House, Quay Street, Manchester.
	Health and Safety Executive, Baynards House, 1 Cheapstow Place, Westbourne Grove, London W2 4TF.

Chapter 12

Employment – Termination of Contract

GETTING STARTED

A contract of employment is a contract like any other contract. In recent years there has been a mass of legislation establishing minimum rights and duties on employers and employees (see Ch. 11); however, the basic contractual rules still apply. A contract of employment may be ended in the same way as any other contract: by performance, by agreement, by frustration, and by breach. It is in the limitation of the employer's right to terminate a contract according to its agreed terms that some of the greatest changes have been made. This has been done by introducing the concept of unfair dismissal – the idea that an employee has a right not to lose his job without a specified fair reason, even where the period of employment has expired or the terms of the contract provide for termination by either side giving the agreed notice. Rights to compensation where a job is lost through redundancy have also been provided.

ESSENTIAL PRINCIPLES

TERMINATION BY THE EMPLOYEE ON GIVING THE CONTRACTED NOTICE

All statements of the main contractual terms (see Ch. 10) should contain a reference to the amount of notice an employee is obliged to give, and entitled to receive, to terminate his contract. An employee is entitled to give his employer notice according to this agreement at any time, without any restrictions as to his reasons.

TERMINATION BY THE EMPLOYER ON GIVING THE CONTRACTED NOTICE

In principle where an employer gives an employee the notice to which he is entitled, either the statutory minimum or his contract notice if this is longer, there is no breach of contract and the employee has no grounds of complaint. In the same way where there is a contract for a fixed term, at the end of the term the contract has been performed. If the employer does not renew the contract the employee cannot complain at common law. However, these rules are now subject to the provisions in the Employment Protection (Consolidation) Act (EPCA) 1978 on unfair dismissal.

Unfair dismissal

The Employment Protection (Consolidation) Act 1978, provides that qualifying employees shall have a right to some form of compensation if they are dismissed unfairly.

This topic is of great practical importance to both employers and employees and is very often the subject of examination questions.

Who is qualified?

Most employees, subject to a normal minimum period of one year's continuous employment or two years' where employment began after 1 June 1985, where at least 16 hours plus a week are worked, or five years' continuous employment where eight hours plus a week are worked. Employees working in a firm which has *never* employed more than 20 employees during the period of their employment are not protected until they have completed *two* years continuous service.

N.B. In the case of dismissal for trade union membership or activities, or for non-union membership, there is no qualifying period at all.

Certain employees are excluded: those normally working outside Great Britain; those at normal retirement age at the date of termination; members of the police and armed forces; registered dock workers; share fishermen; spouses.

What must be proved to recover?

1

That the employee was dismissed.
Dismissal includes:

(a) Termination of the contract by the employer, with or without notice;

(b) The expiry of a fixed term contract of one year or more without it being renewed, unless the employee agreed in writing at the time the contract was made to forego his right to claim for non-renewal.

(c) Termination by the employee in circumstances which are such that he is entitled to terminate the contract without notice by reason of the employer's conduct. This is called **constructive dismissal.**

Constructive dismissal occurs where an employee leaves because of behaviour of the employer amounting to a breach of condition of the contract. This entitles the employee, the innocent party, to repudiate the contract. Although the initiative seems to have come from the employee who has voluntarily given up his job, this is specifically regarded as dismissal.

That the reason for dismissal was not a fair reason.
An employer may be required to give a written statement of the reasons for the dismissal to all employees with one year's service. The Act provides five reasons which are statutorily fair.

(a) *Misconduct.* It will be a question of fact whether the misconduct was sufficiently serious to justify dismissal. The tribunal will take into account all relevant factors such as the employee's previous record, any warning he may have received, the likelihood of the misconduct recurring, the effect on other employees of the misconduct, especially important where there has been breach of safety regulations, and any other relevant circumstances. In principle, dismissal for a first offence without warning is unlikely to be regarded as fair unless the breach clearly demonstrated an intention by the employee no longer to be bound by the terms of his contract. Normally the misconduct complained of will have occurred at work, but misconduct outside work may justify dismissal where an employer can show that it seriously damaged the employee's capacity to carry out his job, e.g. where public confidence in his judgment is reduced.

(b) *Incapacity to do the job for whatever reason.* This covers incompetence, lack of skill, poor performance and ill health. Again it will be a question of degree of *how* incompetent the employee was. Since it is difficult to be competent one day and incompetent the next, at least if there are no medical reasons, it may be quite difficult for an employer to prove that an employee has become unable to perform his task. An employee should normally be warned that his work is not satisfactory and be given an opportunity to improve. Likewise an employee suffering from ill health should be advised of what is required and wherever possible be offered work scaled to suit the disability. Where the incompetence is due to a change in the nature of the job, e.g. the introduction of new technology, an adequate opportunity for retraining must be given.

(c) *Redundancy.* Where an employer needs fewer people to do a certain kind of work, it is fair to dismiss some, but the choice must be made fairly and with adequate notice (see p. 144 following).

(d) *That continued employment of someone in a particular job would break the law.* An obvious example of this would be the dismissal of a driver who had lost his driving licence. Any job which requires an employee to possess a valid permit or professional qualification would be equally dependent on him fulfilling the legal requirement. In such a case the employer has the obligation to try and absorb the employee elsewhere in his business if possible.

(e) *Some other substantial reason.* In this case it is up to the employer to convince the tribunal that the reason justified the dismissal. Examples of such other reasons which have been found to be fair include: personality conflicts; changed duties or conditions which an employee would not accept; or business reorganisation. This may occur at any time in the life of a business but may be particularly likely following the sale or merger of a business.

In addition to specifying which reasons are fair, the EPCA also provides a list of **automatically unfair reasons**. These are:

(a) *Trade union membership or activities, or non-membership of a union.* (Except where there is a closed shop, see below.)
(b) *Pregnancy.* This protection applies to any employee who has been employed for one year at the date of dismissal unless her condition makes it impossible for her to do the job adequately or her continued employment in that job would be against the law. In such a case the employer must offer her any suitable vacancy.
(c) *Sex or race discrimination.*

---

3. *That even if there is a fair reason, the employer acted unreasonably in treating the fair reason as a ground for dismissal.*

This overriding duty to act reasonably on the part of the employer has been interpreted by tribunals as requiring employers to comply with the rules of natural justice and to follow their own disciplinary procedures including giving adequate warnings. Thus an employer should give notice to an employee of any complaint about him; be prepared to hear the employee's side of the story; allow the employee to be accompanied or represented at any disciplinary hearing; take steps to investigate as far as possible any allegations and to take into account any personal mitigating circumstances. The Advisory Conciliation and Arbitration Service (ACAS), has devised a model code of practice for dealing with breaches of discipline. Whereas it is not mandatory to follow this code, which is advisory only, where an employer has no similar code of his own, or has made no attempt to follow the suggested procedures, the tribunal may well hold the dismissal procedurally unfair.

The Closed Shop provisions A 'closed shop' is technically a union-management agreement under which the management agrees with a specified union only to employ union labour in the particular jobs to which the agreement relates. Contrary to the normal rule under which a dismissal for union membership or non-membership is automatically unfair, s.58(3) provides that such a dismissal *is* fair where there is a closed shop agreement and the employee concerned refused to belong to the relevant union. However, it will not be fair if one of the specific exceptions applies. These are:

1. The employee genuinely objects on grounds of conscience or other deeply held personal conviction to being a member of any trade union or of a particular trade union;
2. The employee was employed before the closed shop agreement took effect and had not at any time been a member in accordance with the agreement;

3. The agreement came into effect after 15 August 1980 and has not been approved within the last five years by at least 80% of those covered by the agreement voting in a secret ballot.
N.B. There is no qualifying period of service, or age limit, for employees who wish to complain that they have been unfairly dismissed for non-membership of a union where a closed shop agreement operates. Where an employee is dismissed unfairly in breach of these provisions he will qualify for additional compensation (see below).

TERMINATION BY THE EMPLOYER WITHOUT GIVING THE CONTRACTED NOTICE.

Where the employee has been guilty of gross misconduct amounting to a breach of condition the employer is entitled to repudiate the contract and dismiss the employee without notice. This right to sack an employee is unaffected by any of the unfair dismissal provisions mentioned above. It will be a question of fact whether the misconduct by the employee was sufficiently serious to amount to a breach of condition. Where the breach is held not to amount to a breach of condition and the employer has nevertheless dismissed the employee without notice, the employee may claim at common law in the ordinary courts for damages for wrongful dismissal.

REMEDIES

For unfair dismissal

Complaints of unfair dismissal should be made to an industrial tribunal. This has power to order:

1. Reinstatement. This is an order requiring the employer to take his employee back into the job he was doing before the dismissal.
2. Re-engagement. This is an order requiring the employer to re-employ his employee in a similar job to his original one.
3. Compensation. This will be awarded where the other two are inappropriate or unavailable. It will normally be in two parts, plus a third in some cases:

- *The basic award* – is calculated in the same way as the award for redundancy according to age and length of service and subject to a maximum (see below);
- *The compensatory award* – is designed to compensate the employee for his individual actual or prospective loss, again subject to a maximum, and reducible where the tribunal considers the employee contributed to his dismissal;
- *The special award* – where the reason for the unfair dismissal was membership or non membership of a trade union and the employee had asked for re-engagement or reinstatement but the tribunal had not ordered it or the employer had failed to comply with it. This award is also subject to a maximum and, perhaps more importantly, a minimum – currently £11,000.

For wrongful dismissal

A claim for wrongful dismissal should be brought in the common law courts, i.e. the county court or Queen's Bench Division. The amount recoverable is determined according to the ordinary principles of assessment of damages for breach of contract (see Ch. 7). Thus an employee should recover lost wages for the period of notice to which he was entitled and any other sum specifically foreseen as being the result of breach. His damages may be reduced if they can be shown to have arisen through his failure to mitigate his loss. There is no limit to the amount of money which may be awarded subject to the above.

REDUNDANCY

This occurs where an employer has no further need for work of a particular kind, or work of a particular kind in a particular place. In such a case he will naturally have to reduce his workforce. Any employee who has to be dismissed is classed as redundant. This is statutorily a fair reason for the purposes of unfair dismissal unless the employee can prove that the employer acted unfairly in selecting him for redundancy. However, the employee will be entitled to specific compensation for dismissal on the grounds of redundancy, subject to the following conditions:

1. The employee had been continuously employed for a minimum of two years;
2. He was below the normal retiring age;
3. He normally worked more than 16 hours a week, or more than eight hours if he had been continuously employed for more than five years;
4. He was normally working in Great Britain;
5. He had not specifically agreed in writing to forego his entitlement at the end of a fixed term contract.

Having established that he *is* covered by the provisions the employee must prove that he was dismissed in the same way as for unfair dismissal (see above), and that the ground of the dismissal was redundancy, i.e. the employer no longer had the need for work of his particular kind, or in the particular place he worked.

This includes changes required by internal re-organisation or economy, and changes in job specification. It may also cover periods of 'lay-off' or short time working, i.e. periods of 'no work – no pay' or reduced hours working where below half a normal week's pay could be earned. Where such a reduction has lasted for four consecutive weeks, or for six weeks out of any period of 13 weeks, an employee may give his employer notice and claim redundancy pay. The employer may avoid a liability for redundancy in the case of lay-off by claiming that at least 13 weeks full work will commence within four weeks.

In other cases liability may be avoided by offering an alternative job on the same terms and conditions or by proving that a purchaser of the business has offered suitable alternative employment, and that in either case the employee unreasonably refused such employment. Whether the alternative *is* suitable is a question of fact, relevant factors might be the wages involved, the degree of responsibility compared to the previous job, job prospects, the distance to travel to work and the costs involved. Where alternative employment is offered an employee is entitled to a minimum trial period of four weeks without prejudice to his existing rights. If he accepts the alternative he is treated as never having been dismissed; if he rejects it for good reason he remains entitled to any redundancy pay due on his dismissal.

An employer is under a duty to consult with the recognised unions concerned before making any redundancies. Selection for redundancy must be carried out fairly in accordance with any union agreement.

Compensation

The amount of redundancy pay is related to age and length of service and is calculated as follows:

1. One and a half weeks' pay for each year of employment in which the employee was aged over 41;
2. One week's pay for each year of employment in which the employee was aged between 22 and 40;
3. Half a week's pay for each year of employment between ages 18 and 21.

There is a maximum of 20 years' service which may be taken into account. The statutory entitlement is the minimum, many employers choose to give more. The primary obligation is on the employer to pay, but he may then recover from the Government's Redundancy Fund a percentage refund of the statutory amount due.

RIGHTS ON TRANSFER OF AN UNDERTAKING

Regulations brought into force in 1982 safeguard employees' rights when a business is transferred to a new owner, e.g. by sale or merger, in two ways:

1. Employees who are employed by the original employer at the time of the transfer automatically become the employees of the new employer as if their contracts were originally made with the new employer. The new employer takes over all the employment liabilities of the old employer except criminal liabilities and occupational pensions.
2. If there is an independent trade union recognised for bargaining purposes its representatives must be informed about any measures the new employer intends taking in relation to the transfer which may affect the union members.

USEFUL APPLIED MATERIALS

The majority of the rules in this area are statutory. The most important material is therefore the statutes themselves and any regulations made under them. The following are the most important:

●   Equal Pay Act 1970
●   Sex Discrimination Act 1975
●   Race Relations Act 1976

- Employment Protection (Consolidation) Act 1978
- Employment Act 1980
- Employment Act 1982
- Trade Union Act 1984

The Industrial Relations Law Reports are published decisions of tribunal hearings. However these decisions are not precedents and the Court of Appeal and the Employment Appeal Tribunal have repeatedly warned that they should not be too closely followed. Some decisions of the EAT and the Court of Appeal may be found in the ordinary law reports.

Textbooks and case or source books in the area of employment law or industrial law make good starting points for a student. For a very simple up to date statement of the current law on individual topics of concern to an employee the Department of Employment publish a series of guides to the legislation available free in job centres and citizens advice bureaux.

RECENT EXAMINATION QUESTIONS	It may be useful to spend around ten minutes planning an answer to each question before turning to the outline answers.
Question 1.	An employee alleging unfair dismissal under the Employment Protection (Consolidation) Act 1978 must first prove that he was dismissed. Explain dismissal for these purposes. (DPA 1981)
Question 2.	What are the principal factors that determine whether a dismissal is for redundancy? What protection does a redundant worker get by law? (ICSA 1983)

Question 3.	(a) Termination of a contract of employment by notice is possible but certain obligations are imposed upon an employer who does so. What are these obligations?
	(b) Advise Eric, the employer, whether he is entitled to dismiss the following employees and, if not, the remedies which might be sought against him if nevertheless he does dismiss them:
	   (i) Martin, who has been absent through illness for six months; and
	   (ii) Norman, who is late for work on most days of the week. (ICMA 1982)

Question 4.	(a) In what circumstances is there entitlement to a redundancy payment? (b) A factory is badly damaged by fire and it is expected that it will be four months before production is resumed. The employees are laid off but are told that they will be re-employed later when the factory reopens. Are they entitled to redundancy payments? (ICMA 1981)

OUTLINE ANSWERS

Answer 1.

'Dismissal' for the purposes of the Employment Protection (Consolidation) Act 1978 means:

(a) that the employer terminated the employee's contract directly, with or without notice.

(b) a fixed term contract expired and was not renewed by the employer, and the employee had not agreed in writing at the time the contract was made to give up his right to renewal.
or

(c) the employee resigned in circumstances amounting to constructive dismissal.

Answer 2.

The principal factors which determine whether a dismissal is for redundancy are whether the employer can prove that: he has ceased, or intends to cease, to carry on business, either at all, or in a particular place; or, that his requirements for work of a particular kind have ceased or diminished or are expected to cease or diminish either at all or in a particular place. Clearly to make out these claims the employer should show a clear reduction in his need for the work done by the worker claiming to have been made redundant.

A redundant worker who had been continuously employed for two years is entitled to the following protection: payment of redundancy pay calculated according to age and length of service; a right to reasonable time off with pay during the period of notice to look for an alternative job; right to a four week trial period without loss of accrued rights to try out alternative employment offered by the employer; right not to be unfairly selected for redundancy; right to have a recognised union consulted according to the number of people to be affected in advance of the redundancies coming into effect.

Answer 3.

(a) Termination of a contract of employment by notice is possible at common law but the Employment Protection (Consolidation) Act 1978 lays down the following conditions. An employer who dismisses with or without notice must give written reasons of the dismissal to all employees with one year's service. Those reasons must be one of five fair reasons set out in the Act. Additionally the employer must be able to prove that he acted reasonably in treating the fair reason as a reason to dismiss.

(b) (i) Whether Eric is entitled to dismiss Martin will depend first on what Martin's contract provided in the event of illness. Subject to that E will be entitled to terminate it if he can show there was no real likelihood of M being able to return to carry out his contractual obligations. In this case the contract will either be held frustrated or the dismissal will be fair on the grounds of M's incompetence.

(ii) Whether Eric is entitled to dismiss Norman will depend on whether E has previously warned N that his constant lateness is unacceptable and may lead to dismissal. In principle misconduct is a fair reason for dismissal but warnings should have been given before the dismissal.

If E acts without justification, or unreasonably, provided both M and N have been employed continuously for one year, they will be entitled to claim compensation for unfair dismissal before an industrial tribunal. The tribunal may order, reinstatement, re-engagement or money compensation, as appropriate.

A TUTOR'S ANSWER

Here I present a full answer to question 4.

Answer 4.

(a) To qualify for a redundancy payment an employee must prove that he has been continuously employed for a least two years working 16 hours plus a week, or for five years working eight hours plus per week, that he was below retiring age and that he was dismissed by reason of redundancy. This occurs when an employer dismisses some of his workforce because he no longer needs their particular skill either at all, or in the particular place where they were employed. The right to redundancy pay will be lost if an employee unreasonably refuses an offer of alternative work made by his own or an associated employer. Whether the refusal is unreasonable is a question of fact taking into account all the circumstances. An employee is allowed a minimum trial period of four weeks in an alternative job without loss of accrued rights to redundancy pay should he eventually decline the job.

(b) The employees will be entitled to redundancy pay if they give notice to their employer of their intention to resign and claim redundancy pay after the period of lay-off has lasted for four consecutive weeks. An employer may avoid this liability by counter-claiming that he expects there to be at least 13 weeks full working available within four weeks. In the circumstances, if the factory is to be shut for four months, this is clearly not the case. Subject to the need for a minimum period of continuous employment, the employees are entitled to redundancy payments on giving the appropriate notice.

A STEP FURTHER

Industrial tribunals sit regularly all over the country. They are open to the public, a visit to a hearing is recommended. ACAS, the Advisory, Conciliation and Arbitration Service, publishes a model code of disciplinary procedures which most employers use as a basis for their own internal procedures. ACAS has branch offices all over the country and also publishes other guides. Citizen's advice bureaux are available to help the public and are often called upon to advise in cases of unfair dismissal. Many will represent a client in tribunal proceedings. A visit to one of them and discussion with the officer concerned might be helpful.

The Department of Employment publishes booklets (available at job centres) on individual employment rights which contain the addresses of all the regional offices for redundancy payments, and the ACAS regional centres. Small Firms Centres around the country can also provide advice and help.

In addition to the texts recommended in Chapter 11 the following are suggested for this area:

BASIC READING

Principles of Labour Law (4th edn) Rideout and Dyson, Sweet and Maxwell, 1983.

FURTHER READING OR REFERENCE

Termination of Employment R. Upex, Sweet and Maxwell, 1983.
Law of Unfair Dismissal (2nd edn) Anderman, Butterworths, 1984.
Employment Law Kroner.

USEFUL ADDRESSES

ACAS, Clifton House, 83 Euston Road, London NW1 2RB.

Small Firms, Centre, 8–10 Bulstrode Street, London W1A 5FT
Regional offices can be located via your local telephone directory.

Central Office of Industrial Tribunals, 93 Ebury Bridge Road, London SW1.

Chapter 13   Negotiable Instruments

GETTING STARTED

A man's wealth may consist of various kinds of property, for example his house or other land and his books, clothes and other personal possessions. Additionally he may have intangible, or non-physical assets, for example an account in credit at the bank, shares in a company or the copyright in a book. When the owner wishes to transfer his tangible property, the normal way to do this is by physical delivery or transfer, he simply gives or hands over the property to the new owner.

If the property he wishes to transfer is *not* tangible, e.g. a debt owed to him by the bank, physical transfer is clearly impossible. In this case the law has followed the custom of merchants engaged in trade in allowing the transfer to be made by documents.

In exactly the same way as the basic rule in the sale of goods is '*nemo dat quod non habet*' (see Ch. 8), so in the assignment or transfer of intangible property the basic rule is the same, no one can pass a better title than he already has. Thus the assignee is in the same position as his transferor – any defences, such as fraud or a right of set-off, which could have been used against the original creditor may be used by the debtor against any subsequent assignee of his debt. However, just as there are a number of exceptions to the *nemo dat* rule in the sale of goods, based on commercial necessity and the protection of the innocent purchaser, so there are exceptions to the rule relating to the assignment of intangible property. Negotiable instruments are the exception. Subject to the rules of form and notice, the holder of a negotiable instrument may acquire a better title than his transferor.

ESSENTIAL PRINCIPLES

INTRODUCTION

For commercial convenience traders need to be able to trust their trading partners without having to take extensive precautions. In relation to the transfer of intangible property, in particular rights to money, they developed a set of rules under which a clear title would be guaranteed if certain conditions were fulfilled. These customary rules were adopted by Parliament in a codifying act, the Bills of Exchange Act 1882, which now governs the present law.

The ability to transfer money freely and easily is of enormous importance not only to merchants and traders but to most ordinary people. Examples of negotiable instruments in common use include bank notes and cheques in addition to the more specialised bills of exchange used widely in international trade.

Useful definitions

It may be helpful before considering the rules themselves to distinguish carefully the meaning of the following terms. Examiners asking a question on negotiable instruments often ask for the meaning of some of the following expressions.

- **Transferable.** – The property may be transferred validly from the present holder to another, usually by simple delivery. The transferee takes the same title as the transferor had.
- **Assignable.** – This really means the same as transferable but is used of intangible property, which by definition cannot be delivered. Such property is transferred by assignment. This may be done legally under the Law of Property Act 1925 or equitably outside those provisions. You should learn these rules carefully for the great advantage of negotiable instruments is that they are free from these limitations.

The LPA 1925 s.136 provides for a legal assignment of a *chose in action* (intangible property) by the assignment being:

1. In writing;
2. Of the whole debt (not of part of the sum owed or merely a charge as opposed to outright transfer); and
3. Notice being given to the debtor.

   Such an assignment is effective to give the assignee the right to sue the debtor in his own name without reference to the assignor. The assignee takes the same title the assignor had, and may be subjected to any defences for example, fraud or set-off that the debtor could have raised against the assignor.

An equitable assignment is any assignment outside these provisions. For example an oral assignment, or an assignment of only part of a debt. Such an assignment does not enable the assignee to sue in his own name, he must join the assignor, and again takes the same title.

- **Negotiable.** – The property may be transferred by simple delivery, or delivery and indorsement (signature on the back of the written instrument); no notice need be given to the debtor;

the holder of the document can sue in his own name and most importantly may obtain a title valid at face value, free of any previous defects of which he did not know.

BILLS OF EXCHANGE ACT 1882

This Act codified the then common law on negotiable instruments. It is now the basis of the present law. Section 3 defines a Bill of Exchange as *'an unconditional order in writing addressed by one person to another, signed by the person giving it requiring the person to whom it is addressed to pay on demand, or at a fixed or determinable future time, a sum certain in money to or to the order of a specified person or bearer.'* This definition is very important. Notice particularly the following points:

1. *The order must be unconditional* – a mere request to pay is not enough.
2. *The order must be in writing* – no special form is needed. In practice banks supply their customers with ready-printed cheque forms which are convenient and help both to identify customers and to prevent fraud. However there are no legal rules on the particular form required.
3. *The order must be signed by the person making the order* – known as the drawer.
4. *The order must be addressed by one person to another* – known as the drawee. Where a specific person is named the bill is known as an order bill. If the bill is made payable to bearer it is known as a bearer bill. Where the drawer draws a bill on his own account for payment to himself he is both drawer and payee, the person to whom payment is to be made.
5. *The order must be payable on demand or at a fixed or determinable future time* – if no time is specified the bill is a *demand bill* payable immediately. If a specific date was given or a determinable future time was specified, e.g. 20 days after date, the bill is a *'time' bill*. A demand bill becomes overdue if not presented within a reasonable time. There is no specific limit for this, banking practice is to treat cheques as overdue if not presented within six months. A 'time' bill is overdue if not presented on the date given or within three days.

Examples and use of bills of exchange

In addition to banknotes and cheques with which most people are familiar, the most common use of a bill of exchange is in international trade. It may be used in the following ways:

1. The seller of goods draws a bill on the buyer, who now owes him the price of the goods, ordering the buyer to pay the sum agreed at a future date. The seller sends the bill to the buyer who 'accepts' it by writing 'accepted' across its face and returns it to the seller. The seller may now cash the buyer's order for future payment through a merchant bank or discount house. The bank will pay slightly less than the face value of the bill to compensate

them for the delay before they are able to collect the sum due from the buyer on the agreed date. By this method the seller obtains cash at once, the buyer obtains credit and the bank earns the difference between the sum paid and the sum collected.

2. Alternatively, the buyer may draw the bill on his bank ordering the bank to pay the seller. When payment is due at a future date the same procedure of acceptance and discounting may be followed. If the order is drawn on a bank and is payable on demand, the bill is a cheque and may be cashed at once without the need to accept or discount.

The importance of acceptance

When a bill is payable at a fixed or determinable future time and the holder wishes to negotiate the bill for its face value or to cash it at once, as explained above, it will readily be seen that subsequent holders will be concerned to ensure that the bill will be honoured when the due date arrives. This is achieved by presenting the bill to the drawee for acceptance.

The effect of acceptance is that the drawee becomes liable to honour the bill according to its terms. He undertakes liability to any future holder in due course and cannot set up against them any defences that may have been available to him against the drawer.

Acceptance may be given by the drawee by:

1. Signing the bill and nothing more;
2. Signing the bill and writing 'accepted'; or
3. Signing the bill, writing 'accepted' and giving the date.

Such an acceptance is called a *general acceptance*. Where any qualification is introduced, the acceptance is called a *qualified acceptance*. For example:

1. Conditional – accepted subject to deduction for expenses, or satisfaction with goods.
2. Partial – acceptance for part only of the sum specified, e.g. £3000 not £6000.
3. Local – payable *only* at a particular place.
4. Qualified as to time – payable in six months when the bill said three months.
5. Acceptance by some only of several drawees.

Non acceptance or partial acceptance amounts to dishonour. The holder of such a bill has an immediate right to sue the drawer or any previous endorser.

There is no general rule that a bill *must* be presented for acceptance except where the bill is payable × days after sight (here acceptance is necessary to determine when the bill is due), or the bill itself requires it. The bill may be presented for acceptance by the drawer or any subsequent holder.

TRANSFER AND NEGOTIATION

A bill is negotiated when it is transferred from one person to another in such a manner as to constitute the transferee the holder of the bill: s.31.

A **bearer bill** may be transferred by mere delivery.

An **order bill** may be transferred by delivery plus indorsement (signature on the back).

N.B. Where an order bill is transferred by delivery without indorsement, the transferee acquires the same title as the transferor had, plus the right to have the transferor's indorsement.

Indorsements

There are various kinds of indorsement whose effect you should know:

1. In blank – the bare signature of the indorser. The bill becomes a bearer bill and may now be transferred by simple delivery.
2. Special – signature of the indorser plus an instruction to pay a named person. The bill remains an order bill and it may only be transferred by indorsement by the person now named.
3. Restrictive – signature of the indorser plus an instruction to 'pay X only'. The bill ceases to be negotiable. It may be transferred only to X.

RIGHTS OF THE HOLDER

There are various classes of holder depending on how they acquired the bill. It is important to identify clearly the different categories to define their rights.

1. The Holder – a person in possession of an order bill of which he is payee or indorsee, or the person in possession of a bearer bill.
2. The Holder for Value – a person who holds a bill for which he has given value or for which value has at some time been given.
3. The Holder in due course – a person who takes a bill 'complete and regular on the face of it, before it is overdue, without notice of any previous dishonour, in good faith, for value and without notice of any defect in the title of the person who negotiated it to him': s.29.

The 'mere' holder has the same title as his transferor and has no right to sue on the bill if the bill is dishonoured.

The holder for value has no better title than his transferor, but if the bill is dishonoured he can recover from previous parties. The holder in due course takes free from previous defects in title, for example he will get a good title even though there was a previous fraudulent transfer.

Example

A draws a bearer bill on X bank and pays it to B in sastisfaction of his account. C steals the bill and gives it to D. D negotiates the bill for value to E who then gives it to F. A is the drawer; X bank is the drawee; B is the owner of the bearer bill; C was the holder because he was in possession of a bearer bill, even though B was the owner; D is a holder for value – although the cheque was a gift to D and D did not himself give value, value has at some time been given, in this case by B; D takes subject to B's right; E will be a holder in due course, provided he took without notice and in good faith; E then obtains a good title and is not answerable to B; F is a holder for value and therefore takes the same title as his transferor, E; therefore F has a good title.

DISHONOUR AND LIABILITY

If the drawee refuses to accept and/or pay the bill, the bill is dishonoured. The holder must look elsewhere. He has rights of 'recourse' against all parties to the bill. A party to the bill is anyone who has signed the bill as drawer, acceptor or indorser. A drawee who does not sign as acceptor is not a party and is not liable on the bill. *N.B.* He remains liable to the drawer for any breach of contract involved in non-payment.

The drawer is primarily liable. An indorser who has signed is also liable as a guarantor with a right to recover from the drawer.

A bearer bill may be transferred by mere delivery without indorsement. In this case the transferor does not sign the bill and is therefore not a party to it, and not liable on it *but* by s.58 he warrants *to his immediate transferee* that (a) the bill is what it purports to be, (b) he has a right to transfer it and (c) that at the time of the transfer he is not aware of any facts which render it valueless. He may be liable to his transferee for breach of these promises.

When a bill has been dishonoured notice of dishonour must be given to the drawer and to any indorsers. If the notice is not given they are discharged. The notice must be given within a reasonable time, this means not later than the day after the dishonour. Notice may be oral or written.

Example

A draws an order bill on X bank in favour of B. B signs it, making it by his indorsement in blank into a bearer bill, B gives it to C in payment for services rendered by C. C negotiates the bill for value to D, D gives it to E in satisfaction of an outstanding debt. E presents the bill at the X bank. The bill is then dishonoured. E must immediately give notice of dishonour to A the drawer, and B, the indorser. E can then sue A and/or B as parties to the bill. E cannot sue C because C is not a party to the bill and is not E's transferor. E cannot sue D as a party to the bill because D did not sign it, but E may be able to sue D if D broke any of the warranties implied by s.58, i.e. that the bill was a valid bill, D had a right to transfer it, and did not know that the bill was valueless at the time of transfer.

UNAUTHORISED SIGNATURES

In principle a signature given without authority is not effective. This applies to cases of misuse of authority by an agent and forgery. A signature which purports to be the signature of another is a forgery. As such it is a nullity. No rights are given by it. Thus any forged indorsement is ineffective to pass title. However there may be circumstances where the owner of the forged signature is estopped from denying it. Such circumstances arose in *Greenwood* v. *Martin's Bank* 1933. In this case G's wife forged G's signature as drawer on a number of cheques to withdraw money from his bank account. To avoid embarrassment G did not tell the bank but allowed them to honour the cheques. After his wife's death G sought to reclaim the money from the bank. The court held he was estopped or prevented from pleading the fact of the forgeries by his own previous conduct.

In the case of agents the general rule of agency applies, the principal is only bound where the agent acts within his authority, express or implied, or where the principal is estopped or prevented from denying it. (see Ch. 9). For example, in *Morison* v. *Kemp* 1912 a principal was held not liable on a cheque signed by his clerk 'per pro' his employer which the clerk had used to pay off his personal gambling debts. There was no authority express or implied for such use of the money and indeed the bank should have been suspicious to see money paid into an employee's private account when the cheque was clearly destined for his employer.

The agent will not be personally liable on a cheque as long as he names or identifies his principal and signs 'for an on behalf of . . .', 'per pro . . .' or just 'pp' and the principal's name. In practice all company business *must* be conducted through agents and most businesses, however instituted, depend on some form of delegated authority.

DISCHARGE

A bill may be discharged in three ways:

1. *By payment in due course.* This is the normal way. Where payment is made by the drawee to the holder in good faith and without notice of any defect in title the drawee is discharged from further liability. Where payment is made by an indorser, only the indorser and subsequent parties are discharged.

2. *By material alteration.* Under s.64 if a bill is materially altered, e.g. its amount, date, or time of payment is altered, it is void except against a party who made, authorised or assented to the alteration and subsequent indorsers. **But** – if the alteration is not apparent on its face a holder in due course may enforce the bill as originally drawn against parties prior to the alteration.

   N.B. Accidental damage or alteration is not covered by s.64; such a bill will remain valid as long as its nature and contents are clear.

Example

A draws a bill on X for £10 in favour of B. B fraudulently alters the bill to £110 and indorses it to C who indorses it to D. D has no rights against A or X because s.64 makes the cheque void against them. D can sue B and C, B as the alterer and C as subsequent indorser. If the material alteration were *not* apparent on its face and D were a holder in due course he could sue A and X for the original £10 for which the bill was drawn in addition to B and C for its face value.

3. (a) The acceptor is the holder at maturity;

     (b)   The holder waives or renounces his rights at or after maturity; or

     (c)   The holder has deliberately and apparently cancelled the bill.

CHEQUES

Probably the most widely used form of bills of exchange outside the export world are cheques. *A cheque is a bill of exchange drawn on a bank, payable on demand*: s.73 BEA. Because of these characteristics it is much less frequently negotiated than other forms of bills of exchange. Most cheques are given to the payee and presented by them to their own bank for collection from the drawer's bank.

Certain special rules apply to cheques in addition to the general principles laid down in the Bills of Exchange Act 1882. These are to be found in the Cheques Act 1957 and Banking Act 1979.

Crossings

A crossing, i.e. two parallel lines drawn across the face of a cheque, is an instruction to the banker on whom the cheque is drawn to pay the cheque only into a bank account, not over the counter. There are various forms of crossing:

1.   *General* – this simply requires the paying bank to pay only through another bank.
2.   *Special* – the name of a particular bank is inserted between the lines. The cheque must then be paid into that bank.
3.   *Not negotiable* – the cheque may be transferred or assigned but the transferee will take no better title than his transferor.
4.   *A/C Payee* (only) – this is not a statutory crossing but is sanctioned by use. The bank is instructed to pay only the payee. If it is asked to pay anyone else it should not do so without checking that the proper authority has been obtained. In practice such a crossing renders a cheque virtually non-negotiable and non-transferable.

Protection of the paying bank

The banker has a duty to honour his customers' cheques. If the bank wrongfully fails to honour them or if it pays someone not entitled to payment it will be liable.

The bank's authority to pay may be terminated in several ways:

1.   By an express instruction to stop a cheque.
2.   By notice of the customer's death or unsoundness of mind.
3.   By notice that a receiving order has been made against their customer, or a bankruptcy petition presented.
4.   By service of a court order attaching the customer's funds for disposal by the court.
5.   By injunction.

When payment has *been* made the paying bank is protected in the following ways:

1.   Payment of a bill of exchange 'in due course', in good faith, and

without notice of a defect in the holder's title, discharges the bill and absolves the bank from further liability: s.60 BEA.

2. The paying bank is deemed to have paid in due course even if indorsements are forged or unauthorised. This is extended to the case where there is no indorsement or an irregular indorsement by s.1 Cheques Act 1957.

3. Where a crossed cheque is paid in good faith and without negligence in accordance with the crossing, payment has the same effect as if made to the true owner: s.80 BEA.

4. Where the bank has paid on a cheque where it should not have done so, for example, the cheque had been validly stopped by the drawer, the drawer's signature was forged, or there was a material alteration rendering the cheque void, the bank may be protected from an action by the customer if the customer contributed by his own conduct or negligence to the payment (*Greenwood* v. *Martin's Bank* 1933).

Protection of the collecting bank

The collecting bank would be liable to the true owner if it collected for its customer a cheque to which he had no title. The Cheques Act 1957 s.4 therefore provides if a bank in good faith and without negligence:

1. Receives payment of a cheque for a customer, or
2. Having credited its customer's account with the amount of the cheque, collects payment for itself, the collecting bank does not incur liability by reason only of having collected payment.

In order to take advantage of this protection the bank must prove it was not negligent. This is a question of fact. The following matters may be relevant:

1. When opening an account a collecting bank should normally make reasonable enquiries about the new customer, his identity and references; his place of business or employment.
2. If there are obviously suspicious features on the face of the cheque itself the bank should enquire. For example 'A/C payee' should alert the bank not to permit payment to anyone else without authority. An employee's private account should not without enquiry be credited with a cheque drawn in favour of his employer. In *Underwood* v. *Bank of Liverpool* 1924 the bank was held liable for collecting a cheque in favour of a company for the private account of the managing director.

Where a collecting bank is held liable for conversion of a cheque the damages it has to pay may be reduced for contributory negligence by the plaintiff: Banking Act 1979.

USEFUL APPLIED MATERIALS

Most of the rules governing negotiable instruments are contained in the Bills of Exchange Act 1882 and the Cheques Act 1957. Reference should be made directly to them, again an annotated copy is likely to be most useful.

There are in addition decided cases which could be helpful in understanding the statutory rules. A number are considered here in addition to those noted in the text.

1

London Joint Stock Bank v. *Macmillan and Arthur* 1918
A customer owes a duty to his banker when drawing cheques to take care. Where he does not the bank is not liable for money wrongly paid out. In this case M signed a bearer cheque leaving the space to enter the amount in words blank, and entering £2 in the space for figures. A rogue wrote in the words 'one hundred and twenty pounds' and altered the figures accordingly. The rogue presented the cheque and the bank cashed it. The bank was held entitled to debit the customer's account because of his negligence.

2

Slingsby v. *District Bank* 1931
Where a bank pays out wrongly on a customer's cheque it will not be allowed to debit his account in the absence of the customer's negligence.

Here a customer left a gap between the payee's name and the printed words 'or order'. A rogue altered the cheque by inserting after the payee's name 'per pro X and Y'. He then indorsed and cashed the cheque. The bank was held unable to debit their customer's account because he had not been negligent.

N.B. It may be that today a similar gap might be found to have facilitated the fraud and might therefore be regarded as negligence.

Basic textbooks on commercial law, or more particularly banking law and practice, will refer the student to a wide range of further authorities and examples.

For immediate study look closely at your own cheque book, the form and the words. Most banks supply crossed cheques as a matter of course, look out for variations in the crossings. A bank note from the Bank of England is a promissory note, look at the instructions written on it.

RECENT EXAMINATION QUESTIONS

It may be useful to spend ten minutes planning an answer to each question before turning to the outline answers.

Question 1.

(a) Describe the essential characteristics of negotiable instruments and give examples of instruments which are negotiable.

(b) Bodger, a director of the 'Do-All' Co, received a cheque for £100,000 drawn by a customer in favour of the company. He took this cheque to his bank and paid it into his personal account. The cashier made no objection, merely saying, 'Of course, Mr Bodger, I know you are a director of the company'. Bodger later drew out the £100,000, closed his account and absconded. Advise the 'Do-All' Co.   (ICSA 1983)

Question 2.

(a) Define a bill of exchange and explain its function. How does it differ from a cheque?

(b) Explain the effect of the following crossings on a cheque:
  (i) Two parallel lines with the name of a banker between them;
  (ii) The words 'not negotiable';
  (iii) The words 'A/C Payee'. (ACCA 1981)

Question 3.

(a) Explain and illustrate the indorsements that can appear on a bill of exchange.

(b) K draws a cheque for £500 in favour of L as payment for goods received. L indorses the cheque and negotiates it to M. M does not indorse the cheque but negotiates it to P in good faith. K is dissatisfied with the goods and stops the cheque.
  (i) Can P recover his £500?
  (ii) Would it make any difference if M knew K had stopped the cheque? (ACCA 1984)

Question 4.

(a) Explain what is meant by a bill of exchange and for what purposes it may be used. What is the difference between a holder in due course and a holder for value?

(b) R draws a cheque in favour of S for £50. The cheque was stolen by T who forged S's signature as an indorsement and obtained £50 in cash from a garage. The garage paid the cheque into their account with the Blue Bank. The Blue Bank then obtained the value of the cheque from the White Bank where R had his account.

Discuss the legal position. (ACCA 1983)

OUTLINE ANSWERS

Answer 1.

(a) Negotiable instruments have the following characteristics: they may be transferred by simple delivery, or delivery plus indorsement (signature on the back of the written instrument); no notice of the transfer need be given to the debtor; the holder of the instrument may sue in his own name; the holder in due course may obtain a better title than his transferor.
Examples of instruments which are negotiable are bills of exchange, cheques and promissory notes

(b) In principle, the collecting bank is liable to the true owner if the bank collects for its customer a cheque to which he has no title. On the facts of this problem B had no title and the 'Do-All' Co will be able to sue the bank for the £100,000. However the Cheques Act 1957 s.4 protects a bank if it collects in good faith and without negligence. If the bank is able to prove it was not negligent it should not be liable to the company. However it appears the bank was negligent in paying the cheque made out to the company into B's private account. The 'Do-All' Co should therefore be advised to sue the bank for the lost money.
Underwood v. *Bank of Liverpool* 1924.

Answer 2.   (a)   Give definition of bill of exchange in the BEA 1882.
A bill of exchange is used to transfer rights to money. It is particularly used in the export business to finance international trade. The drawer is able to discount his bill once accepted and the drawer does not have to pay until the date due. A cheque is a bill of exchange drawn on a bank and payable on demand. It is normally used simply to transfer money owed to the drawer by the bank to the payee.

(b)   (i)   This is a special crossing instructing the paying bank to pay only the banker named.

(ii)   The transferee cannot obtain a better title than his transferor.

(iii)   This is not a statutory crossing but is widely used in practice. It is an instruction to the collecting bank to pay the money only into the account of the named person.

Answer 3.   (a)   A bill of exchange is a negotiable instrument which may be transferred by simple delivery or by delivery plus indorsement. A bearer bill is transferred by delivery, an order bill requires the signature of the payee on the back in addition. The indorsement may take one of the following forms:

Indorsement in blank – a simple signature which converts an order bill into a bearer bill.
Special indorsement – a signature plus a further instruction to pay another named person. The bill remains an order bill.
Conditional indorsement – a signature subject to conditions, e.g. pay X if the goods are satisfactory.
Restrictive indorsement – signature plus a restrictive condition e.g. pay X only.

(b)   (i)   If L negotiates the cheque to M by simple indorsement the bill will become a bearer bill. A bearer bill may be negotiated by mere delivery. M may therefore negotiate the cheque to P without signing it. If P is the holder in due course P may recover the £500 from K, the drawer, or from any previous party to the cheque. L is a party to the cheque because he indorsed it and therefore L is liable on it. M is not a party and is not so liable. Since K appears to be insolvent since his bank has dishonoured his cheque, P would be advised to sue L who is liable as an indorser.

(ii)   Although M is not a party to the cheque as P's immediate transferor M warrants to P that the cheque is a valid cheque, that he, M, had a right to transfer it, and that he did not know of any matter which rendered it valueless. If M *knew* that K had stopped the cheque before he negotiated it to P, M would be in breach of this warranty and would thus also be liable to P.

Answer 4.

(a) A bill of exchange is an unconditional order in writing addressed by one person to another signed by the person giving it, requiring the person to whom it is addressed to pay on demand or at a fixed or determinable future time a sum certain in money to or to the order of a specified person or bearer. Bills of exchange are governed by the Bills of Exchange Act 1882.

A bill of exchange is a negotiable instrument which may be transferred by simple delivery or delivery plus indorsement. In appropriate circumstances it is able to pass a superior title to that of the transferor.

A holder for value is a person in possession of a bill as holder, i.e. as payee or indorsee if the bill is an order bill, for which value has at some time been given, though not necessarily by him. Such a holder takes the same title as his transferor. A holder in due course is one who takes a bill complete and regular on its face, before it is overdue, without notice of any previous dishonour, in good faith, for value and without notice of any defect in the title of the person who negotiated it to him. Such a holder takes free from any previous defects in title.

A bill of exchange is used to transfer rights to money, where a future date is used for payment. A bill of exchange is widely used in the export trade to provide security to the seller and credit to the buyer by the use of discounting bills. A cheque is a bill of exchange drawn on a banker and payable on demand. It is widely used domestically to transfer money.

(b) R is the drawer of the cheque, S is the payee of an order bill. T has no title to the cheque since he stole it. He is not the holder since he is not the payee or indorsee. A forged signature is a nullity and has no effect. Therefore the endorsement of S's signature by T is ineffective, and the bill does not become a bearer bill. Therefore the garage are not holders and do not take any greater right than their transferor. T had no title, therefore the garage has no title.

The drawer is primarily liable on a cheque. S would normally, as the true owner of the cheque, be entitled to enforce it against R but under s.80 BEA the drawer is discharged from further liability if a crossed cheque is paid in accordance with the crossing. S therefore has no further claim against R.

S may sue either T as the thief and forger, or the garage for conversion of his cheque. The garage could then try to recover from T.

There will be no liability on the part of either bank because of the statutory protections. A paying bank, White in this example, which pays a cheque in the ordinary course of business is protected if there is any irregularity in the indorsement: s.60. A collecting bank, Blue in this case, is not liable in conversion to the true owner S provided they acted in good faith and without negligence in collecting for their customer, the garage.

A STEP FURTHER	Banks are a useful source of material, most of them produce publicity material for the benefit of their customers, e.g. Union Bank of Switzerland publish a free pamphlet on Bankers' Commercial Credits. The Department of Trade and Industry produce a wide range of material designed to help exporters, including the various methods of payment available. The London Chamber of Commerce and the British Institute of Export would also be able to help. Many local chambers of commerce have export groups and may run periodic courses for the benefit of members.
BASIC READING	*Guide to Negotiable Instruments* (7th edn) Richardson, Butterworths, 1983. *Commercial Law* R. M. Goode, Penguin (Part Three), 1982. *Charlesworth's Mercantile Law* (14th edn), Stevens (Part Six), 1984.
FURTHER READING OR REFERENCE	*The Law of Bills of Exchange* (25th edn) Sir J. B. Byles, Sweet and Maxwell, 1983.
USEFUL ADDRESSES:	British Overseas Trade Board, 1 Victoria Street, London SW1H OET. Department of Trade and Industry, 1 Victoria Street, London SW1H OET. HMSO, 49 High Holborn, London WC1. International Chamber of Commerce, Centre Point, 103 New Oxford Street, London WC1A 1QB. London Chamber of Commerce and Industry, 69 Cannon Street, London WC4N 5AB. Midland Bank Group, International Trade Services, 120 Cannon Street, London EC4N 6AB.

Chapter 14

General Principles of Tort

GETTING STARTED

The word tort comes from the French and means 'a wrong'. Torts in English law cover infringements of legal rights or a failure to comply with a duty arising outside of contract. The commission of a tort entitles the injured party to obtain a legally enforceable remedy, usually damages.

It is possible for the same action to give rise to more than one legal consequence. It is frequently the case that a tortious action can also be a crime. For example, theft and criminal damage are crimes but they can also be the torts of trespass to goods and conversion.

In addition, there can be liability both in contract and tort for the same injury. The employee who is injured while at work may be able to base his claim on a number of grounds – negligence, breach of statutory duty and breach of his contract of employment. The employer may also be prosecuted if he has committed a criminal offence under the Health and Safety at Work etc. Act 1974.

The variety of torts is seemingly unlimited. They protect both the person and his property. They include trespass to the person, land and goods, private nuisance, breach of statutory duty, deceit, defamation and negligence to name only some. Because of this vast range, this area of law is sometimes called the law of torts.

In this chapter the student will be introduced to the general principles which underlie the law of tort and be provided with a short introduction to a number of torts. These general principles do not normally form the basis of a complete question but frequently the student is expected to show that he can use these principles effectively.

ESSENTIAL PRINCIPLES

This section will concentrate on the general rules of tort. The authorities referred to are included in the section, 'Useful Applied Materials'.

WHO CAN COMMIT A TORT?

The general rule is that any legal person, natural or artificial (e.g. a company), can commit a tort. A person who commits a tort is called a tortfeasor. If more than one person commits the same tort, either because they act together or because one person is vicariously liable (see below) for another's tort, they are joint tortfeasors and their liability is said to be joint and several. This means that they are both liable for the tort and the injured party can proceed against either of them to obtain compensation. If, however, a person suffers damage because of the independent actions of more than one person, his car, for example, is negligently struck at the same time by two different motorists, then these defendants will remain separate tortfeasors.

WHEN DOES LIABILITY ARISE?

For a person to be liable in tort he must usually have committed a particular act combined with a particular mental state (*Fowler* v. *Lanning* (1) 1959)

Some torts do not require any particular mental element but only the commission of a particular act. These are known as torts of strict liability. They include:

1.   The tort of *Rylands* v. *Fletcher* (2) 1868 (see p. 171);
2.   Breaches of certain statutory duties. Certain statutes, such as the Factories Act 1961, have been interpreted by the courts as imposing strict liability.

TORTS ACTIONABLE PER SE

Although the plaintiff must usually show that the defendant's actions have resulted in him suffering damage, some torts are actionable per se, that is without proof of material loss or damage. Simply the fact that the defendant has committed the tort is sufficient for the plaintiff to be entitled to a remedy. In law this is expressed as *injuria sine damno*, (an infringement of a legal right without damage). Torts which are actionable per se are trespass to the person, land or goods, libel and certain forms of slander.

MOTIVE AND LIABILITY

With regard to liability, motive is generally irrelevant. A good motive will not make an unlawful act lawful, nor a lawful act unlawful (*Bradford Corp* v. *Pickles* (3) 1895). In certain circumstances, however, the presence or absence of malice may be important either to establish the commission of a tort, such as deceit or private nuisance, or to defeat a defence such as the defences of fair comment or qualified privilege in defamation.

VICARIOUS LIABILITY

The person who commits a tort is always liable for its consequences. In addition, if anyone has authorised the commission of a tort he is also liable.

A person can also be held indirectly liable for another's torts. This form of liability is called vicarious liability and arises within certain relationships. For example, a principal may be vicariously liable for the torts of his agent or one partner may be vicariously liable for the torts of his other partners committed in the course of partnership business.

Employer and employee

The most important example of vicarious liability is the relationship between the employer (master) and his employee (servant). *The rule is that an employer is vicariously liable for the torts of his employee if they are committed in the course of the employee's employment.* If the employee is doing what he is employed to do, then even if he carried out his duties dishonestly or improperly, the employer will still be liable (*Limpus* v. *London General Omnibus Co* (4) 1862; *Beard* v. *London General Omnibus Co* (5) 1900).

Sometimes an employer is vicariously liable even though he had expressly forbidden what the employee did. If the employer's prohibition is only as to the way in which the employee should do his job, the employer is normally still vicariously liable (*Rose* v. *Plenty* (6) 1976). If, however, the prohibition specifically forbids certain types of duties, then it is likely that the employer will not be vicariously liable (*Twine* v. *Bean's Express* (7) 1946).

An employer is not vicariously liable if the employee commits a tort while on a 'frolic of his own', (*Hilton* v. *Thomas Burton (Rhodes) Ltd* (8) 1961). If, when he committed the tort he was not acting as an employee, there will be no liability on the part of the employer.

Employees are occasionally loaned to other employers. If this happens then it must be decided whether control of that employee's work has passed to the other employer or remained with the original employer. The employer who is responsible for the employee will be the one vicariously liable if that employee commits any torts (*Mersey Docks & Harbour Board* v. *Coggins and Griffith (Liverpool) Ltd* (9) 1947).

Independent contractors

An employer can be liable for the torts of an independent contractor, but only in certain situations. An independent contractor is someone who has a contract for services in contrast to an employee who has a contract of service.

The employer will be personally liable in the following circumstances:

1. The independent contractor was employed to do something unlawful; or
2. The employer authorised or subsequently ratified the independent contractor's tort; or
3. The employer was negligent in the way he selected the independent contractor or he did not give him proper instructions.

The employer will be vicariously liable for the torts of his independent contractors in the following situations:

1. The independent contractor was employed to do something extra hazardous; or
2. The independent contractor was employed to do dangerous work on or adjoining the highway. In those circumstances the employer is liable for any foreseeable damage; or

3. The employer was under a strict statutory or common law duty, (as under *Rylands* v. *Fletcher* (2)), which he cannot avoid by delegation.

IMMUNITY FROM TORTIOUS LIABILITY

The general rule is that anyone can sue and be sued in tort. However, certain persons either have absolute immunity from liability or immunity in certain circumstances. Thus, although they can commit torts, they cannot be compelled to compensate the injured party.

1. *The Crown* – the Queen in her personal capacity has complete immunity in tort. This does not apply to the rest of the Royal Family nor to members of her government or civil service (Crown Proceedings Act 1947);
2. *Diplomatic immunity* – those who can claim diplomatic immunity, such as foreign ambassadors, royal sovereigns and their staff, have complete immunity;
3. *Minors* – those under the age of 18 are fully liable in tort, although they must sue through their 'next friend' and defend an action through their *guardian ad litem*'. However, a minor may sometimes avoid liability because he is considered incapable of forming the necessary mental element required for the tort.

    Further, a minor cannot be held liable in tort in order to make him indirectly liable on an unenforceable contract. Thus, he cannot be sued in deceit for fraudulently misrepresenting his age (*Leslie Ltd* v. *Sheill* (10) 1914).

    Parents cannot be held responsible for their child's tort unless they are vicariously liable, (for example, the child is the parent's employee), or they authorised the tort or were negligent (*Bebee* v. *Sales* (11) *1916*).
4. *Persons suffering from mental disorder* – mental disorder does not in itself give immunity from liability but it can affect a person's ability to form the required mental element for a particular tort.

GENERAL DEFENCES

There is no liability if no tort has been committed even if the plaintiff has suffered as a result of the defendant's actions (*Bradford Corporation* v. *Pickles* (3) 1895). The phrase which is used to describe such situations is *damnum sine injuria*, (loss without a legal wrong).

Further, there will no liability if the plaintiff cannot establish, on a balance of probabilities, that the defendant committed the tort alleged.

In addition to the above, certain general defences have been created. The defendant can also plead any special defences appropriate for the particular tort for which he is being sued. The general defences include:

1. Volenti non fit injuria (Consent to run the risk of injury)	This is probably the most important general defence. *The defendant has to show that the plaintiff knew of the risk and expressly or impliedly consented to run the risk, understanding that if he was injured he would not have a legal remedy.* Whether the plaintiff consented depends on the facts of each case. No consent is given by the plaintiff simply because he knew of the risk – sciens (knowing) is not volens (willing). For this reason it is difficult to establish this defence against an employee who will lose his job if he refuses, (*Smith* v. *Baker & Sons* (12) 1891; *Bowater* v. *Rowley Regis Corporation* (13) 1944). Further, volenti is less likely to be a defence if the plaintiff was injured while fulfilling some legal or moral duty such as coming to the rescue of a person placed in danger because of the negligent act of the defendant (*Haynes* v. *Harwood* (15) 1935).
2. Contributory negligence	See Negligence, Ch. 15.
3. Self defence	The defendant will not be liable if he can prove that he only used reasonable and necessary force to defend himself, another, or property.
4. Mistake	The general rule is that mistake is no defence. However, it may sometimes be a good defence to an action based on false imprisonment if the defendant can show that he reasonably believed he had the right to make the arrest. Mistake is also a defence to malicious prosecution if the defendant can establish that the prosecution was brought under a mistaken but reasonable belief in the plaintiff's guilt.
5. Inevitable accident	The accident could not have been foreseen or prevented by a reasonable man (*National Coal Board* v. *J E Evans & Co (Cardiff) Ltd* (16) 1951). This defence is not available if the tort is one of strict liability.
6. Act of God	This defence is similar to the defence of inevitable accident except that the cause was a natural event which could not have been foreseen. This defence can be used in torts of strict liability (*Nichols* v. *Marsland* (17) 1876).
7. Necessity	The essence of this defence is that, although the defendant committed a tort, he did so in order to prevent a greater harm (*Cope* v. *Sharpe* (18) 1912).
8. Statutory authority.	Statutory authority gives complete protection from liability as long as the act, which is authorised by legislation and its necessary consequences, is done with reasonable care.
REMOTENESS OF DAMAGE	The rules governing remoteness of damage determine for what damage the defendant must compensate the plaintiff. If the defendant's actions are intentional then all the damage which flows from his act will not be too remote. In other circumstances it will depend on whether the damage was reasonably foreseeable. This topic is discussed in detail in the chapter on Negligence (see Ch. 15).

LIMITATION OF ACTIONS (LIMITATION ACT 1980)

Damage to property

If the plaintiff's action is based on damage to property then the plaintiff has six years to bring his claim from the date the cause of action arose.

Personal injury claims

If the plaintiff wishes compensation for personal injuries, with or without property damage, he must bring his claim within three years from the date the cause of action arose or the date he became aware of the serious nature of his injury and the identity of the defendant.

Torts actionable per se

The cause of action arises when the tort is committed.

Torts requiring damage

The cause of action dates from the moment when that damage occurred.

Torts of a continuing nature

Each incident gives rise to fresh cause of action. This could be the case in an action based on trespass to land or private nuisance.

Actions concealed by fraud

Time does not begin to run, if the cause of action is concealed by fraud, until that fraud is or could have been discovered.

DEATH

It used to be the case that death extinguished rights and liabilities in tort. This rule was changed by the Law Reform (Miscellaneous Provisions) Act 1934 which allows an action to be brought or defended by the deceased's estate. In addition, under the Fatal Accidents Acts 1846–1976 (as amended), certain dependants of the deceased also have a right to bring an action for the financial loss they have suffered as a result of the death, if the deceased could have sued for the injury he had received, if he had lived.

REMEDIES

The most common remedy is damages, monetary compensation. The general purpose of damages is to put the plaintiff back in the position he would have been in if no tort had been committed. Damages are usually assessed on the basis of being equal to the plaintiff's loss. This is not too difficult when the plaintiff has suffered only property loss but it can be extremely difficult to assess when the plaintiff has suffered personal injury.

In addition, or as an alternative to damages, the court may grant an injunction to prevent a tort or its repetition.

EXAMPLES OF TORTIOUS LIABILITY	The intentional unlawful direct interference with a person or his liberty. Trespass to the person takes three forms:
Protection of the person	1. *Assault* – causing another reasonably to fear the immediate infliction of force upon himself;
Trespass to the person	2. *Battery* – the application of force against another; and
	3. *False imprisonment* – restricting another's freedom of movement even for a very short time.
Protection of land and property	
Trespass to land	The intentional unlawful direct interference with the land of another.
Trespass to goods	The intentional unlawful direct interference with another's goods.
Conversion	Dealing with another's goods in a way inconsistent with his rights of ownership over those goods, such as selling or damaging them. The torts of conversion and trespass to goods are frequently committed at the same time.
Rylands v. *Fletcher* 1868	This case established a strict liability tort. A person is liable if he brings onto his land and keeps there anything not natural to that land which is likely to do damage if it escapes, and it does escape and causes damage.
Private nuisance	The unlawful interference with another's use or enjoyment of his land. This tort includes both physical damage to property and interference with the occupier's health and enjoyment of his property.
Protection from false statements	A defendant is liable for this tort if he knowingly or recklessly makes a false statement of fact intending the plaintiff to rely on it, the plaintiff did rely on the statement and thereby suffered damage.
Deceit	
Injurious falsehood	The malicious making of a false statement derogatory of another's goods or title which causes damage.
Economic torts	The intentional and unjustified interference with a contract made between others to induce a breach of that contract.
Interference with contractual relations	
Passing off	Misleading others into believing that one's goods or business are those of another.
The torts of negligence and defamation	These torts are discussed in detail in Chapters 15 and 16.

USEFUL APPLIED MATERIALS

The cases described in this section are listed in the order in which they were mentioned in the 'Essential Principles' section.

1

Fowler v. *Lanning* 1959

Unless the tort is one of strict liability, the plaintiff must establish that the defendant committed the tortious act with the appropriate mental element.

  The plaintiff was shot by the defendant. He sued for trespass to the person but in his pleadings he did not allege that the defendant had acted either intentionally or negligently. He therefore had not established that any tort had been committed.

2

Rylands v. *Fletcher* 1868

Lord Blackburn's ratio established a new tort of strict liability, ' . . . the person who for his own purposes brings on his land and collects and keeps there anything likely to do mischief if it escapes, must keep it in at his peril, and, if he does not do so, is *prima facie* answerable for all the damage which is the natural consequence of its escape'.

  An independent contractor was engaged to build a reservoir. The reservoir was built over some disused mine shafts, although no one was aware of that fact. The reservoir was filled with water which flooded the disused shafts and entered the plaintiff's working mine. Although the defendant had not acted intentionally, recklessly or negligently he was still personally liable for the damage. He could not delegate the responsibility for the damage onto the independent contractor.

3

Bradford Corporation v. *Pickles* 1895

The defendant's motive is usually irrelevant in determining liability.

  Pickles wished to sell some land to Bradford Corporation, but at his price. In order to force them to buy he prevented water, which percolated from his land, from reaching the corporation's water supply. The corporation sued, but, although it had suffered damage, Pickles had not committed any tort. No liability.

Vicarious liability

4

Limpus v. *London General Omnibus Co* 1862

An employer is vicariously liable for the torts of his employee if they are committed in the course of his employment.

  A bus driver had been forbidden to race his bus. He raced his bus and caused an accident. His employers were held vicariously liable for the employee's tort as when the tort was committed the employee was doing what he was employed to do.

5

Beard v. *London General Omnibus Co* 1900

An employer is not vicariously liable for the torts of his employee if they are not committed in the course of his employment.

  A bus conductor drove a bus and caused an accident. His employers were not vicariously liable since when he drove the bus he was not acting in the course of his employment.

6

Rose v. Plenty 1976

An employee is still acting in the course of his employment even if he acts contrary to instructions as to how he does his job.

A milkman was prohibited from using children to help him to deliver milk. He ignored this instruction and a child was injured while helping him to deliver milk. The employers were vicariously liable, notwithstanding their prohibition, as the employee was still acting in the course of his employment.

7

Twine v. Bean's Express 1946

An employer is not vicariously liable if the consequence of disobeying his prohibition results in the employee acting outside the course of his employment.

A driver gave a lift to a hitch-hiker who was injured while travelling as a passenger in the lorry. The employers were not vicariously liable as the employee was acting outside the terms of his employment when he gave the lift.

8

Hilton v. Thomas Burton (Rhodes) Ltd 1961

The employer is not vicariously liable if when the employee committed the tort he was on a frolic of his own.

The defendant's employee had an accident while returning from a cafe. The employer was not liable as, at the time of the accident, the employee was on a frolic of his own.

9

Mersey Docks and Harbour Board v. Coggins and Griffith (Liverpool) Ltd 1947

If an employee is loaned to another employer, the employer who assumes control over that employee is vicariously liable for any torts he commits during the course of that employment.

A crane excavator and its operator were hired on condition that the hirers be regarded as the employee's employer during the time of hire. The employee was negligent while working the crane. The hirers were vicariously liable.

Minors

10

Leslie Ltd v. Sheill 1914

A minor cannot be held liable in tort in order to enforce an unenforceable contract.

A minor misrepresented his age in order to borrow money. He could not be sued for breach of contract. The plaintiff tried to enforce the contract by suing the minor for deceit. His action failed.

11

Bebee v. Sales 1916

A parent will be liable for his child's torts if the child was able to commit the tort because of his parent's negligent supervision.

A 15-year-old boy was given an airgun. He damaged a window with the gun but was still allowed to keep it. The father was liable when the boy later injured another child's eye with the gun.

Volenti **12**	*Smith* v. *Charles Baker & Sons* 1891 Knowledge of the risk does not mean the plaintiff consented. An employee was injured while at work when a stone dropped from a crane. The employers argued that he was volens as he knew of the risk. Although it was accepted he had known of the risk, the court held that he did not thereby consent to run that risk.
13	*Bowater* v. *Rowley Regis Corporation* 1944 The consent must be freely given. An employee was ordered to take out a dangerous horse, notwithstanding his protests. He was injured when the horse bolted. The employers could not rely on the defence of volenti.
14	*ICI* v. *Shatwell* 1965 Employees may, in appropriate circumstances accept the risk of injury at work. Here a shot-firer was held volenti to the risk of danger incurred when, with a companion, he deliberately breached safety instructions.
15	*Haynes* v. *Harwood* 1935 The defence of volenti cannot be used against a plaintiff who has come to the rescue of the defendant or another person who is placed in danger by the defendant's tort. A cart was left unattended and the horse drawing the cart bolted. The plaintiff was injured while stopping the horse which was heading towards a group of children. The defence of volenti could not be used. It would have been different if there had been no danger of personal injury, as in *Cutler* v. *United Dairies (London) Ltd* 1933 where a horse bolted in an empty field.
Accident **16**	*National Coal Board* v. *J E Evans & Co (Cardiff) Ltd* 1951 The defence of inevitable accident can be used if the defendant can prove he could not foresee or control the event. An electricity cable was damaged. The defendants were able to use the defence of inevitable accident since they were unaware of the cable and could not have known of its presence.
Act of God **17**	*Nichols* v. *Marsland* 1876 The defendant can plead Act of God to avoid liability for strict liability torts. An unusually heavy rainfall caused some artificial lakes to flood. This rainfall was held to be an Act of God and there was no human liability.
Necessity **18**	*Cope* v. *Sharpe* 1912 If the defendant committed a tort in order to avoid greater harm he may be able to rely on the defence of necessity. In order to prevent a fire spreading the defendant trespassed onto the plaintiff's land to build a fire break. He had acted reasonably in the circumstances and was not liable.

The following recent examination questions illustrate the type of question asked on general principles of torts. It may be useful to spend around ten minutes planning an outline answer to each question before turning to the outline answers.

Question 1.

To what extent is fault an element in tortious liability?   (ILE 1982)

Question 2.

(a) An employer is vicariously liable for the negligent acts of his employees but not for those of an independent contractor. Discuss.

(b) Road Contractors Limited engages a number of drivers to move earth and rubble during the construction of a motorway. Each driver provides his own lorry and payment is made on a piece-work basis subject to guaranteed minimum earnings. During prescribed hours of work the drivers are subject to control by the company's supervisors.

One driver overloads his lorry contrary to instructions given by a supervisor and this is the cause of an accident in which a third party is injured. Advise Road Construction Limited as to its possible liability.   (ICMA 1975)

Question 3.

It is said that if a person consents to assume the risk of injury he will not have a remedy if an injury is suffered. Explain this statement and outline the circumstances in which consent will not be accepted as a defence.   (ICMA 1982)

OUTLINE ANSWERS

The following are suggested outline answers to questions 1 and 2.

Answer 1.

Usually the plaintiff must prove that the defendant committed the act required of the tort together with the appropriate mental state; intention, recklessness or negligence (*Fowler* v. *Lanning*). If no tort has been committed, even if the plaintiff has suffered loss, there is no liability (*damnum sine injuria*).

If the tort is one of strict liability the commission of the act is itself sufficient to create liability. If the tort is actionable per se the plaintiff does not have to show that he suffered any actual loss.

The actual tortfeasor is always liable. A person can also sometimes be vicariously liable for the torts of another. Some persons have immunity from tortious liability. Some defendants are at 'fault' but still avoid liability becuse they can rely on a general defence such as volenti or a defence associated with a particular tort.

Fault must be distinguished from motive. A bad motive does not create liability nor does a good motive excuse a tortious act (*Bradford Corporation* v. *Pickles*).

Answer 2.

(a) If an employee has committed the tort of negligence during the course of his employment and not while he is on a frolic of his own, the employer, who is in control of the employee, will be vicariously liable for the employee's tort. The general rule is that an employer is not vicariously liable for the torts of an independent contractor except in certain circumstances.

(b) If the driver has committed a tort, Road Contractors Limited may be vicariously liable. If the driver was an employee, then they will be liable if he committed the tort in the course of his employment even if he was acting improperly, such as acting contrary to instructions (*Rose* v. *Plenty*). If, however, the instructions actually limited the scope of his employment, he would not have been acting in the course of his employment when he drove with an overloaded lorry (*Twine* v. *Bean's Express*).

If the driver was an independent contractor, Road Contractors Limited would be vicariously liable only in certain specific situations; the work was extra hazardous, the work involved dangerous activity on or near the highway or Road Contractors Limited was under strict liability.

Road Contractors Limited could be personally liable for the driver's tort if the driver as an independent contractor was given negligent instructions by the company's supervisor or the company was negligent in choosing this particular driver.

A TUTOR'S ANSWER

Students are frequently asked to discuss the defence of *volenti*. The following is a full answer to Question 3.

Answer 3.

Volenti non fit injuria is one of the general defences available in tort. If the defendant can establish that the plaintiff knew of the risk and consented, either expressly or impliedly, to run that risk then, even if the defendant has committed a tort against the plaintiff, he will not be liable. For example, if a player in a rugby match is injured while the game is being played according to the rule book, he cannot claim compensation as he is volenti his injury. It would be different if he was injured in an incident on the playing field not permitted by the rules, e.g. a deliberate foul. Whether a plaintiff consented to run the risk of injury is a question of fact in each case.

Sciens (knowing) is not necessarily consent (*willing*) (*Smith* v. *Charles Baker & Sons*). The consent must be freely given. An employee may be aware of the risk he is running but he does not thereby normally consent to run that risk if the only alternative is unemployment (*Bowater* v. *Rowley Regis Corporation*). Sometimes, however, even an employee may consent to run the risk of injury (*Imperial Chemical Industries Ltd* v. *Shatwell*).

Usually *volenti* cannot be used as a defence against a rescuer who has been forced to act because the defendant has placed either himself or another in fear of the danger of imminent personal injury (*Haynes v. Harwood*). The situation is different if there is no risk of physical injury (*Cutler* v. *United Dairies (London) Ltd*).

A STEP FURTHER

BASIC READING

There are a number of standard textbooks on tort. These include:

Tort Law, R. W. Dias & B. S. Markesinis, Clarendon Press, 1984.
Winfield & Jolowicz on Tort (12th edn) W. V. H. Rogers, Sweet & Maxwell, 1984.
Students might find the discussion in these texts useful:
Tort (3rd edn), David Baker, Concise College Texts, Sweet & Maxwell, 1981.
Tort, Geoffrey Samuel, Nutshells series, Sweet & Maxwell, 1979.

FURTHER READING OR REFERENCE

Students who are interested in how this area of law may develop are advised to read:

Royal Commission on Civil Liability and Compensation for Personal Injury (the Pearson Report), Cmnd. 7054, HMSO.
Foundations of the Law of Tort (2nd edn), G. Williams and B. A. Hepple, Butterworths, 1984.
Accidents, Compensation and the Law, P. S. Atiyah, Weidenfeld and Nicolson, 1980.

Chapter 15   Negligence

The term negligence is like a chameleon for its meaning changes according to the situation in which it is used. To the layperson the word could be translated as simply carelessness, but in the study of law, the word negligence has come to mean the tort of negligence. Although its development really only started some 50 years ago, negligence has become the most important tort. There are two reasons for this: first, most claims for compensation, either for personal injury or property damage, are based on this tort and secondly, there is no limit to the number of negligent situations which can arise. As Lord Macmillian said in *Donoghue* v. *Stevenson*(1), 'The categories of negligence are never closed'.

Students should not assume, however, that every careless action will give rise to liability. In order to prove that a defendant is liable the plaintiff must establish that the three elements of the tort are present:

1. The defendant owed the plaintiff a legal duty of care;
2. The defendant was in breach of that duty of care; and,
3. The plaintiff suffered loss as a result of the defendant's breach.

Each element of the tort must be firmly settled upon the shoulders of the element preceding it. Thus, a defendant can be as negligent as he wishes if he does not owe a duty of care to the plaintiff. Even if he owed a duty of care, if there has been no breach the defendant will not be liable. Further, although the plaintiff may prove that the defendant acted negligently, if his negligence has not caused the plaintiff's loss, or if that loss was too remote, the defendant will not be liable. Finally, even though the defendant has acted negligently, he will escape the noose of liability if he has a defence.

Under the 'Essential Principles' section each element of the tort of negligence will be discussed in detail. In addition, a section has been included on the rules of remoteness, since, although these rules are applicable to all torts, they are chiefly examined in questions on negligence. Negligence is a product of the common law and its principles have been developed through judicial decisions. Authorities are given for the various legal principles mentioned and are included in the 'Useful Applied Materials' section.

ESSENTIAL PRINCIPLES

THE DUTY OF CARE

This is the most commonly examined element of the tort. The question of whether a duty of care exists within any particular relationship is a question of law. Prior to 1932 the categories of negligence were closed – certain specified acts and omissions, and no others, were regarded as negligent. This was because there was no recognised general principle underlying the duty situations. In *Donoghue* v. *Stevenson* (1) 1932 (the case of the snail in the ginger beer bottle) Lord Atkin formulated the 'neighbour principle', thus establishing a general test for determining the existence of a duty of care.

Lord Atkin stated the principle as:

'You must take reasonable care to avoid acts or omissions which you can reasonably foresee would be likely to injure your neighbour. Who, then in law is my neighbour? . . . persons who are so closely and directly affected by my act that I ought reasonably to have them in contemplation as being so affected when I am directing my mind to the acts or omissions which are called in question.'

Judges have used this neighbour principle to establish whether a duty of care exists in any particular situation. Lord Reid in *Home Office* v. *Dorset Yacht Co* (3) 1970, a case concerned with damage caused by Borstal boys who had escaped, emphasised that the neighbour principle was not a mechanical formula but a 'statement of principle'. 'Reasonable foreseeability' is not the only criteria for establishing the existence of a duty of care, policy considerations are of equal importance.

Recognition of the relationship between proximity and policy was more recently restated in *Anns* v. *Merton London Borough Council*(4) 1978 where Lord Wilberforce set out a two-stage approach to determine if a legal duty of care exists:

1. Is there a sufficient relationship of proximity between the parties so that a prima facie duty of care arises?;
2. If the first question is answered in the affirmative, are there any considerations which ought to negate, or reduce or limit the scope of the duty of care or the class of persons to whom it is owed or the damages to which a breach of it may give rise?

Policy has been a crucial factor in determining whether a duty of care exists in such areas as negligent misstatement, pure economic loss, nervous shock and occupiers' liability to trespassers and these areas are frequently the subject of examination questions. In such cases judges have argued that it is not in the public interest that a duty of care should be recognised. The principal argument usually given to support such decisions is known as the 'floodgates' argument – if a particular grievance were recognised then countless litigants would be able to bring claims demanding compensation. The courts would be 'flooded' with claims. As the American judge Cardozo said, there would be liability for 'an unlimited amount for an unlimited period to an unlimited number'.

Associated with the floodgates argument are other supporting arguments. These include the fear of numerous or exaggerated claims and the difficulties in proving such claims or determining the amount of compensation. Further, one defendant might have to bear the brunt of many claims which should either be borne by society as a whole or the citizen should accept his loss as one of the risks of living in a community. These arguments were stated in Lord Denning's judgment in *Spartan Steel and Alloys Ltd* v. *Martin & Co (Contractors) Ltd* (6) 1973.

The specific areas where policy has played an important part include:

The duty of care and pure economic loss	In general a plaintiff only receives compensation for damage to person or property and such economic loss which arises as a consequence of such damage. Pure economic loss, that is financial loss not arising from damage to property or personal injury, has not usually been recoverable because the courts have held that no duty of care was owed and/or the loss was too remote. This attitude is being challenged (*Junior Books* v. *Veitchi Co Ltd* (7) 1982).
The duty of care and negligent misstatement	There has always been liability in negligence for careless statements which have caused damage to person or property but for policy reasons limitations have been placed on awarding compensation for careless statements causing only economic loss. The obiter dicta in *Hedley Byrne & Co* v. *Heller & Partners Ltd* (8) 1964, as modified by subsequent cases, established that there could be liability. The student should remember that if a statement is made fraudulently liability would lie in the tort of deceit.
The duty of care and nervous shock	To obtain damages a plaintiff must prove that he has suffered some legally recognisable loss. This can include mental injury. The courts have never in the past shown great enthusiasm for claims based on nervous shock for the various policy reasons previously mentioned. The case of *McLoughlin* v. *O'Brian* (13) 1982 may indicate a change of attitude.
The duty of care and occupier's liability	Section 2(2) of the Occupiers' Liability Act 1957 imposes on an occupier a 'common duty of care' to all his lawful visitors to take reasonable care to see that they are reasonably safe in using the premises for the purposes for which they are allowed to be there. This Act did not include liability for trespassers. In *British Railways Board*

v. *Herrington* (14) 1972 the courts recognised that the occupier owed a
'duty of humanity' to trespassers.

The liability of occupiers to nonlawful visitors is now governed by
the Occupiers' Liability Act 1984. An occupier is under a duty if the risk
is such that in all the circumstances he would be reasonably expected to
give some protection. When the duty arises the occupier must '. . .
take such care as is reasonable in all the circumstances of the case to see
that (the person to whom the duty is owed) does not suffer injury on the
premises by reason of the danger concerned'.

BREACH

*If a duty of care is established the plaintiff must then prove that the
defendant was in breach of that duty. This is a question of fact not law.
The standard of care required is that of the ordinary reasonable man.*
The reasonable man is not perfect. It is not expected that he will never
make a mistake in judgment. He must, however, take reasonable care.

An objective test is applied. To determine whether a defendant
has come up to the reasonable man standard the question asked is not
did he do his best but did he come up to the standard which would have
been achieved by a prudent and reasonable man acting in the same
circumstances.

If a man claims no special expertise then he is only judged by the
standard of the ordinary reasonable man (*Wells* v. *Cooper* (17) 1958). If
he claims some special skill or knowledge then he must be judged by the
standard of a reasonable man having such expertise. The defendant in
those circumstances does not have to be the very best in his field, nor
does he always have to agree with all his colleagues, but he must at least
follow recognised approved practices (*Bolman* v. *Friern Hospital
Management Committee* (18) 1957).

A court, when determining the question of breach, may consider
such factors as:

1. Was the injury foreseeable? (*Roe* v. *Minister of Health* (19) 1954);
2. The balance between the likelihood of injury and the burden
    placed on the defendant in taking precautionary steps (*Bolton* v.
    Stone (20) 1951). The greater the risk the greater the care
    required. If the defendant is dealing with dynamite he is obliged to
    take more care than if he is dealing with lead.

    If the defendant could have taken precautions which would
    have cost little either financially or in terms of time or labour, he
    will probably be found negligent if, in those circumstances, he has
    failed to take such precautions.

    Associated with this is the rule that a reasonable man must
    consider the particular characteristics of those who may be
    affected by his actions (*Paris* v. *Stepney BC* (22) 1950). More care
    may be needed to protect children (*Glasgow Corporation* v.
    Taylor (25) 1922).
3. Sometimes necessity may justify taking what would otherwise be
    an unreasonable risk (*Watt* v. *Hertfordshire County Council* (24)
    1954).

Res ipsa loquitur (The thing speaks for itself)

The general rule is that the plaintiff must prove that the defendant has been negligent. In certain situations, when the maxim *res ipsa loquitur* applies, the balance of proof will shift to the defendant to prove that he was not in breach of the duty of care. If the defendant can show this then he will not be liable.

In order for the maxim to apply certain conditions must be fulfilled:

1. The cause of the damage must have been under the defendant's or his servant's control;
2. The defendant must have had knowledge which the plaintiff did not possess;
3. The accident would presumably not have occurred but for the defendant's or his servant's negligence.

The maxim would apply, for example, if a barrel of flour fell out of a window (*Byrne* v. *Boadle* (26) 1863).

CAUSATION

It is necessary for the plaintiff to show that the defendant's breach was the cause of his damage. Usually this presents no problem. Sometimes, however, even though the defendant has been negligent his negligence is not the operative cause of the plaintiff's losses. For instance, in *Barnett* v. *Chelsea and Kensington Hospital Management Committee* (27) 1969 the patient died because of arsenic poisoning not because the hospital doctor failed to examine him.

The test used by the courts to determine questions of causation is the hypothetical 'but for' test – would the damage have occurred but for the negligent act?

Nova causa (or novus actus) interveniens (An intervening act)

A *nova causa interveniens* will break the chain of causation. A *nova causa interveniens* must be unforeseeable and outside the defendant's control (*McKew* v. *Holland and Hannen and Cubitts (Scotland) Ltd* (33) 1969). Such a break in the chain of causation may be a natural event or the result of a conscious act by a third party or even by the plaintiff.

The defendant can not ordinarily escape liability by claiming a break in the chain of causation in cases where the plaintiff has had to escape from danger created by the defendant's negligence or where the plaintiff has gone to the rescue of someone placed in danger because of the defendant's negligence.

REMOTENESS

For a plaintiff to obtain damages in negligence he must show that he suffered loss as a result of the defendant's breach. A plaintiff's losses, however, may be extensive. For what losses the defendant must compensate the plaintiff is determined by the rules governing remoteness of damage. These rules are not limited to the tort of negligence. Damage which is intended, for instance, is never too remote. Because the element of remoteness is frequently examined in questions on negligence, these rules are discussed in this chapter.

The general rule on remoteness was established in the Privy Council case *Wagon Mound (No 1)* (29) 1961. *A defendant is only liable to compensate a plaintiff for the type of damage which was reasonably foreseeable as a result of his tort.* An objective test is applied. This principle is, however, subject to qualifications:

1. *The defendant must take his victims as he finds him – the* '**egg-shell skull' rule**. If injury to the plaintiff is reasonably foreseeable then the defendant will be liable for the full effects of the injury even if these are increased by the plaintiff's particular characteristics (*Smith* v. *Leech Brain & Co Ltd* (32) 1962).
2. *The kind of injury and the way it was inflicted need only be of a type which was reasonably foreseeable*; its exact nature or method of infliction does not have to be foreseen. (*Hughes* v. *Lord Advocate* (30) 1963);
3. *If damage of the kind foreseen occurs that damage will not be too remote notwithstanding that the extent of damage done is greater than anticipated* (*Vacwell Engineering Co Ltd* v. *B D H Chemicals Ltd* (31) 1971);
4. *Policy considerations may limit the damages recoverable.*

DEFENCES

Even if the plaintiff is able to prove negligence, the defendant may still have a defence. The most common defences used to avoid liability are *volenti non fit injuria* (see Ch. 14) and *contributory negligence*.

Contributory negligence

If the plaintiff is in any way to blame for his own loss his damages will be reduced as is 'just and equitable' in accordance with s.1(1) Law Reform (Contributory Negligence) Act 1945. Thus, if the defendant fails to wear a seatbelt or crash helmet his damages will be reduced accordingly as he would have failed to have taken reasonable care for his own safety.

N.B. Vicarious liability: This topic is discussed in detail in Chapter 14. It is not uncommon, however, particularly in questions involving negligent employees, for the examiner to expect the student to discuss vicarious liability. *Simply put, vicarious liability means one person is liable for another person's tort because he is in a particular relationship with the tortfeasor.* The employer, for example, is vicariously liable for his employee's torts if they are committed in the course of the employee's employment. This is in addition to the employee's personal liability.

USEFUL APPLIED MATERIALS

The principles of negligence have been primarily established through case law. A student should support any general rule used with appropriate cases. It is essential to give the ratio of any case cited. This is far more important than trying to impress the examiner by reciting the facts of the case in detail. The facts are really only important to the parties in dispute, the legal principle of the case is important to the development of the law. Sometimes the two are inextricably intertwined so that explaining the legal principle can only be accomplished by giving the facts.

In this section the authorities are listed with reference to the area for which they are relevant. Some cases have significance for more than one area. Relevant statutes are also mentioned.

DUTY OF CARE

1

(M'Alister or) Donoghue v. *Stevenson* 1932

The case which established the 'neighbour principle' as well as recognising a manufacturer's duty of care to the ultimate consumer.

Mrs Donoghue went to a cafe with a friend who purchased a bottle of ginger beer. When poured, the decomposed remains of a snail came out of the bottle and she suffered shock and severe gastro-enteritis. Held that 'a manufacturer of products which he sells in such a form as to show that he intends them to reach the ultimate consumer in the form they left him with no reasonable possibility of intermediate examination, and with the knowledge that the absence of reasonable care in the preparation or putting up of the products will result in injury to the consumer, owes a duty to the consumer to take reasonable care, although the manufacturer did not know the product to be dangerous and no contractual relations exists between him and the consumer'.

2

(Hay or) Bourhill v. *Young* 1942

No duty of care is owed to an 'unforeseeable' plaintiff. This case illustrates the distinction between legal proximity and physical proximity.

A motor accident occurred which was heard but not seen by the pregnant plaintiff. She claimed that as a result of the noise of the accident and the blood she saw, she later gave birth to a still-born child. Held that she was not entitled to compensation as she was not a reasonably foreseeable plaintiff.

3

Home Office v. *Dorset Yacht Co Ltd* 1970

An important case which illustrates the wide sweep of the neighbour principle as a general test.

Borstal boys escaped when the officers in charge of them were in bed. They took a vessel and collided with a yacht which they boarded causing more damage. The Home Office was held to owe a duty of care to the Dorset Yacht Co.

4

Anns v. *Merton* 1977

This case contains the statement of Lord Wilberforce which emphasised the importance of policy in negligence. The case discussed the differences between a careless inspection of foundations by the council and a decision not to inspect at all.

The local authority was held to owe a duty of care to occupiers of premises to ensure the building's foundations were adequate.

5

Dutton v. *Bognor Regis UDC* 1972

A professional person who gives advice as to the safety of buildings is a neighbour not only to those to whom he gives the advice but also to anyone else who might suffer damage if the advice is given negligently.

The second owner of a house discovered that it was built on a rubbish tip. The foundations had been inspected and passed. Held the inspection was negligent and a duty of care was owed to subsequent occupiers of the property.

Pure economic loss

6

Spartan Steel and Alloys Ltd v. *Martin & Co (Contractors) Ltd* 1972

In this case Lord Denning outlined the various policy reasons why defendants should not be liable for pure economic loss, e.g. that claims for pure economic loss would be limitless and that the loss of electricity was a hazard the whole community had to risk.

A claim for damages was made against a highway contractor whose servants negligently damaged an electricity cable causing a factory to stop production. One melt in the furnace was damaged and four other melts could not be processed. Held compensation was payable only for the melt in the furnace and not for the other melts which were pure economic loss.

7

Junior Books Ltd v. *Veitchi Co Ltd* 1982

This case established that in certain circumstances compensation can be given for pure economic loss. Lord Roskill expressed the opinion that *Spartan Steel* was wrongly decided.

Veitchi Co Ltd were subcontractors and thus had no contract with Junior Books Ltd. They negligently laid the flooring in the latter's factory who claimed the cost of repairs and loss of profits. Held the loss of profits, although pure economic loss, was recoverable because of the close legal proximity of the parties.

Negligent misstatement

8

Hedley Byrne & Co v. *Heller & Partners Ltd* 1964

The case which created liability for careless statements in negligence causing economic loss.

The plaintiifs were advertising agents who wanted information as to the creditworthiness of one of their clients. The defendants, who were merchant bankers, were asked to give a reference. They did so but gave it 'without responsibility'. On the basis of this reference the plaintiffs entered into several contracts on behalf of their client. The client went into liquidation and the plaintiffs were left with debts. They sued the bank on the basis that the reference was negligently given. Held that the merchant bank was not liable because the reference contained the disclaimer.

Obiter dictum – there may be liability for a negligent misstatement if the parties are in a special relationship where one of the parties relies on the special skill and judgment of the other and the latter knew or ought to have known that he was being relied upon. In such circumstances a duty of care is imposed upon that person to make his statements carefully.

9

Mutual Life Assurance v. *Evatt* 1971
This Privy Council case has been interpreted as limiting liability for negligent misstatement to those persons who hold themselves out as having a particular skill or expertise.

E asked MLA for advice concerning certain investments. Acting on that advice he invested money unprofitably. Held MLA was not liable as it was not in business to give such advice.

Nervous shock

10

Dulieu v. *White and Sons* 1901
Damages are recoverable for nervous shock resulting in physical injury even if no direct physical injury is suffered.

D suffered nervous shock when a vehicle ran into a public house although she was not actually struck by the vehicle.

11

Hambrook v. *Stokes* 1925
Fear for another's safety may result in nervous shock for which a duty of care may be owed.

A woman saw a 'runaway' lorry and mistakenly believed her children to have been injured by it. She suffered shock which later resulted in her death.

12

Chadwick v. *British Transport Commission* 1967
It is foreseeable that a rescuer may suffer nervous shock.

A voluntary rescue worker suffered nervous shock after assisting at a train disaster for which he was given compensation.

13

McLoughlin v. *O'Brian* 1982
A duty of care is owed to a plaintiff who is in a particularly close relationship to those injured and is also in close proximity in time and space to the accident.

A duty of care was owed to a mother who, although not at the scene of a road accident in which members of her family were injured or killed, saw members of her family in various states of shock and injury at the hospital a short time later. As a consequence she suffered nervous shock. She was entitled to compensation.

Occupier's liability

14

British Rail Board v. *Herrington* 1972
House of Lords recognised that occupiers have 'a duty of humanity' to trespassers.

N.B. This case has now been superceded by the Occupiers' Liability Act 1984.

H, a six year old boy was severely injured on BRB's electric line. The House of Lords held that although H was a trespasser, because BRB knew that children frequently reached the line via a broken fence, which they had failed to repair, they therefore owed a minimum 'duty of humanity.'

BREACH

15

Nettleship v. *Weston* 1971
The defendant is in breach of his duty of care if he does not come up to the standard of the reasonable man.

A learner driver had an accident in which his passenger was injured. Held that he was liable as, although he was doing his best, he had not driven at the level expected of a reasonable driver.

16

Wooldridge v. *Summer* 1963
An error in judgment does not necessarily mean that the defendant has fallen below the standard of care required. If he has not, the defence of volenti need not be considered.

A professional photographer was injured when one of the horses in a competition went out of control. Held that, although the rider had made an error of judgment in the way that he had ridden, this did not constitute a breach.

17

Wells v. *Cooper* 1958
The defendant must come up to the standard of the ordinary reasonable man doing that particular job.

A do-it-yourself carpenter refixed a door handle. The handle came away when it was pulled because the screws used were not adequate. Held that such a repair did not call for an expert and the DIY man had come up to the standard required for this small repair job.

18

Bolman v. *Friern Hospital Management Committee* 1957
A person who holds himself out as having a particular skill or expertise must come up to the standard of a reasonable person having those qualities.

A doctor gave electro-convulsive therapy to a patient who suffered injury as a result. Held that the doctor had not fallen below the standard required in the manner in which he had given such treatment, although it was not a universally accepted method.

19

Roe v. *Ministry of Health* 1954
The damage must be foreseeable. A reasonable man, even if he is a professional, is only expected to have such knowledge as is available at the time of the incident.

Two patients were given an anaesthetic. The ampoules in which the anaesthetic was contained had invisible cracks and the anaesthetic was contaminated. As a result both patients were paralysed. Held that there was no liability as the injury was unforeseeable. In 1947, when the accident took place, no one was aware of the possibility of invisible cracks in ampoules.

20

Bolton v. *Stone* 1951

The likelihood of injury is a factor which the reasonable man must consider in deciding what precautions are necessary.

A pedestrian was hit by a cricket ball during a match. Held that considering all the circumstances – the distance from the wicket to the fence, the infrequency in which balls had been hit out of the ground and the upward slope of the ground itself – the fact that no precautions had been taken to prevent such accidents did not mean that the defendant had fallen below the standard of care required. The risk of such injury happening was so low that a reasonable man would not have been expected to take precautions.

In determining the likelihood of injury the reasonable man takes into consideration any factors or personal characteristics which he knows about his 'neighbour'.

21

Haley v. *London Electricity Board* 1965

A blind pedestrian was injured when he fell into an excavated hole left unattended by the London Electricity Board. Precautions had been taken which were sufficient to prevent a sighted pedestrian from falling into the hole but the electricity board was held liable for not doing enough to ensure the safety of reasonably foreseeable blind pedestrians.

22

Paris v. *Stepney Borough Council* 1951

A one-eyed employee lost his sight as a result of an accident at work. This would not have happened if the employer had supplied goggles. Held that, although the council would not have been expected to supply goggles to a normally sighted employee, in the circumstances it had not acted reasonably in failing to supply goggles to this particular employee.

23

Latimer v. *AEC* 1953

There must be a balance between the degree of risk and the burden of taking precautions.

AEC reopened their factory after it was flooded and did all they could to make the floor safe. Nevertheless, L fell and was injured. AEC were not liable as it would have been unreasonable for them to have kept their factory closed.

24

Watt v. *Hertfordshire CC* 1954

An emergency can sometimes necessitate risks being taken.

A fireman was injured on the way to an emergency when a piece of equipment slipped. The lorry on which he was travelling was the only vehicle available but it was not equipped to carry the equipment. The council was not liable in the circumstances.

25

Glasgow Corporation v. *Taylor* 1922

More care may be needed to act reasonably in protecting young children.

A child died after eating poisonous berries growing on a tree in a park. The berries were an allurement and the corporation was liable even though the child was a trespasser.

Res ipsa loquitur	If a situation occurs which cannot be explained but can only presumably have happened because of the defendant's negligence the maxim *res ipsa loquitur* will apply.
26	*Byrne* v. *Boadle* 1863 A barrel of flour fell from a warehouse injuring a pedestrian. The inference was that someone had been negligent. *Res ipsa loquitur* applied.
CAUSATION **27**	*Barnett* v. *Chelsea Hospital Management Committee* 1969 The defendant's breach must be the cause of the plaintiff's damage. A doctor negligently failed to examine a man who later died of arsenic poisoning. Although the Committee were in breach of their duty of care, B died of the poisoning and not because he was not examined. No liability.
28	*McWilliams* v. *Arrol Ltd* 1962 The test used to determine causation is the 'but for' test. An employee died at work. He would not have died if he had been wearing a safety belt. Such belts were not supplied by the employer. However, it was decided that even if a safety belt had been available the employee would not have worn one. There was no liability.
REMOTENESS OF DAMAGE **29**	*The Wagon Mound (No 1)* 1961 A defendant is only liable for the type of damage which was reasonable foreseeable. A wharf at Sydney Harbour was damaged by fire after oil which had been discharged from the Wagon Mound ignited. Although it was foreseeable that the wharf would be damaged by fouling as a result of the oil, the fire damage was not foreseeable and was too remote.
30	*Hughes* v. *Lord Advocate* 1963 Only the type of damage done needs to have been reasonably foreseen; its specific nature or the exact means by which it was inflicted do not. Two boys entered a canvas shelter covering an unattended manhole taking one of the warning paraffin lamps with them. While in the shelter one of the boys tripped over the lamp and an explosion occured injuring the boy. His damage was not too remote as damage by fire was foreseeable.

31	*Vacwell Engineering Co* v. *BDH Chemicals* 1971 Even though the damage done is much greater than expected if the type of damage was reasonably foreseeable, it is not too remote. BDH Chemicals were held liable for damage which was done by a much greater explosion than was foreseen.
32	*Smith* v. *Leech Brain* 1962 The defendant must take his victim as he finds him. An employee suffered a burn on his lip due to negligence. This injury was foreseeable and resulted in the employee's death as it encouraged his predisposition to cancer. The employers argued that his death was too remote a consequence of the burn but the court held that the employers were liable.
Nova Causa (or Novus Actus) Interveniens **33**	*McKew* v. *Holland, Hannen & Cubitts* 1969 The plaintiff's own actions can break the chain of causation. McK suffered a leg injury caused by his employer's negligence. That injury was made worse when he fell while descending some stairs at a flat. Held the way he negotiated the staircase was a *nova cause interveniens* and his employers were not responsible for the further injury he suffered.
DEFENCES **Volenti**	See cases listed in Chapter 14.
Contributory negligence	A plaintiff may be contributorily negligent if he does not take care of his own safety.
34	*Froom* v. *Butcher* 1976 A plaintiff who is injured in a motor accident may be contributorily negligent if he was not wearing a seatbelt.
35	*Sayers* v. *Harlow UDC* 1958 S was locked in a public toilet. She attempted to escape but fell trying to climb out using the toilet roll as a hoist. Her damages were reduced because of the way she attempted to rescue herself from her predicament.
36	*Jones* v. *Boyce* 1816 A plaintiff is not contributorily negligent if he makes a reasonable decision in the agony of the moment. A passenger reasonably believed that the coach on which he was riding was going to overturn. He jumped off and was injured. The coach did not overturn. Held no contributory negligence because he acted in the agony of the moment.

RECENT EXAMINATION QUESTIONS

Because negligence is such an important tort it is frequently the subject of examination questions. Usually two types of questions are asked; the essay question requiring the student to discuss some specific aspect of the tort such as the 'neighbour principle', and the problem question where the student must place himself in the shoes of the person or persons he has to advise. Frequently a negligence question will include both an essay and a problem. If only a problem is presented it normally will involve a number of situations for the student to unscramble. One of these questions is usually included to allow the student to give a straightforward explanation of the tort while the remainder are intended to provide the student with the opportunity to discuss certain particular aspects of the tort such as the concept of the reasonable man.

The student should be aware that, although an examination question may concentrate on negligence, the question may also contain references to other torts such as trespass to land or private nuisance. If that is the case, the student will also have to discuss those other torts unless the question is limited to a discussion of the tort of negligence.

The following illustrate the type of questions most commonly asked. The student should discuss each question from all perspectives. He should not present his answer in absolute terms but should indicate all the possible conclusions to the problem. It may be useful to spend around ten minutes planning an answer to each question before turning to the outline answers.

Question 1.

Advise Thomas whether an action for negligence is likely to succeed against each of the parties in the following cases, explaining the relevant principles of law involved:

(a) Albert, a practising accountant, upon whose advice Thomas made an investment which proved to be worthless.
(b) Bernard, a barrister, who represented Thomas in a recent case and who conducted the case badly.
(c) Charles, a car driver, whose car skidded and crossed on to the wrong side of the road where it collided with Thomas's car.
(d) David, a demolition worker, who carelessly injured a fellow worker thereby causing Thomas, who was passing at the time to suffer nervous shock. (ICMA 1977)

Question 2.

Susan owns a factory which manufactures furniture. Advise Susan as to her liability in tort in each of the following situations:

(a) One day a prospective customer visits the factory and trips over some timber which has been left in one of the gangways; the customer breaks his ankle.
(b) An employee, while sitting at his work bench is injured when a piece of timber falls from a hoist carrying timber from one part of the factory to another.

(c) A second employee is out in the van delivering furniture when he knocks over a pedestrian on a pedestrian crossing.   (DPA 1983)

Question 3.

(a) What are the essential features of the tort of negligence? Explain what is meant by the term 'remoteness of damage'.

(b) While Alan, a self-employed businessman, is driving to the station on his way to an important meeting in London, he is involved in a collision with another car driven by Tim. The accident was caused by Tim's negligent driving and, as a result, Alan suffers a broken leg and severe lacerations to his face. He also suffers from shock and, because he was unable to attend the meeting in London, he loses a valuable contract.
    Advise Alan as to the damages he may claim from Tim.
    (ACCA 1981)

Question 4.

Ben has only three hours practice in learning to drive when he asked Tom to accompany him on a practice drive. Tom, who had earlier advised Ben to invest in Potters Plum Pudding Co, agreed to accompany him but only when told by Ben that he held a valid foreign driving licence. Ben had no such licence. Ben's car mounted a pavement, crashed into the doorway of Mary's shop, badly injuring Tom. Falling masonry caused a stock of matches in the shop to ignite and the consequent fire spread to Graham's adjacent garage. There was an explosion which damaged the windows of Heathcliffe College a mile away.
    Ben has lost several hundred pounds in the investment in Potters Plum Pudding Co.
    Advise Ben as to his legal position.   (AEB 1983)

OUTLINE ANSWERS

Answer 1.

Thomas must be advised whether he has a prima facie case in each situation.

(a) The student must discuss liability for negligent misstatements as stated in *Hedley Byrne* v. *Heller*. It is not certain whether Albert owed a duty of care to Thomas since we do not know if the advice was given in the course of Albert's business (see *Mutual Life and Citizens' Assurance Co* v. *Evatt*) or on a social occasion.

(b) For policy reasons barristers are not liable for negligent statements made in connection with litigation (*Rondel* v. *Worsley* . This immunity also includes pre-trial work closely connected with the court case (*Saif Ali* v. *Mitchell (Sydney) & Co*). As the word 'represented' is used in the question, it is probable that Bernard will not be liable.

(c) Charles, as another road user, owed Thomas a duty of care (*Nettleship* v. *Weston*). The question is, did the car skid because

Charles fell below the standard of a reasonable driver driving in those circumstances? If he did not, then there will be no liability even though Thomas' car was damaged.

(d) Compensation can be awarded for nervous shock but only in limited circumstances. Was Thomas reasonably foreseeable, or was he unforeseeable like the pregnant fishwife in *(Hay or) Bourhill* v. *Young*? Was Thomas personally in any danger (*Dulieu* v. *White*)? He did not suffer his injury because he was coming to the rescue of the injured worker as was the case in *Chadwick* v. *British Transport Commission*. He is not in a close relationship with the injured worker as in *Hambrook* v. *Stokes Bros.*. Thus, it appears unlikely that Thomas will be able to obtain compensation for his injury.

Answer 2.

This question will be answered only in terms of negligence. In the examination the student would also need to discuss breach of statutory duty (e.g. Factories Act 1961).

(a) If the customer is a lawful visitor, Susan, as the occupier, would owe him a 'common duty of care' under the Occupier's Liability Act 1957. If the customer is not a lawful visitor liability is governed by the Occupiers' Liability Act 1984.

(b) Susan, as the employer, owes a duty of care to her employees. The maxim *res ipsa loquitur* appears to apply (*Byrne* v. *Boadle*). It would be highly unlikely that Susan could use the defence of *volenti non fit injuria* (*Smith* v. *Baker*). The employee does not seem to have been contributorily negligent.

(c) The injured pedestrian must prove that the employee was negligent. If, at the time the employee was delivering furniture he was acting in the course of his employment, Susan will be vicariously liable for her employee's tort.

Answer 3.

(a) The student should briefly explain:
  (i) the defendant must owe the plaintiff a duty of care;
  (ii) the defendant must be in breach of his duty of care;
  (iii) the plaintiff must have suffered damage as a result of the defendant's breach.

  'Remoteness of damage' refers to such of the plaintiff's losses for which the defendant must compensate. Remoteness is not limited to the tort of negligence but, like negligence, is dependent on the concept of reasonable foreseeability. The student must explain the ratio of the *Wagon Mound* case and those cases which modify it. The student should also mention that damage intentionally done is never too remote.

(b) Tim owed a duty of care to Alan and his negligent driving has resulted in Alan suffering damage. Tim is liable to compensate Alan for the type of damage he suffered which was reasonably foreseeable (*Wagon Mound*); the broken leg and lacerations. In addition Alan suffered shock. Sometimes nervous shock has been held too remote an injury but this would probably not be the case here. Even if Alan has an emotional temperament the rule is that the defendant must take his plaintiff as he finds him (*Smith* v. *Leech Brain*). The loss of the valuable contract is economic loss. As this loss is a consequence of Alan suffering his physical injuries, it may not be too remote unless it is held by the court as not reasonably foreseeable.

A TUTOR'S ANSWER

Question **4** is typical of many negligence problem questions. Before answering this question the student should outline each character's position vis-à-vis each of the other parties. When answering the question the student should first state the legal position and then apply the law to the facts.

Answer 4.

Tom, Mary, Graham and Heathcliffe College all have potential claims against Ben in the tort of negligence. Ben may have a potential claim against Tom based on the advice Tom gave him.

To prove a claim in negligence a plaintiff must prove, on a balance of probabilities, the three elements of the tort; that the defendant owed the plaintiff a duty of care, that the defendant was in breach of that duty and as a result of the breach the plaintiff has suffered loss.

In *Donoghue* v. *Stevenson* Lord Atkin stated a general principle which has been seen as underlying all duty situations. This is the 'neighbour principle', a person must 'take reasonable care to avoid acts or omissions which you can reasonably foresee would be likely to injure your neighbours . . . who then, in law is my neighbour? . . . persons who are so closely and directly affected by my act that I ought reasonably to have them in contemplation . . .'

Tom will have to prove that Ben owed him a duty of care and applying the neighbour principle it could be argued that Ben could reasonably foresee that if he drove negligently Tom as his passenger might be injured.

If Ben owes a duty of care to Tom then it must be decided if he was in breach of that duty of care. The standard of care applied to determine breach is the standard of the reasonable man. This is an objective test. The question is, did the defendant come up to the standard which an average man would have achieved in the circumstances in which the defendant acted. In the case of Ben and Tom this means did Ben come up to the standard of a reasonable driver. If Ben did achieve this standard then there will be no breach and he will not be liable.

It is no defence for Ben to argue that he was doing his best or that he was only a learner driver. As Lord Denning said in *Nettleship* v. *Weston* ' . . . if a driver goes on the wrong side of the road. It is no answer for him to say: 'I was a learner-driver . . . I was doing my best . . .' The civil law permits no such excuse. It requires of him the same standard of care as any other driver.'

If Ben has been in breach of his duty of care to Tom, then it is apparent that Tom's injuries were caused by Ben's action; the element of causation is fulfilled.

Further, as regards Tom's injuries, the test for remoteness as established in the *Wagon Mound* (1) case is also satisfied as Tom's injuries could be said to be of a type which was reasonably foreseeable as a result of Ben's tort.

Ben might try to escape liability by using the defence of *volenti non fit injuria*. However, for this defence to succeed the defendant would have to prove that the plaintiff knew of the risk and freely consented to run the risk. It might be argued by Tom's counsel that Tom did not freely consent as Ben had led him to believe that he was a qualified driver by telling him he had a valid foreign driving licence.

Ben might also argue that Tom was contributorily negligent by not checking, for example, to see if he did have a driving licence. If this is accepted by the court, Tom's damages will be reduced as is 'just and equitable' in accordance with the provisions of the Law Reform (Contributory Negligence) Act 1945.

Ben also appears liable to Mary for the property damage done to the doorway of her shop if his driving is found to be negligent on the same principles as discussed above. However, the second damage of the fire both to her property and to Graham's adjacent garage as well as the damaged windows to Heathcliffe College might be argued by Ben to be too remote.

As stated above, the Privy Council in the case of the *Wagon Mound* (1) held that a defendant is only liable to compensate a plaintiff for the type of damage which was reasonably foreseeable as a result of his tort. This general rule has been further qualified. In *Hughes* v. *Lord Advocate* it was held that the kind of injury and the way in which it was inflicted need only be of a type which was reasonably foreseeable; its exact nature or method of infliction does not have to be foreseen. The question then is would a reasonable man have foreseen that falling masonry might start a fire?

Further Ben might argue, for example, that the explosion was a *novus actus interveniens* and thus breaking the chain of causation being unforeseeable and outside his control.

Regarding Ben's claim against Tom, it is assumed that Tom had no contractual arrangement with Ben to give him financial advice, that Tom was not in any fiduciary relationship with Ben nor did Tom give his advice with the intention of deliberately deceiving Ben. If the above assumptions are correct, then Tom's only action would be to bring a claim for negligent misstatement.

The *obiter dictum* in *Hedley Byrne & Co* v. *Heller & Partners Ltd* says that there can be liability for a negligent misstatement if the parties are in a special relationship where one of the parties relies on the special skill and judgment of the other and the latter knew or ought to have known that he was being relied upon. In such circumstances a duty of care is imposed upon that person to make his statements carefully.

If there is a special relationship then Tom will be liable. But if his remarks were only made casually on a social occasion this is unlikely.

Further, the Privy Council in *Mutual Life Assurance* v. *Evatt* limited liability for negligent misstatement to those persons who hold themselves out as having a particular skill or expertise. If this decision is followed then Ben will have to show that Tom had such skill or expertise or held himself up as having such skill or expertise to give such advice.

A STEP FURTHER

BASIC READING

All general textbooks on tort contain chapters on negligence. It is useful to use a casebook in conjunction with a textbook.

A selection of standard textbooks follows:

Tort (3rd edn), David Baker, Concise College Texts, Sweet & Maxwell, 1981.

Tort Law, R W Dias and B S Markesinis, Clarendon Press, 1984.

The Law of Torts (6th edn) J Fleming, The Law Book Company Limited, 1983.

Winfield & Jolowicz on Tort (12th edn), W V H Rogers, Sweet & Maxwell, 1984.

The Law of Torts (7th edn), H Street, Butterworths, 1983.

A Casebook on Tort (5th edn), T Weir, Sweet & Maxwell, 1983.

FURTHER READING FOR REFERENCE

Detailed commentary on the tort of negligence can be found in *Charlesworth & Percy on Negligence* (7th edn), Sweet & Maxwell, 1983.

Chapter 16   Defamation

The tort of defamation is a legal balancing act. The tort consists of making an untrue statement which damages the reputation of another. The tort's purpose is to protect a person's reputation but its defences reflect the need for freedom of expression.

The tort is composed of two torts; libel and slander. Libel is a defamatory statement in permanent form. It is a mistake, however, to believe that libels are only written statements. Pictures, cartoons, signs, paintings and even wax effigies have been held to be libels. Libel also includes films, radio and television broadcasts as well as public performances of plays.

Slander is a defamatory statement in transient form. The spoken word is the most usual and obvious example of slander, but there is nothing to stop a mime artist, for example, from making a slanderous remark through his gestures.

The boss who dictates a letter containing a defamatory statement is making a slanderous remark. When the letter is typed and sent, he may be liable for libel.

Although libel and slander are similar, there are certain important differences. For example, slander is only a tort while libel can be both a crime and a tort. More importantly, libel is actionable *per se* while slander generally is not. This means that a plaintiff who bases his action on libel does not have to prove that he suffered actual damage as a result of the defamatory statement. In an action based on slander a plaintiff must usually establish that he has suffered some material loss, such as loss of employment, as a result of the defamation. Injured feelings, reputation or pride are not losses which can be compensated.

Slander is actionable *per se* in certain circumstances. These are:

1. The imputation that the plaintiff has committed an imprisonable offence;
2. The imputation that the plaintiff is suffering from a contagious or infectious disease;
3. The imputation that a female plaintiff is not a virgin, is an adulterer or a lesbian (Slander of Women Act 1891);
4. An imputation calculated to disparage the plaintiff in any office, profession, calling, trade or business held or carried on by him at the time the defamation was made (Defamation Act 1952 s.2). Such a statement might question the plaintiff's honesty, competence or integrity.

Defamation is one of the few civil matters where a jury is used. Matters of law are decided by the judge while matters of fact are determined by the jury. An action for defamation can only be commenced in the High Court.

ESSENTIAL PRINCIPLES

To succeed in defamation the plaintiff must prove that the statement was defamatory, that it refers to him and that it was published. As mentioned above, if the action is based on slander then generally the plaintiff must additionally establish actual damage or loss. The plaintiff is not obliged to prove that the defamatory statement was false. However, if the defendant can establish that the statement was substantially true he will have a complete defence. This section will concentrate on explaining the elements of the tort and the various defences. Except for the Defamation Act 1952 and a number of other statutes, the tort has developed and been defined through court decisions. The relevant authorities are cited in the section on 'Useful Applied Materials'.

THE ELEMENTS OF THE TORT

The statement must be defamatory

There is no established yardstick by which the defamatory quality of any statement can be determined. Lord Atkin in *Sim* v. *Stretch* (1) 1936 suggested the test: '*Would the words tend to lower the plaintiff in the estimation of right-thinking members of society generally?*'. The phrase 'right-thinking members of society' has never been defined but it is assumed to mean reasonable people. As established in *Byrne* v. *Deane* (3) 1937, a plaintiff is not defamed simply because those who receive the statement think less well of him unless their reaction is the same as that expected of the general mass of respectable citizens.

Lord Atkin's test would include defamatory statements which refer to a person's honesty or morality. But his definition is incomplete for it does not, for example, include a statement alleging a woman has been raped or a reference to a person's mental state. Because of its inadequacies, Lord Atkin's test should be supplemented by the test applied in *Youssoupoff* v. *Metro-Goldwyn Mayer Pictures Ltd* (2) 1934, (where the plaintiff was depicted as having been either raped or seduced by the mad monk Rasputin), i.e. *that the statement would cause ordinary, reasonable members of society to shun or avoid the plaintiff.*

Mere abuse is not enough to satisfy either test. For a statement to be defamatory the plaintiff's reputation must actually have been attacked and injured. People, as a result of the defamatory statement, would look upon him with repulsion and or contempt.

Reputation is not the exclusive attribute of a living person. Businesses, for example, have commercial reputations that can also be defamed (*South Hetton Co* v. *NE News* (12) 1894). It is not possible to defame the dead.

The context in which the words are used is all important in determining whether the statement is defamatory. Situations and values change and what may be defamatory in one context may not be in another. For example, describing someone as a 'mole' or 'grass' will have different connotations depending on when and where the words are used. Sometimes the context in which the statement is made prevents it from being defamatory.

The defendant's intentions are irrelevant. A defendant is liable for a defamatory statement whether or not he intended to defame the plaintiff, unless he can establish a defence such as unintentional defamation. Further, the defendant does not have to be aware of the defamatory nature of his statement, nor can he argue that nobody believed the statement.

Whether a statement is defamatory is a two-part process; the judge decides whether the words are capable of being defamatory and the jury decides if they in fact defame the plaintiff.

In order to be defamatory the statement must be false.

Innuendo	A statement may be defamatory from the ordinary or primary meaning of the words used. It can also be defamatory because of a secondary meaning. This secondary, or hidden meaning, is called innuendo.

Innuendo can arise in two situations:

1. The words have a defamatory meaning because of extraneous facts of which the person receiving the statement is aware, (*Tolley* v. *J S Fry and Sons Ltd* (6) 1931).
2. The words used are capable of more than one meaning. A statement such as 'she drinks' could have several interpretations, of which some could be defamatory.

The statement must refer to the plaintiff	The plaintiff must establish that the statement could be taken as referring to him. He does not have to be specifically named or expressly referred to but he must be reasonably identifiable. It is irrelevant whether the defendant intended to refer to the plaintiff or not. It was decided in *Newstead* v. *London Express Newspapers Ltd* (9) 1940 that a true statement about one person could be defamatory of another. Further, even if the maker of the statement intended it to refer to a fictitious character such a statement could still be

defamatory of a living person, as was the case in *Hulton* v. *Jones* (8) 1910.

The judge must consider whether the statement was capable of referring to the plaintiff. The jury decides whether the words in fact were understood by reasonable people to whom they were published to have referred to the plaintiff.

A class of persons can be defamed but only if it is small enough for the words to refer to each member of the class. Thus, to say that 'all solicitors are liars' is not specific enough, but it might be if the statement was made with reference to the solicitors in a particular village.

The statement must be published to a third party

Publication occurs when the defendant communicates the statement to at least one other person other than the plaintiff. There is no liability for publishing a statement to one's spouse but publication to the plaintiff's spouse is actionable. It is necessary that the person receiving the statement can understand it. A defamatory statement spoken in French to someone who does not speak that language would not be a publication to that person unless it was translated.

Publication does not have to be intentional but merely foreseeable. Thus, if the defendant has written a defamatory statement on the back of a postcard it is to be expected that the card may be read by more than just the person to whom it was addressed. It is foreseeable that a letter may be opened and read by the plaintiff's spouse or secretary unless it is marked personal or confidential.

Every person who repeats a defamatory statement, even innocently, incurs potential liability in defamation. Thus, the secretary who repeats the defamatory contents of the letter dictated to her by her boss to her friends over lunch is publishing the defamation afresh and could also be held liable. Further, not only is the writer of a libel liable but also his publisher, the printer, and the bookseller who stocks his book on the basis that they have all communicated the statement, although they may be able successfully to plead the defence of unintentional defamation.

DEFENCES

A defendant may plead that the tort has not been committed or that the plaintiff consented (volenti) to the making of the defamatory statement. In addition to these defences certain special defences, which are discussed below, have been developed to protect a defendant from liability. It may be possible for a defendant to use more than one defence.

Justification

It is a complete defence to show that the statement is true no matter how maliciously it was made. Minor inaccuracies do not deprive the defendant of this defence as long as these are not significant. For example, a defendant could still use this defence if he had said that the plaintiff had been dismissed from his employment because he stole £500 from his employer when he actually stole £400.

It is possible for a statement to contain more than one

defamatory remark. The Defamation Act 1952, s.5 states that a defendant does not lose the defence of justification even though he cannot establish the truth of every allegation as long as those allegations not proved to be true do not materially injure the plaintiff's reputation having regard to the truth of the other allegations.

A defendant cannot use the defence of justification simply because he believed the words to be true. The statement must actually be true.

There are two exceptions to this defence; an injunction may be granted to prevent the disclosure of confidential information, and by s.8 of the Rehabilitation of Offenders Act 1974 a spent conviction cannot be published maliciously, even if true.

Fair comment

The purpose of this defence is to protect the expression of opinions. *A defendant will not be liable if he can show that his statement, being only one of opinion and not fact, was made in good faith on a matter of public interest.* The opinion must be based on facts which were correct.

The term 'public interest' includes the public activities of government officials and the way in which the nation's affairs are conducted both politically, economically and culturally. It may also include the conduct of public personalities but not necessarily their private lives.

Although motive is generally irrelevant in tort, **if the defendant is shown to have been motivated by malice or deliberate ill will the defence will fail.** The defence can still be used, however, notwithstanding that the opinion expressed by the defendant was unreasonable, as long as it is accepted that he honestly held that opinion and was not malicious.

Privilege

Privilege is divided into two types; absolute and qualified privilege.

(a) Absolute privilege

If a statement is protected by absolute privilege the maker of that statement has complete protection even if the plaintiff can prove that the defendant made the statement maliciously and without any foundation. Because this is potentially unfair, the defence is limited to those situations where freedom of expression is considered more important than an individual's reputation.

Absolute privilege applies to statements made:

1. In Parliamentary proceedings or contained in documents published by order of Parliament or contained in reports given to and made by the Parliamentary Commissioner and Local Commissioners;
2. During judicial proceedings by those connected with those proceedings; e.g. the judge, witnesses, advocates or jurors;
3. In contemporaneous reports of judicial proceedings contained in newspapers or published on radio or television which are fair and accurate unless their publication is prohibited.
4. Communications between Government Ministers on matters of state.

(b) Qualified privilege	*If the defendant can show that he made the defamatory statement because he had a moral, social or legal obligation to do so and the statement was only published to those who had a similar obligation to receive the statement, he will be able to rely on the defence of qualified privilege.* The element of reciprocity is crucial to this defence. *Further, the defence will fail if the defendant acted maliciously* when making the statement in that he did not honestly believe in the statement's truth or he acted from an improper motive. But a prejudiced view, honestly held, does not destroy the defence.

This defence covers such situations as the giving of references, necessary business communications, complaints to government departments and professional bodies, and communications between a solicitor and his client. The defence also applies to fair and accurate reports of proceedings in Parliament, and judicial proceedings.

Unintentional defamation or offer of amends

As mentioned above, a person may be liable for a defamatory remark even though he acted innocently and was unaware of the statement's defamatory nature. Publishers, printers, booksellers, newsagents and even libraries (*Vizetelly* v. *Mudie's Select Library Ltd* (5) 1900) can all be held liable for a libel contained in a book or article even if they do not know of its libelous content.

Now such 'innocent' disseminators can claim *the defence of* **unintentional defamation** *created by s.4 of the Defamation Act 1952 if they can show that they were unaware and could not have known that the defamatory statement referred to the plaintiff, that it was not defamatory either in the ordinary sense of the words used or by innuendo and they did not act negligently in publishing the statement.* Under this section the defendant can make an offer of amends to the person defamed. By this offer the defamer is obliged to publish a suitable apology and correction and take all necessary steps to notify those who may have already received the statement. If the offer is accepted there is no further liability; if it is refused then the defendant can defend by showing that he published innocently, an offer was made as soon as possible once the defamatory nature of the words was known and the originator of the words had not acted maliciously.

Remedies and mitigation

Damages are the usual remedy used to compensate the plaintiff for loss of reputation. If the plaintiff's action is based on libel or those cases of slander which are actionable *per se*, then damages are 'at large' and the plaintiff is entitled to receive substantial damages without proving any material loss. The court has power to award the plaintiff parasitic damages in respect of his injured feelings and *aggravated* damages to take into consideration the circumstances in which the defamatory statement was made. In addition, *exemplary damages* may be awarded to 'punish' the defendant for anticipating making a greater profit for publishing the defamatory remark then he would have to pay in damages.

In addition to damages, or as an alternative, the court may be prepared to grant an *injunction* to prevent a repetition of the defamatory statement.

The defendant may attempt to *mitigate* by submitting evidence that he was provoked into making the defamation, that the plaintiff had a bad character before the statement was made, or that he has apologised to the plaintiff.

| USEFUL APPLIED MATERIALS | When explaining the principles of defamation it is necessary to refer to authorities. Although the following list of cases is not exhaustive, it includes the most frequently quoted. |

The statement must be defamatory

1

Sim v. *Stretch* 1936
A defamatory statement is one which lowers a person's reputation in the estimation of right-thinking members of society generally.

The plaintiff alleged that a telegram contained a libel; namely that he had borrowed money from his housemaid and had not paid her wages. The court held that the words were not defamatory of him.

2

Youssoupoff v. *MGM Pictures Ltd* 1934
It is defamatory to publish a statement which would cause reasonable ordinary people to shun or avoid the plaintiff. Further, this case established that the contents of a film are capable of being a libel.

A Russian princess sued MGM which had produced a film implying that she had either been raped or seduced by Rasputin. They were held liable.

3

Byrne v. *Deane* 1937
If 'right-thinking' members of society would not think less of the plaintiff because of the statement, then even if some people do he is not defamed.

A member of a golf club told the police about illegal gaming machines at the clubhouse. A poem was posted on the wall of the clubhouse which effectively referred to the member as an informer. He sued but it was held that 'right-thinking' people would have applauded his actions. He had not been defamed.

4

Slazengers Ltd v. *Gibbs & Co* 1916
The context in which the statement is made is important in determining whether the statement is defamatory.

It was held defamatory to refer to S Ltd as a German firm during World War I.

5

Vizetelly v. *Mudie's Select Library Ltd* 1900
MSL Ltd were held liable for publishing defamatory material in their circulating library even though they were unaware of the libel.

N.B. Such a defendant would now have the protection of s.4 Defamation Act 1952.

Innuendo	*Tolley* v. *J S Fry and Sons Ltd* 1931
6	Extrinsic factors may make an otherwise innocent statement defamatory.
	An amateur golfer successfully sued Fry Ltd for publishing an advertisement bearing his name and likeness without his consent as this could lead people to believe that he had compromised his amateur status.
7	*Cassidy* v.*Daily Mirror* 1929
	If the statement is defamatory it does not matter that the defendant did not know it was.
	A story and photograph was published telling of the engagement of Miss X to C's husband. C successfully established that the story implied that she was an immoral woman who had cohabited with a man without being married to him.
The statement must refer to the plaintiff	*Hulton* v. *Jones* 1910
	The defendant may refer to the plaintiff unintentionally.
8	An article was published which referred to 'Artemus Jones', a churchwarden at Peckham, who was believed to be a fictitious character. There was no Artemus Jones in Peckham but there was a barrister of that name elsewhere who was awarded damages for the libel by showing that some of his friends thought the article was about him.
9	*Newstead* v. *London Express* 1940
	An article reported that a Camberwell man named Harold Newstead aged 30 had been convicted of bigamy. This was true. There was, however, in Camberwell another Harold Newstead about which the statement was untrue. The latter received damages for libel.
10	*Knupffer* v. *London Express Newspaper* 1944
	If a group is too large no individual plaintiff can be referred to unless specifically identifiable.
	An article alleged that an association of political refugees numbering some 2000 were going to be used by Hitler to rule Russia. A member of this group sued but it was held that the article could not be taken as specifically referring to him.
The statement must be published to a third party	*Theaker* v. *Richardson* 1962
	The defendant is liable for a publication even if it is unintentional if he could have foreseen it.
11	The plaintiff's husband opened a sealed letter addressed to his wife. The defendant was held liable for the publication.
A company may sue in libel	*South Hetton Co.* v. *NE News*1984
12	An action by the SH Co for libel upheld by the Court of Appeal in respect of a statement injuring its trade or business.

DEFENCES

Justification

13

Alexander v. *NE Railway* 1865

To use the defence of justification the words only have to be substantially true.

The railway published a poster stating that A had been convicted of failing to pay his rail fare and had received a sentence of three weeks' imprisonment or a fine. He had only received two weeks' imprisonment but that did not defeat the defence of justification.

Fair comment

14

Thomas v. *Bradbury, Agnew & Co Ltd* 1906

To rely on the defence of fair comment the defendant must not have acted maliciously.

A reviewer in his review of T's biography made certain unfavourable comments about T's literary ability. The defendants were not able to rely on the defence of fair comment as the reviewer's remarks were made maliciously.

Qualified privilege

15

Watt v. *Longsdon* 1930

There must be a legal, moral or social duty to make and receive the statement.

A company manager wrote a letter containing serious allegations about an employee. The letter was shown to the employee's wife and to other directors. The defence of qualified privilege protected the publication to the directors but not the publication to the employee's wife.

RECENT EXAMINATION QUESTIONS

Examination questions on defamation are frequently presented as problems which require the student to explain both the plaintiff's position and the defendant's defences. Such questions are often combined with an essay question, such as asking the student to explain the differences between libel and slander. This 'combination' style of questioning allows the students to demonstrate both his powers of memory and analysis. The following are typical of the questions asked on defamation. It may be useful to spend around ten minutes planning an answer to each question before turning to the outline answers.

Question 1.

(a) Outline the differences between libel and slander.

(b) Miss Jones is called to the office of Mr Brown the managing director of her company. Mr Brown accuses her of stealing from the petty cash and says, 'You are a disgrace to the company and you are dismissed. I won't tolerate dishonest employees'. Mr Brown's secretary, Miss Evans, is listening at the door and overhears his remarks. Miss Jones is so upset she rushes from the room, trips on a loose floorboard and breaks her arm. Miss Evans immediately goes to the canteen and discusses what she has heard with her friend Doris.

Discuss. (Exclude the provisions of the Health and Safety at
Work etc Act from your answer.)   (DPA 1981)

Question 2
    (a) Define defamation. What are the chief differences between the
         two forms which defamation may take?
    (b) Ten years ago Tony was released from a term of imprisonment. He
         has 'gone straight' ever since. George, who bears him a grudge,
         tells his present employer that Tony is an ex-convict. The
         employer consequently gives him notice of dismissal. Explain
         whether Tony can sue George for damages.   (ACCA 1975)

Question 3.
Elias is extremely disgruntled with his solicitor, Jeb. He sends a letter
to Jeb in which he states, 'you are totally incompetent and if it were not
for the illegal use of your clients' moneys you would have been
bankrupt long ago.' The letter was read by Elias's wife who had typed
it, and is opened and read by Jeb's secretary. Has Jeb any claims in tort
against Elias? If he has, are there any defences available to Elias?
Would your answer be any different if the letter to Jeb was contained in
an envelope marked, 'Private and Confidential'?   (ILE 1982)

OUTLINE ANSWERS
These outline answers indicate how to use the material presented in the
other sections. Although the questions may sometimes include the
commission of other torts, the answers will only discuss defamation.

Answer 1.
    (a) Defamation consists of two torts; libel and slander. Libel is a
         defamatory statement made in a permanent medium and slander
         is a defamatory statement made in transient form.
             Libel is actionable *per se*; no material loss need be shown to
         obtain damages. In certain circumstances slander is actionable *per
         se*. If the slander is not actionable *per se* material loss must be
         shown; e.g. loss of a commercial contract or tenancy agreement.
             Libel can be a crime and a tort, slander only a tort.
    (b) Miss Jones's action is in slander as Mr Brown's statement was
         spoken. She would have to prove:

    1.   That the statement was defamatory;
    2.   That the statement referred to her;
    3.   That the statement was published. Publication must be to a third
        party, not just the plaintiff. Publication does not have to be
        intentional as long as it could have been foreseen. Could Mr Brown
        have foreseen Miss Evans at the door? By repeating the statement
        Miss Evans also publishes it and becomes liable;
    4.   Slander is normally only actionable if material loss can be shown,
        such as loss of a job. However, in this case the remark may be
        actionable *per se* as her boss has implied that she has committed an
        imprisonable offence, theft, and, further, his words may be
        considered to be calculated to disparage Miss Jones in the office
        she held at the time of publication.

If the accusation is substantially true, Miss Jones did steal from the petty cash, the defence of justification can be used. Further, if Mr Brown's opinion, 'you are a disgrace to the company . . .' is considered to have been made in good faith regarding a matter of public interest and based on facts which are true the defence of fair comment is available.

(A student would also discuss Miss Jones's potential claim for compensation for her personal injury by considering an action based on negligence or breach of the employer's implied or express contractual obligations to his employee).

Answer 2.

(a) Defamation is a civil wrong (a tort). It is an attack on a person's reputation. Lord Atkin in *Sim* v. *Stretch* gave the test, would the words tend to lower the plaintiff's reputation in the estimation of right-thinking members of society generally. In *Youssoupoff* v. *MGM Pictures Ltd* the test was would the plaintiff be shunned or avoided as a result of the remark.

For the rest of this answer the student is referred to the outline answer to question 1a.

(b) Tony would have to prove:

1. That the statement was defamatory; stating he was an ex-convict would probably be sufficient to lower his reputation;
2. That the statement referred to him;
3. That the statement was published; which it was to Tony's employer.
4. It is not clear how the statement was made since we only know that George told the employer of Tony's previous conviction. If George 'told' by writing a memorandum to the employer, the statement would be libel; if he gave the information orally then it would be slander. If the statement was slanderous, then, unless it is a statement which comes under the exceptions, material loss must be shown, for example, loss of a job. Since George's words relate to an imprisonable offence and may also disparage Tony in his present office, it is possible that this slander is actionable *per se*.

George may be able to use the defence of justification. However, if Tony's conviction was 'spent' and provided George acted maliciously he cannot use this defence (Rehabilitation of Offenders Act 1974). Or he might be able to use the defence of qualified privilege.

A TUTOR'S ANSWER

The following is a full answer to Question **3**. The answer discusses a number of topics which are frequently examined.

Answer 3.

Elias may be liable to Jeb in the tort of defamation. Elias' statement may be a libel as it is in permanent form. Jeb would have to show that the statement was defamatory. Accusing Jeb of incompetence and dishonesty as well as a breach of professional standards, would fulfil the test set by Lord Atkin in *Sim* v. *Stretch* – 'would the words tend to lower the plaintiff in the estimation of right-thinking members of society generally?'

The statement must be shown to have referred to Jeb, the plaintiff, and that would undoubtedly be the case here where the letter is sent to him.

The libel must be published, that is communicated, to a third party. This does not include communication by the defendant to his wife. Thus, there is no communication to Elias' wife when she reads the letter. There may, however, be a publication to Jeb's secretary when she opens the letter, for, although this publication was not intentional on Elias' part, it was foreseeable.

As Elias' statement may be libellous, and therefore actionable *per se*, Jeb is under no obligation to show that he suffered any material loss. It is sufficient that his reputation has been attacked.

Elias may have a number of defences. If his statement is substantially true then he will be able to rely on the defence of justification. Alternatively, he might argue that his statement was fair comment; that is that it was made in good faith on a matter of public interest and based on facts which were true. If this defence is to succeed then Elias must not have written the statement maliciously and he must honestly believe in the opinions expressed.

As Elias' communication was to his solicitor he may also be able to rely on the defence of privilege. It has not been absolutely decided whether the defence is one of qualified or absolute privilege. In *More* v. *Weaver* 1928 the Court of Appeal considered it to be absolute. If the privilege is absolute there will be no liability even if Elias acted maliciously. If the privilege is qualified then the defence will be defeated if it is shown that the statement was made maliciously. If it is argued that the communication was made on a privileged occasion then the communication to Jeb's secretary would not destroy the defence as the publication to her was in the usual course of business (*Edmonson* v. *Birch & Co Ltd* 1907).

If the letter had been in an envelope marked 'private and confidential' then there could not possibly have been any publication and therefore no liability in defamation would have arisen.

A STEP FURTHER

A student interested in doing further research on this tort might read: *Gatley on Libel and Slander* (8th edn), Philip Lewis, Sweet and Maxwell, 1981; or *Defamation*, Duncan & Neill, Butterworths, 1978 in addition to any of the standard textbooks on tort. He may also wish to consult *Current Law* and the various law reports, as well as the *Report of the Committee on Defamation*, (the Faulks Report) Cmnd. 5909, 1975.

BASIC READING

All general textbooks on tort contain chapters on defamation. A student might look at:

Tort (3rd edn), David Baker, Concise College Texts, Sweet & Maxwell, 1981.
Tort Law, R W Dias & B S Markesinis, Clarendon Press, 1984.
The Law of Torts (6th edn), J Fleming, The Law Book Company Limited, 1983.
Winfield & Jolowicz on Tort (12th edn), W V H Rogers, Sweet & Maxwell, 1984.
The Law of Torts (7th edn), H Street, Butterworths, 1983.

FURTHER READING OR REFERENCE

Gatley on Libel and Slander (8th edn), Philip Lewis, Sweet & Maxwell, 1981.
Defamation, Duncan & Neill, Butterworths, 1978.
Report of the Committee on Defamation (the Faulks Report), Cmnd, 5905, 1975.

USEFUL ADDRESS

The Press Council, 1 Salisbury Square, London, EC4.

Table of Statutes

Table of Cases

Index